Approaches to Teaching the Works of Robert Louis Stevenson

Approaches to Teaching World Literature

For a complete listing of titles, see the last pages of this book.

Approaches to Teaching the Works of Robert Louis Stevenson

Edited by

Caroline McCracken-Flesher

The Modern Language Association of America

New York 2013

Library of Congress Cataloging-in-Publication Data
Approaches to teaching the works of Robert Louis Stevenson / edited by Caroline
McCracken-Flesher.
p. cm.—(Approaches to teaching world literature series ; 124)
Includes bibliographical references and index.
ISBN 978-1-60329-121-7 (hardcover : alk. paper)—
ISBN 978-1-60329-122-4 (pbk. : alk. paper)
1. Stevenson, Robert Louis, 1850–1894—Study and teaching. 2. Stevenson, Robert Louis,
1850–1894—Criticism and interpretation. I. McCracken-Flesher, Caroline.
PR5496.A67 2013
828'.809—dc23 2012030658

Approaches to Teaching World Literature 124
ISSN 1059-1133

Cover illustration for the paperback edition:
The Wreck of the Covenant, by N. C. Wyeth, 1913. "It was the spare yard I had got hold of,
and I was amazed to see how far I had travelled from the brig." Oil on canvas.
Brandywine River Museum. Bequest of Mrs. Russell G. Colt, 1986

Published by The Modern Language Association of America
26 Broadway, New York, New York 10004-1789
www.mla.org

CONTENTS

Theoretical Contexts

Literary Contexts

Classroom Conventions and Challenges

ACKNOWLEDGMENTS

This book owes its inception to the MLA as host to a critical mass of colleagues who have avidly discussed Stevenson, his texts, and his teaching in recent years, each from his or her own very different cultural, literary, theoretical, and pedagogical perspective. Colleagues aplenty helped the book along: in particular, Fiona Wilson, Ian Duncan, Matthew Wickman, Kenneth McNeill, and Nancy Gish. Stevenson conferences, too, bore up this project. In connection with such conferences, I thank Richard Dury, Richard Ambrosini, Martin Danahay, and Ann Colley. Stevensonians en masse helped hone the book: Eric Massie, Penny Fielding, Alex Thomson, and Julia Reid. Senior scholars like Roger Swearingen, Rory Watson, Jenni Calder, Barry Menikoff, Wendy Katz, Gordon Hirsch, and Stephen Arata were unfailingly generous in sharing their knowledge and offering advice that was always gentle and aimed at the best interests of those who read this book. Colleagues far removed from Stevenson in their studies, such as Hap Veeser and Robert Caserio, were enthusiastic, challenging, and energizing supporters. The faithful members of the MLA, from all parts of the curriculum, who returned their survey sheets guided the construction of the volume.

The Scottish Literature Discussion Group of the MLA provided much encouragement—indeed, it provided, in the person of John Corbett, the challenge that produced this book. Duncan Jones and Gwen Enstam, the superlative staff at the Scottish Writing Exhibition in America and Europe, listened carefully to the needs of visitors to their booth and directed them and their ideas to this project. Scott Hames and Eleanor Bell assembled a Stevenson panel at the MLA and recognized the desire for more that it evoked in its audience.

All those who have contributed—and, for the cause, borne with my heavy-handed editing—deserve thanks, especially the many who come from outside the community of Stevenson, Scottish literature, or Victorian scholars. In field, they range from queer theory to modernism to travel studies to linguistics to Romanticism; in location, they range from Australia to Edinburgh to Wyoming to Hawai'i.

Last but never least, the book owes thanks to our librarians and especially those in interlibrary loan at the University of Wyoming. Maggie Farrell, the library director, and Kaisja Calkins, English subject librarian, together magicked the Tusitala Edition out of their recession-era budget. A great librarian is more precious than rubies. As is a supportive editor: thank you, Sonia Kane and James Hatch.

PREFACE

"Has my face changed?"
—Robert Louis Stevenson

Robert Louis Stevenson is the stealthiest and most subversive of authors. Although he was a late Victorian and died over a hundred years ago, his work still circulates energetically and internationally among popular and academic audiences, and among young and old. The most unexpected people can quote him unknowingly: "I have a little shadow," "Faster than fairies, faster than witches," "Man is not truly one but truly two"—Stevenson echoes through our daily speech. Yet even when his popular audience knows it is quoting him, it seldom knows much about him or about his reach beyond the thing quoted. Often the case is the same in the classroom: *Strange Case of Dr Jekyll and Mr Hyde* dominates in our syllabi, but scholars like Jenni Calder fight a rearguard action to show that Stevenson wrote about duality as a Scot; professors raised on Kate Greenaway wonder where the darkness of his children's poetry could come from, not realizing he grew up in a strict Presbyterian household; Americanists recommend the Henry James side of the debate on "The Art of Fiction" without recognizing James's excitement at being challenged by Stevenson. This undiscovered quality of Stevenson makes him an ongoing revelation in the classroom. The greatest disruption to ideas of genre comes from the realization that an author too easily pigeonholed into classes as an unproblematic writer of fantasy or boys' fiction does not actually fit those categories. Substantial reworkings of America as an idea come from a sickly author imagined by his contemporaries to have crossed the continent in search only of a woman (his wife to be, Fanny Osbourne) or of a style—the languid, mildly entertaining voice that mesmerized them in his earlier travelogues so that they often missed his more disturbing substance.

Recently scholars working in Scottish literature at the MLA, especially those who cross the many divisions of literary study (Romanticists, modernists, afficionados of genre fiction, queer theorists, and so on), noted among our colleagues a great enthusiasm for Stevenson. A Robert Louis Stevenson panel in 2006 hosted in its audience psychoanalysts; Americanists; scholars of science fiction, fantasy, the gothic, the novel, literary theory—to name but a few—alongside Stevensonians. The Scottish Writing Exhibition was besieged by colleagues interested in the range of Stevenson texts. This development is accompanied by an upsurge in Stevenson's popularity outside the academy. In 2005, Lionsgate released *Jekyll and Hyde* (the tagline was "Think you know the story?"); the BBC featured James Nesbitt as Jekyll two years later (Mackinnon and Lipsey). *Kidnapped* (2007) and then *Jekyll and Hyde* (2008) became the "book of the city" for Edinburgh as UNESCO City of Literature. Publishers' lists blossomed with new issues of standard texts: *Kidnapped* became a graphic novel—not for the first time, since it was also a *Classics Illustrated* comic, but certainly for the first time in Scots and Gaelic as well as in English; Barnes and Noble not only released Stevenson's novels in many of their series, they even offered them in a blockbuster tome of seven at a time. Stevenson meanwhile has surged in scholarship: the 1990s publication of the author's letters, by Bradford A. Booth and Ernest Mehew, is soon to be followed by Edinburgh University Press's New Edinburgh Edition of *The Collected Works of Robert Louis Stevenson*. Numerous recent biographies (e.g., McLynn; Harman, *Myself* and *Robert Louis Stevenson*; and Gray, *Robert Louis Stevenson*) and publications like Penny Fielding's *Edinburgh Companion to Robert Louis Stevenson* help span the distance between the popular and scholarly reputations of the author. Yet even as our colleagues across the curriculum teach and enjoy *Treasure Island*, *Jekyll and Hyde*, *Travels with a Donkey*, or another Stevenson of their choice, we increasingly hear them lament a lack of support for their work.

Guided by the MLA survey in preparation for this Approaches volume, our contributors aim to share pedagogical approaches that allow the richness of these and other texts to enter the many possible classroom homes for Stevenson. Survey participants admired the wide variety of his publications and requested help understanding and teaching them in all their multiplicity. Many commented on the increasing interest and relevance of Stevenson's travel and South Seas writing; others reembraced the energy and challenge of his adventure stories; a sizable group sought new ways to understand *Jekyll and Hyde*; some saw Stevenson shifting within our convergence culture and its media; some noted the complexity of a writer capable of both *A Child's Garden* and *Weir of Hermiston*. In the survey, Stevenson showed up in courses on the novel, Romanticism, children's literature, Scottish literature, modernism, genre fiction, travel literature, the gothic, queer studies . . . the list goes on and on. Indeed, both in and between survey responses, a discourse of "teaching the conflicts" in Stevenson stood out. An author so varied in his productivity and his audiences invites disagreement and debate. But inevitable conflict constitutes a pedagogical opportunity.

With this in mind, *Approaches to Teaching the Works of Robert Louis Stevenson* embraces the range of Stevenson's texts and their many overlapping and clashing cultural and literary contexts. It attempts to connect students' love for an author celebrated in popular culture to their educational needs and enthusiasms. Thus scholars from across the curriculum demonstrate the challenges and possibilities that texts as various as *A Child's Garden of Verses*, *An Inland Voyage*, *In the South Seas*, *The Wrecker*, and "The Bottle Imp" offer to established courses and suggest for courses yet to come. This book offers additional support by echoing the form of previous Approaches volumes. It seeks first to suggest materials, then to explain general background and raise large questions, and finally to provide pedagogical strategies for particular problems, texts, and types of classes. Instructors can use the essays of this volume to focus on an issue or theme, to study a particular text in depth, or to weave back and forth according to their interest or fascination with Robert Louis Stevenson—making further scholarly and pedagogical opportunities for themselves and their students. Those new to teaching Stevenson will find the support of information, sources, and ideas; those who have long known one facet of Stevenson may complicate their teaching with another; those who are Stevenson experts should find much that is new as they read essays generated from all points of the curriculum by colleagues who each know Stevenson in a very different way.

An author beloved of Henry James, Vladimir Nabokov, and Jorge Luis Borges merits our attention in the classroom as well as in our research or private reading. But equally, an author so beloved can never fully be addressed in a book such as this. Like all MLA Approaches volumes, *Approaches to Teaching the Works of Robert Louis Stevenson* benefits from the generous sharing of ideas between colleagues, but those ideas, interacting in other classrooms, will no doubt generate new Stevensons, new reasons for us and for our students to line up with Henry James, Vladimir Nabokov, and Jorge Luis Borges. With Borges, may we find Stevenson both literary and a pleasure.

Part One

MATERIALS

Introduction

"There is but one art, to omit."
—Robert Louis Stevenson

Robert Louis Stevenson lived in Edinburgh, Bournemouth, Davos, Saranac Lake, Monterey, and the South Seas—to name but a few of his abodes. Scotland, England, America, and Samoa all claim him for their places and their literatures. His books are hailed in numerous fields: Scottish studies, the postcolonial, modernism, science fiction, children's writing, travel studies. Given the tendency of literary criticism to bring different works into focus in different periods and given the range of Stevenson's writing, it is a changing picture, too. *David Balfour* (known as *Catriona* in the United Kingdom) is gaining ground as the critical eye switches from adventure (*Kidnapped*) to politics; *Virginibus Puerisque* comes to the fore as we turn to consider modes of gender determination; *The Wrecker* emerges through a poststructural perspective and today's convergence culture that celebrates collaboration; "The Bottle Imp" fades in and out of view through the colonial-postcolonial gaze. The editions and anthologies of Stevenson's works, from his own lifetime to today, position themselves differently for each generation's diverse and inclusive market: children, romance readers, scholars, readers of travel, and so on. Not surprisingly, then, Stevenson both belongs in and can trouble any course or curriculum. Moreover, the materials bearing up our teaching are varied and challenging in themselves.

The discussion of materials below draws on suggestions from an MLA survey conducted in preparation for this volume to orient readers with regard to the changing perspectives, authoritative sources, and emerging emphases of Stevenson studies. The materials given here are not exhaustive; rather, they provide a road map that points to greater detail elsewhere—not least in this book's list of works cited. Also, essays in the "Approaches" section themselves provide extensive biographical and historical materials that will not be duplicated here. That is, this section follows Stevenson's "one art" and necessarily omits. But it hopes nonetheless to give the lay of the land that readers can then traverse according to their own enthusiasms.

Literary Criticism

Stevenson's reputation has been high culture and low populist; Romantic and modern; British, Scottish, and American; and up and down. It has been characterized in any number of ways, often all at the same time. The *Critical Heritage* volume of essays edited by Paul Maixner offers an invaluable resource to track the early conflicts and vagaries in Stevenson's literary interpretation and value. Among the newspaper reviews (Stevenson's succession of travel writings are called charming, irresponsible, the work of a stylist, grotesque [e.g., 379–83]) and parodies from *Punch* ("Story of the Bore," featuring Mr. Hidanseek [208–10]), letters from Stevenson's correspondents manifest complex responses from the author's literary cohort and his rather bemused family. Stevenson's father reacts proudly to *Travels with a Donkey*—"very bright"—but shows growing concern with his son's "irreverent uses of the name of God"—a concern with the indecorous and inappropriate that would lead him to suppress Stevenson's report of his travels to America in *The Amateur Emigrant* (64). W. E. Henley's letters and reviews show the enthusiasms and later resistances of a less able collaborator (76, 494–500); Henry James moves from fascination with a young poseur (who is nonetheless charming) to appreciation when Stevenson questions his literary theories to ongoing delight in the author's works and their challenge to established norms (57, 143). Interestingly, many of these debates maintain today: Janet Adam Smith in 1948 and, more recently, Glenda Norquay (*R. L. Stevenson* and *Robert Louis Stevenson*) probe the James-Stevenson relationship for its contribution to ideas of the real and romance, of literary cohorts and competition. In this volume, Scott Hames continues that discussion.

Still, there are tides in Stevenson criticism. Few authors have so met the moment for sentimental biography. The sickly child with a penchant for adventure who fled parental control and went across America in pursuit of a not yet divorced woman and then died in the South Seas is irresistible fodder for such books (edited according to the decorum of the times, of course). Notably, such biographies of Stevenson were often memoirs: Fanny Van de Grift (Osbourne) Stevenson and Stevenson's stepson, Lloyd Osbourne, both contributed to the genre, as did friends and passing acquaintances. Books with firsthand information are crucial resources but should be carefully checked against more authoritative biographies and editions of letters. Aligned with these biographical memoirs is a curious subgenre: both thoughtful travelers and aspiring bohemians have assertively followed in the author's footsteps, locating themselves oddly within Stevenson's places of memory from Edinburgh to Saranac to distant Samoa. Such books at their best activate discourses of authenticity and memory as they go (see Rankin; Holmes). They demonstrate the continuing interest in Stevenson's life as a locus for engagement with the author and occasionally yield insights, but for the most part they show only how Stevenson has spawned imitators and a practice of adaptation through repetitive journeying—an intriguing phenomenon in itself.

Another fascination with Stevenson that began early and echoes today revolves around the problem of romance. James recognized the value in Stevenson's romancing and its challenge to the literary norms of their moment as the two authors debated the art of fiction (see J. Smith; Norquay, *R. L. Stevenson* and *Robert Louis Stevenson*). Yet most contemporary reviewers found themselves perplexed. When Stevenson contributed evenhandedly to the *Cornhill* and *Young Folks*, they praised the art of tall tales like *The Dynamiter* (Maixner 196) yet also worried that *Jekyll and Hyde* "overshoots the mark . . . by being not merely strange, but impossible" (202) and waited for the author to get over his unfortunate proclivity to write of adventure for boys and use his talent instead to produce art. T. Watts-Dunton expressed this opinion in his comment on *Kidnapped*, "It seems to be considered necessary that the schoolboy of the period should be supplied with a new story of adventure for every day in the week. It also seems to be considered necessary that men of genius should be told off [assigned] to write them—men who, like . . . Mr. Stevenson, are sorely needed to produce stories for men and women" (Maixner 240). It was this conundrum—could one write for children and accomplish adult art?—that drove Stevenson not out of circulation but out of critical reputation through the modern period. But it was also through such writing that Stevenson reentered the canon. In fact, it may be through romance that he enjoys his liveliest literary reputation today.

Edmund Wilson tried to chivvy Vladimir Nabokov out of his admiration for Stevenson: "Stevenson is second-rate. I don't know why you admire him so much—though he *has* done some rather fine short stories. . . . I didn't like *Treasure Island* even as a child." Nabokov countered, "You approach Stevenson from the wrong side. Of course *Treasure Island* is poor stuff," and he praised *Jekyll and Hyde* (Nabokov and Wilson 209, 210). Jorge Luis Borges adored Stevenson for what others considered the flaws of his predecessor's romance. In fact Stevenson becomes Borges's test of readerly sensibility. Quoting "Home is the sailor, home from the [sic] sea, / And the hunter home from the hill," words laden with adventure and nostalgia, Borges declared, "Well, if those words will not ring out for you, I can say nothing whatever. If Stevenson fails, what can I do?" (152). Borges appreciated Stevenson's London for its unreality in those unlikely tales of *The New Arabian Nights* and touted that most irreducible attribute of the author, his bravery—often the crux of "boys' own" stories. Borges particularly loved that playful, unpredictable, and until recently seldom read novel, *The Wrecker*. And here we find a key to Stevenson, a problem sorted out by Alan Sandison in 1996 and recent writers like Hames and Roderick Watson in this book: critical tradition has preferred to read Stevenson through binaries derived from his debate with James, yet neither James nor he reductively privileged either romance or realism. In fact, Stevenson, in his debates and his texts—including his romance writing—was often an abstract modernist (consider the musical shaping of *The Ebb-Tide*) or a proto-postmodernist (consider *The Wrecker*).

In growing appreciation of this complexity, critics of recent years have increasingly and unashamedly accepted Stevenson as an accomplished and innovative writer of genre fiction—one who manifests and extends the possibilities of popular forms. Linda Dryden considers the variety of Stevenson's popular writing, while Robert Irvine connects it to issues of class; Lisa Honaker and also H. Aram Veeser (in this volume) ponder romance, empire, and masculinity; William Gray pursues Stevenson as fantasist (*Death*); Robert Mighall and Judith

Halberstam both reconnect him to the gothic; Jean-Pierre Naugrette examines his role in detective fiction. The most consistently and deeply developed reconsideration of Stevenson as writer of genre fiction—and of genre fiction as rewritten by Stevenson—comes in science fiction studies. Here, *Jekyll and Hyde* remains to the fore, with Julia Reid (*Robert Louis Stevenson*) and Allen MacDuffie delving deeper into contemporary science and particularly into medicine. And this is where a persistent and powerful strain of Stevenson criticism now intensifies even further.

Stevenson, as one of the first writers knowingly to take a psychoanalytic perspective on and through his characters—most obviously but not solely in *Jekyll and Hyde*—has always attracted Freudian readings. Stephen Heath's "Psychopathia Sexualis" and Susan Sontag's imaginative recreation in *I, Etcetera* are the most prominent Freudian readings, but movies have long recognized the psychoanalytic aspect of *Jekyll and Hyde*, and the films by Rouben Mamoulian (1931), Victor Fleming (1941), and Roy Ward Baker (1971) privilege it. Newer criticism approaches this phenomenon through the history of medicine and in nuanced ways: Reid situates Stevenson within the discourse of fin de siècle science (*Robert Louis Stevenson*); Anne Stiles considers ideas of the double brain. Most importantly, our growing understanding of Stevenson's nineteenth-century medical context offers new perspectives on the range of his texts and has reenergized biographies of the author. Luisa Villa nicely demonstrates the weaving together of textual and biographical analysis through this mode of thinking, reading oedipality across Stevenson and his works.

New historical and psychological perspectives have ramped up scholarship of Stevenson as a writer for children. Ann Colley's "'Writing towards Home'" paves the way and is expanded upon by Reid in "Childhood and Psychology." Such perspectives also yield a deeper understanding of Stevenson's Scottishness—often invisible to early critics, reconsidered by David Daiches in his writings on Stevenson, expressed again by Jenni Calder (*Robert Louis Stevenson* and *Stevenson and Victorian Scotland*), argued analytically by Caroline McCracken-Flesher ("Thinking"), further researched by Barry Menikoff (*Narrating*), and theorized by Matthew Wickman. This theorizing, which in turn informs the postcolonial perspective on Stevenson, points to him as a travel writer aligned with Herman Melville (see Buckton) and suggests in him a sensibility as refined as Joseph Conrad's (see Kucich; Colley, "Robert Louis Stevenson's South Sea Crossings" and *Robert Louis Stevenson*; Jolly, *Robert Louis Stevenson*). Though Edmund Gosse declared after reading *In the South Seas*, "it is very nice to *live* in Samoa, but not healthy to *write* there. Within a three-mile radius of Charing Cross is the literary atmosphere, I suspect" (223), today we can see that Stevenson has made a substantial contribution to the literature and the criticism of the colonial and postcolonial (see Hill in this volume).

Stevenson is frequently adapted—and not just through *Jekyll and Hyde* or *Treasure Island*. I have theorized *Jekyll and Hyde*'s transposition from fiction into film ("Cultural Projections"), Brian Rose has reviewed extensively the films that adapt *Jekyll and Hyde*, and Martin Danahay and Alex Chisholm have traced the novel's stage adaptations. But *The Wrong Box* and *The Ebb-Tide*, never mind *Kidnapped*, *St. Ives*, and *The Suicide Club*, have all undergone adaptation that is innovative and deserves critical attention. Stevenson's writing for children, particularly *A Child's Garden of Verses*, is perhaps the most adapted of his work. The verses, jointly and severally, have been reformulated in the most interesting modes and media. Barbara Chatton in this volume begins the work of analyzing the challenges to text and audience of such adaptation. Stevenson as adapted, given our convergence culture and the speeds and opportunities allowed by the Internet, constitutes a part of our field destined only to grow.

Oliver Buckton's *Cruising with Robert Louis Stevenson* indicates where Stevenson criticism is heading now. Edited volumes by William Veeder and Gordon Hirsch, William Jones (*Robert Louis Stevenson*), Richard Ambrosini and Richard Dury, and Penny Fielding indicate the variety of Stevenson's works and of the critical perspectives on them. But since Elaine Showalter's *Sexual Anarchy*, Stevenson's role within the discourse of queer theory continues to build. We understand more and more not just the indeterminacies and opportunities expressed through Stevenson the bohemian author but also the theoretical interventions he performed through his deliberate boundary crossing as a writer—and the rearrangements in our scholarly thinking that boundary crossing can achieve today.

Editions

Stevenson poses a challenge to the researcher even as he constitutes an opportunity for the popular reader: he published all over the place. His works are available in many editions and easily accessible secondhand books (even in first editions) and as trade paperbacks. But what is the teacher or scholar in search of an authoritative text to do?

As an essayist and short story writer, Stevenson placed pieces in journals ranging from *Longman's Magazine* ("A Gossip on Romance") to *Temple Bar* ("A Lodging for the Night"), the *Cornhill* ("Child's Play"), and the *Portfolio* ("Notes on Edinburgh"). He gathered these pieces into volumes, revising as he went: "Child's Play" ends up in *Virginibus Puerisque*; "Notes on Edinburgh" becomes *Edinburgh: Picturesque Notes*. He serialized his most famous novels in publications like *Young Folks* (*Kidnapped*) before they were published as volumes in Britain and then the United States—or sometimes in the United States and then Britain. In his later years, he was sending revisions back to Britain from Samoa, where they were processed by his sometimes interfering (if long-suffering) friend and literary editor Sidney Colvin. Obviously, the possibility for variation between texts is substantial. Here, scholars are tremendously assisted by Roger Swearingen's magisterial and precise volume *The Prose Writings of Robert Louis Stevenson: A Guide*. Swearingen tracks Stevenson's prose from its manuscripts through its serializations and anthologized forms to its authoritative editions, carefully identifying archives as he goes.

For teaching purposes, it is possible—even recommended—to allow students to search the various online marketplaces for cheap or obscure Stevenson editions. This project can lead to interesting discussion about textual variation in class, but one caveat is crucial: beware the abridged volume (except perhaps in English education classes, where it can have a practical value). There are substantial and scholarly editions of many frequently taught Stevenson texts. *Jekyll and Hyde*, as edited by Katherine Linehan (Norton, 2003), Dury (Edinburgh, 2004), and Danahay (Broadview, 2005), benefits from the particular resources of each publishing house, and each edition serves a specific classroom purpose—Dury's, for example, having a fuller apparatus, is directed more to scholarly research. For those interested in textual comparison, Stevenson's Scottish texts are available in a useful array of editions. Barnes and Noble reprints a variety of early editions, with source texts for *Kidnapped* and *Catriona* in the Library of Essential Reading chosen according to the author's last sustained revision, so far as it can be established. Menikoff uses the *Young Folks* publication of *Kidnapped* for his edition (Huntington, 1999). Classes that would benefit from a solid introduction can use the Oxford and Penguin texts, many of which are prefaced by essays from major Stevenson scholars. Those wanting to venture beyond the Stevenson canon might turn to Kennedy and Boyd's new series of Stevenson's obscure but rising texts, such as *The Wrecker*. One can select according to classroom need and interest.

There are many collected editions of Stevenson. For classroom use, paperback anthologies such as Menikoff's *The Complete Stories of Robert Louis Stevenson* and Roger C. Lewis's *The Collected Poems of Robert Louis Stevenson* are most useful. Those wanting to consider the wider range of Stevenson's work or his less known titles will want to turn to the older collected editions, which are easily accessible in American public and university libraries. I recommend in particular the edition used for all the citations in this volume, *The Works of Robert Louis Stevenson*, the Tusitala Edition, in thirty-five volumes.

The New Edinburgh Edition of *The Collected Works of Robert Louis Stevenson* will be the authoritative edition when it appears in a few years. With its careful consideration of manuscripts and early editions and its extensive scholarly apparatus, it will be *the* resource for scholars.

Stevenson on Stevenson

Stevenson discussed not only his life but his works and his theories of art, philosophy, and almost anything else in his letters. He pursued these thoughts in many important essays. Stevenson's letters are easily accessible. There are numerous early and fragmentary volumes listed at www.robert-louis-stevenson.org/letters. These helpfully give insights from Stevenson's correspondents when they are the volume editors—see for instance Stevenson's *Vailima Letters*, edited by Colvin. *The Letters of Robert Louis Stevenson*, edited by Bradford Booth and Ernest Mehew, is the authoritative edition—extensive, scholarly, thoroughly indexed, and the reference for this Approaches volume (cited as *Letters*). This is the book for research, but for more casual use or general reading, students will appreciate Mehew's *Selected Letters of Robert Louis Stevenson*. Letters more recently discovered are listed at www.robert-louis-stevenson.org.

The most useful essays by Stevenson on his work and its theories are "Ordered South" (1874; *Works* 25: 61–72); the essays in *Familiar Studies of Men and Books* (1882), particularly "Victor Hugo's Romances" (1874; 27: 1–23), "The Gospel according to Walt Whitman" (1878; 56–79), and "Henry David Thoreau" (1880; 80–105); from *Memories and Portraits* (1887), "The Foreigner at Home" (1882; 29: 1–11), "A Gossip on a Novel of Dumas's" (110–18), "A Gossip on Romance" (1882; 119–31), and "A Humble Remonstrance" (1884; 132–43); and, in *Across the Plains* (1892), "A Chapter on Dreams" (1888; 30: 41–53). Uncollected pieces include "A Note on Realism" (1883; 28: 69–75), "Books Which Have Influenced Me" (1887; 62–68), "Popular Authors" (1888; 28: 20–32), and "My First Book: *Treasure Island*" (1894; 2: xxiii–xxxi). Many are now available online. The Web site www.robert-louis-stevenson.org gives authoritative texts for the collected volumes, and new texts are constantly being uploaded there for use. Janet Adam Smith provides full texts for Stevenson's debate with James, and Norquay anthologizes Stevenson's literary opinions (*R. L. Stevenson on Fiction*).

Biographies

Biographies of Stevenson range from the "I remember him" type to magisterial works. A 1922 offering from Rosaline Orme Masson, daughter of David Masson, who was professor of rhetoric and English literature at Edinburgh University, is titled *I Can Remember Robert Louis Stevenson*. That it is much reprinted indicates an audience even today for the sentimental biography of the 1920s. The most valuable books of this type are by Stevenson's wife, Fanny Van de Grift (Osbourne) Stevenson, and his stepson, Lloyd Osbourne—not because they are less emotionally invested texts (quite the contrary) but because they give firsthand information. Over the years, authoritative Stevenson biographies have accumulated. Each also reflects its moment and special concerns, but each has its strengths. Daiches's *Robert Louis Stevenson and His World* is the most accessible for junior students. It carries Daiches's Edinburgh investment and is appropriately and liberally illustrated. Other giants in the field are J. C. Furnas's *Voyage to Windward*, James Pope Hennessy's *Robert Louis Stevenson*, Calder's

Robert Louis Stevenson: A Life Study, Frank McLynn's *Robert Louis Stevenson*, and Claire Harman's *Myself and the Other Fellow*. More objective evaluations are always in the works, yet the most interesting biographies are often the most invested—indeed, there is hardly a biographer of Stevenson without an ax to grind. Consider McLynn's opening assertion that he writes "in the firm conviction that Robert Louis Stevenson is Scotland's greatest writer of English prose," which he follows with the de rigueur gesture of demolishing Walter Scott (1). With this caveat about fond relatives and biased biographers, I recommend Margaret Mackay's *The Violent Friend: The Story of Mrs. Robert Louis Stevenson*, always reliable to stimulate argument. For those who prefer their biography unsullied by opinion, there is no better resource than J. R. Hammond's *A Robert Louis Stevenson Chronology*, which simply and elegantly outlines dates and events, indexed with works, people, and places.

Archives and Museums

The crucial guide to archives is Swearingen's *Prose Writings of Robert Louis Stevenson*. Any serious research on Stevenson's writing starts here and, with W. F. Prideaux's bibliography, then moves outward through major manuscript resources and early editions housed at Yale (Beinecke Library), Princeton, Harvard, the Huntington Library, and the National Library of Scotland. Many of these collections are now searchable online. (For the National Library of Scotland, visit www.nls.uk; for Princeton, www.princeton.edu/~rbsc/databases/; for the Huntington Library, http://catalog.huntington.org/. Consult www.robert-louis-stevenson.org for a descriptive list of further holdings.) Print catalogs include George L. McKay's six-volume reference for Yale, Harvard's *Catalogue of Books and Manuscripts of Robert Louis Stevenson in the Library of the Late Harry Elkins Widener*, and Princeton's *Robert Louis Stevenson: A Catalogue*, by A. D. Wainwright.

Many museums feature works and artifacts related to Stevenson. The Writers' Museum in Edinburgh places Stevenson in the pantheon of Scottish writers, alongside Robert Burns and Walter Scott (see www.edinburghmuseums.org.uk/Venues/The-Writers--Museum.aspx). The historic district in Monterey, California, features a number of properties related to Stevenson, including the Stevenson House (www.parks.ca.gov/default.asp?page_id=963). The Silverado Museum in Saint Helena, California, is rich in manuscript material and memorabilia from Samoa (www.silveradomuseum.org). In the nearby Robert Louis Stevenson State Park, one can follow the Stevenson Memorial Trail to the top of Mount Saint Helena. Saranac Lake, where Stevenson took the cure with Dr. Trudeau, boasts the Robert Louis Stevenson Memorial Cottage and Museum (www.robertlouisstevensonmemorialcottage.org/main.html). Stevenson's last home, in Samoa, houses the Robert Louis Stevenson Museum—with access to his grave (www.rlsmuseum.com/). The Robert Louis Stevenson Web site maintains links to these various museums. This is one British author for whom American students can go on a field trip—either in person or online.

Art and Photography

Study of Stevenson is borne up by a wealth of visual material, much of it available online. As a beloved only child in the early days of photography, he was much photographed. Images from 1854 show him in the elaborate skirts of the time; photographs from the 1870s show him as a languid, rather self-dramatizing student and in his (brief) bewigged career in the law. There are photographs by the handful from the South Seas voyages, for Lloyd Osbourne and Stevenson were fascinated by photography themselves (see Colley in this volume). In addition, because he was well known when relatively young, Stevenson was much painted and sculpted. There are famous portraits by John Singer Sargent and a medal by Augustus Saint-Gaudens. The gallery at www.robert-louis-stevenson.org contains many of these photographs, though for copyright reasons it displays fewer portraits. (But portraits too are easily findable online.)

Study of Stevenson's works is enriched by consideration of the illustrations that liberally supported them. *Kidnapped* was illustrated in *Young Folks* and illustrated anew by William Hole for later editions. (Hole also provided massive friezes for the Scottish National Portrait Gallery.) Sometimes Stevenson advised on illustration. Much of that collaboration is visible in the Stevenson Web site's archive (*The Works of Robert Louis Stevenson*). These illustrations have begun to be considered in relation to Stevenson, contemporary publication, and in their own right. Richard Hill takes the lead in these studies. There is also a trove of illustration in which Stevenson was not involved—and some of that illustration might be considered through theories of adaptation. N. C. Wyeth's color-saturated illustrations played an important role in the perception of Stevenson's texts, particularly in the United States in the early twentieth century. Story, new technology, and mass production combined to produce editions of extraordinary richness, changing and energizing the relation among text, illustration, reader, and author in ways that would not be matched until the heyday of film. Wyeth's illustrations, still often reprinted in Stevenson editions, are available online at www.ncwyeth.org/.

Popular Culture Resources

Because popular culture resources for Stevenson are without limit, I point only to the most important. First are the illustrations discussed above, just coming into their own as a subject for study; they are tremendously useful in the classroom. Illustrations of *Jekyll and Hyde* (there is a nice collection of them in Veeder and Hirsch) allow students to see how this overdetermined text oddly invites reconception as successive generations of readers try to give nuance to the opposition between Jekyll and Hyde. Films, almost beyond counting, allow a similar tracking: students can see how a story of transformation has invited and challenged depiction at the cutting edge of special effects; they can debate the cultural values inherent in the way a movie replots evil; they can consider how production values are also cultural values in the corporate project as they remark how often *Jekyll and Hyde* is remade and for what audiences. Films of particular importance are the 1920 version with John Barrymore (dir. John Stuart Robertson), the 1931 Mamoulian version, the 1941 Victor Fleming film with Spencer Tracy, Jerry Lewis's 1963 *The Nutty Professor*, Baker's 1971 *Doctor Jekyll and Sister Hyde*, and William Crain's 1976 *Dr. Black, Mr. Hyde*. Of quirky interest are versions directed by Jerry Belson, Terence Fisher, Charles Jarrott, Charles Lamont (with Bud Abbott and Lou Costello), Scott Pembroke (with Stan Laurel), Stephen Weeks (with Peter Cushing and Christopher Lee), David Wickes (with Michael Caine), David Winters (with Kirk Douglas), and James Wood. Danahay, in this volume, points to films of other texts, and Dury maintains a growing list at www.robert-louis-stevenson.org.

Children's versions of Stevenson works are particularly challenging, for they abridge, excerpt, illustrate, and put the text to music. These changes of course raise questions of adaptation, but such questions are complicated by issues of audience, community, and commerce. See Barbara Chatton's essay in this volume for some concerns and approaches. The many versions of *A Child's Garden of Verses* are especially interesting, along with comic and graphic novel versions of books like *Kidnapped*. William Jones's *Classics Illustrated* offers ways to understand Stevenson in early comics. Alan Grant's *Kidnappit*, "The First Graphic Novel in Scots" (Fitt; also released in modern English [Grant] and Gaelic [MacDhomhnaill] and supported by Scottish Arts agencies and projects), provides stellar material through which to discuss the politics of adaptation and the role of literature in constructing and maintaining an imagined community.

Electronic Resources

Stevenson has a large and growing online presence. Richard Dury has long maintained the Stevenson *Newsletter*, now transferred to the *RLS Site*, and has set up the *EdRLS Newsletter* so that colleagues may track the development of the New Edinburgh Edition. That edition itself promises to put its raw data online. Increasingly, substantial Stevenson collections are making materials electronically available. See the Web site for the Thomas Cooper Library at the University of South Carolina (*Robert Louis Stevenson*) and for the National Library of Scotland (www.nls.uk).

High school teachers will find the resources at the Association for Scottish Literary Studies Web site especially helpful (www.arts.gla.ac.uk/scotlit/asls/TeachNotes.html). The association publishes teaching notes on major Scottish texts and includes both *Kidnapped* and Stevenson's shorter fiction in its repertoire. The e-zine *The Bottle Imp*, named for a Stevenson story, gives introductions to Scottish literature in general and to Scottish contributions to specific literary genres (www.arts.gla.ac.uk/ScotLit/ASLS/SWE/TBI/). Stevenson features in many of its issues.

The primary online resource for Stevenson, and one providing portals to other authoritative sites, is www.robert-louis-stevenson.org, run by Linda Dryden from Napier University, Edinburgh. The site gives access to Stevenson works, biography, art, and photography. It numbers his friends, maps his travels, and reviews museums and collections. In addition, it archives the *Journal of Stevenson Studies*, providing PDF files of previous issues. On it Dury maintains his ongoing bibliography of Stevenson studies. This site should be the first stop for students and researchers working online, closely followed by the Thomas Cooper Library's "Islands" of Stevenson information.

Societies, Conferences, Journals

The academic study of Stevenson goes into overdrive every two years, in conferences that have wandered from Stirling to Edinburgh to Bergamo—and that will surely get to Samoa someday. Stevenson clubs, connecting popular and academic readers, prevail in places linked to the author. For instance, there is an Edinburgh Robert Louis Stevenson Club and a Monterey RLS Club. The Stevenson Society of America is based in Saranac Lake. News on societies and clubs, their meetings and conferences, is kept up-to-date at www.robert-louis-stevenson.org.

Maps

Maps are an integral part of Stevenson's life and art. The author was an incorrigible wanderer—traveling by canoe (*Inland Voyage* [*Works* 17: 3–124]) or hiking (*Travels with a Donkey in the Cevennes* [125–273]), shipping out with the emigrants from the Clyde and across America, and sailing around the South Seas. One rainy day in Braemar, his stepson claimed, "I happened to be tinting a map of an island. . . . [Stevenson] was soon elaborating the map and naming it. I shall never forget the thrill of Skeleton Island. . . ! [Or] when he wrote down the words 'Treasure Island' at the top right-hand corner!" (2: xviii [*Treasure Island*]).

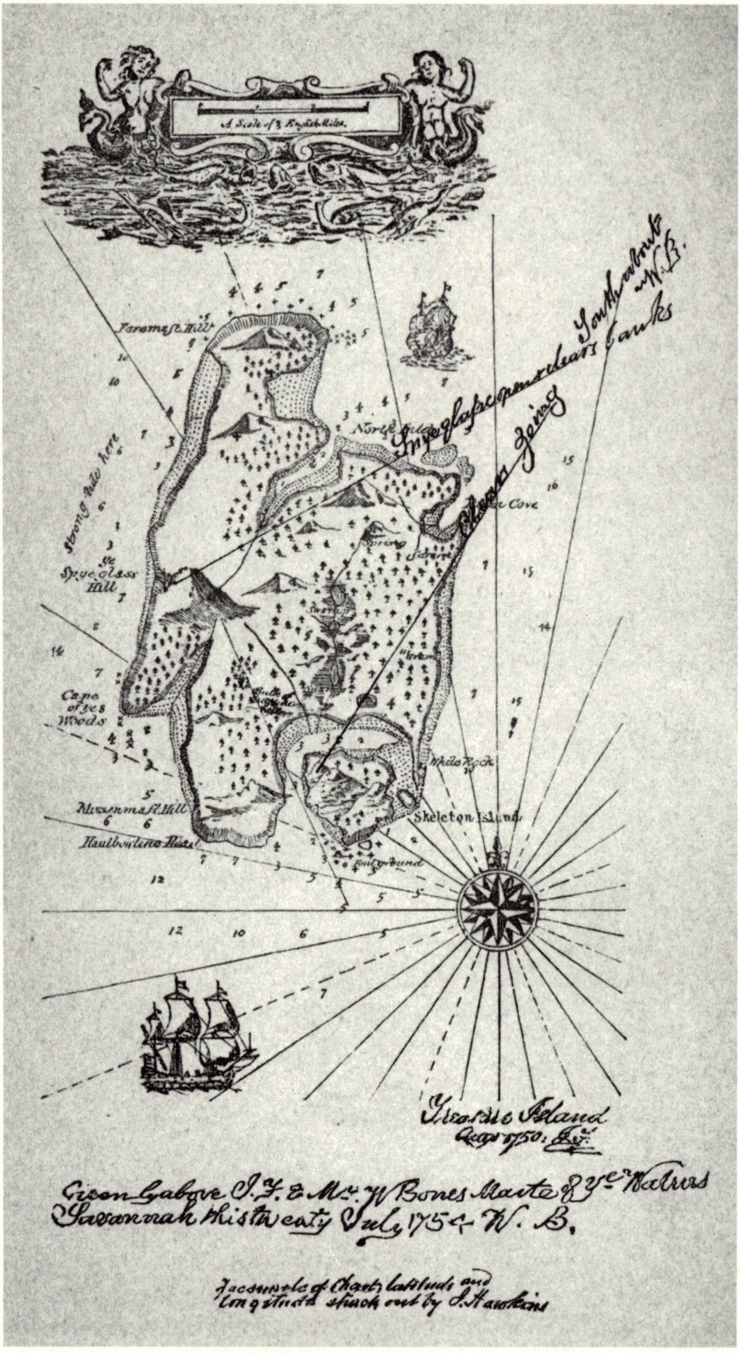

Fig. 1. Stevenson's map for *Treasure Island* (*Works* 2: frontispiece). Beinecke Rare Book and Manuscript Library, Yale University

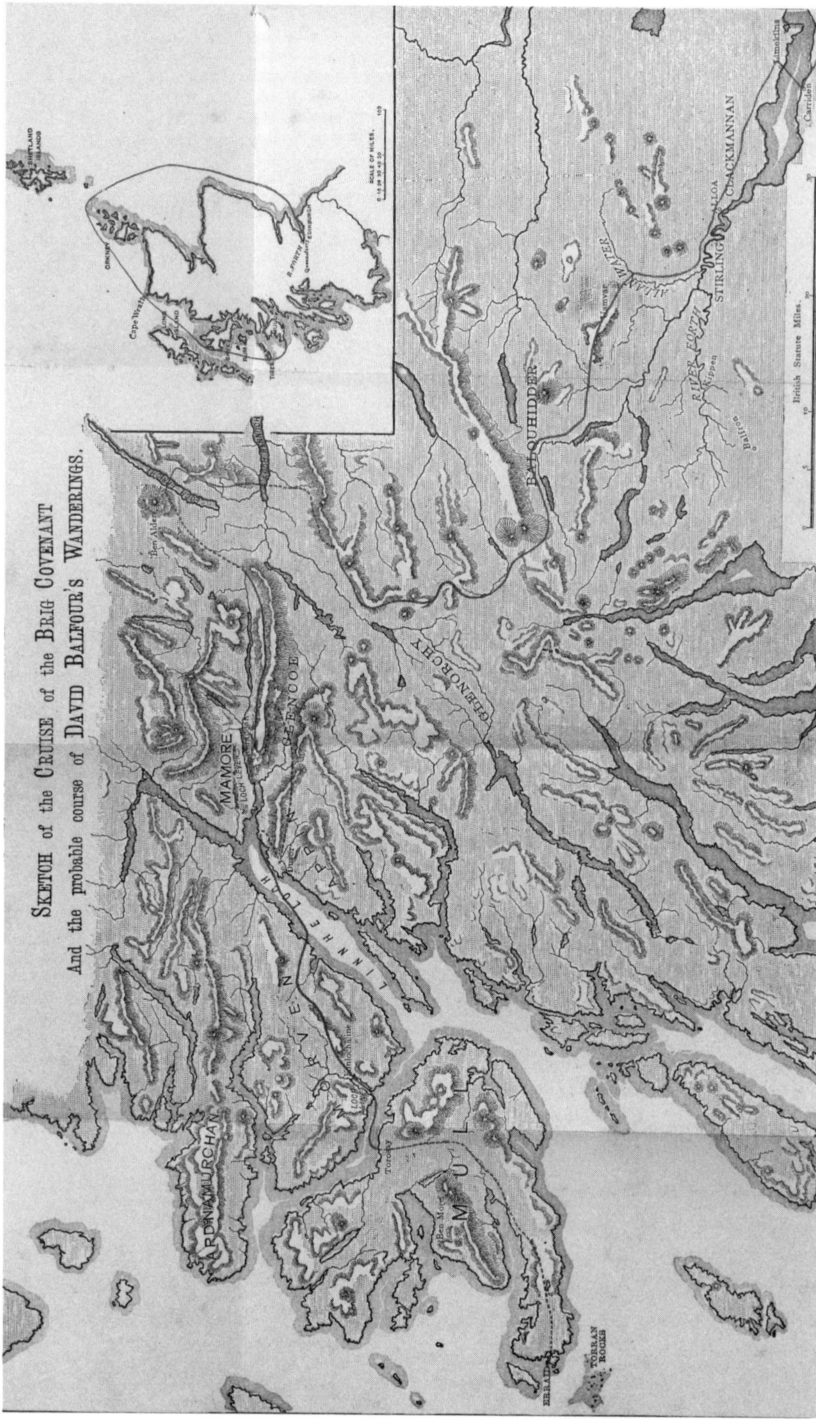

Fig. 2. David Stevenson's maps for *Kidnapped*, as requested by Robert Louis Stevenson (*Works* 6: back insert). Beinecke Rare Book and Manuscript Library, Yale University

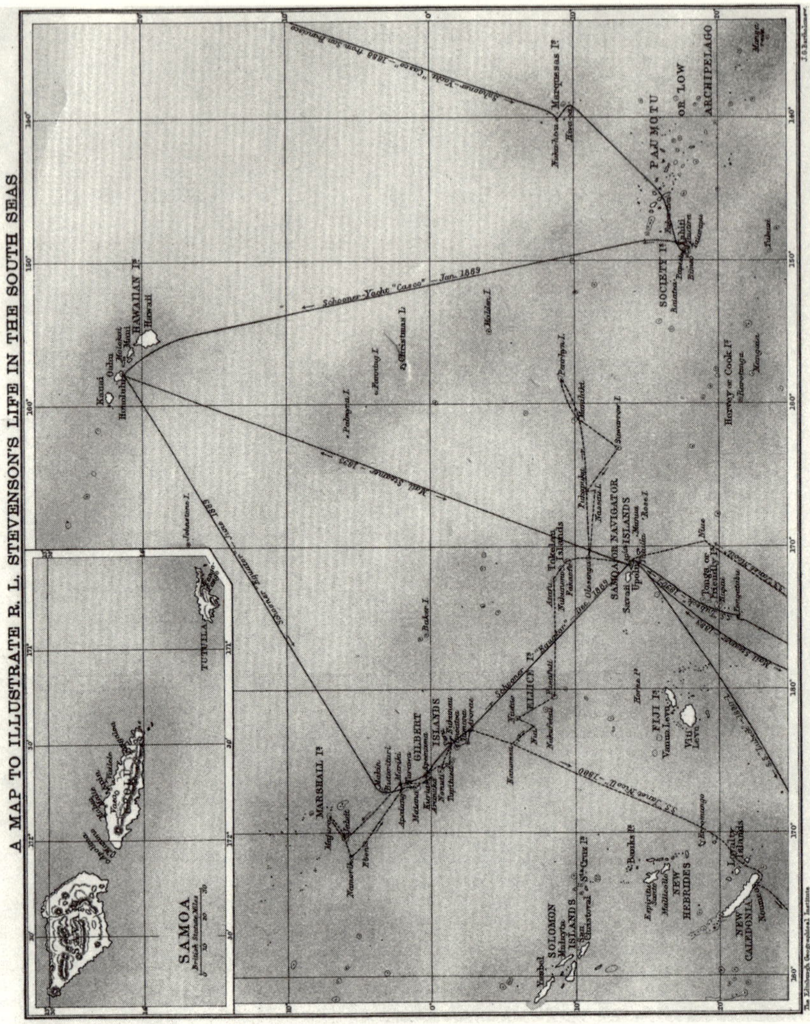

Fig. 3. Stevenson's travels in the South Seas (*Works* 20: front insert). Beinecke Rare Book and Manuscript Library, Yale University

Stevenson claimed the map as his (xxv), but in either case *Treasure Island* began with a map. Later, Stevenson would give remarkably precise instructions for the map to support *Kidnapped*, detailing the location of David Balfour's shipwreck (to be rendered in red on an inset map) and considering how to demonstrate the confusions of David's travels through Scotland on the large map: "a red line is to show the wanderings of my hero. . . . It must be sometimes dotted to show uncertainty. . . . If room can be found all the places I have named, might be named" (*Letters* 5: 230–31). Stevenson's maps often are included in editions of his works; if they are not included, they are well worth retrieving online and studying in class in relation to the discourses of fantasy and history, of the real and the romance, that his writings tend to disturb. The Robert Louis Stevenson Web site is building sets of maps from Stevenson's texts (see its page *In the Footsteps of Robert Louis Stevenson*) and also provides information about actual places. Three maps are the most famous: Stevenson's map for *Treasure Island*; "The Sketch of the Cruise of the Brig Covenant," from *Kidnapped*; and the route of his South Seas travels. They raise important questions about composition, travel, imagination, and history.

Chronology

For fuller detail, see Hammond's *Chronology*. This descriptive chronology covers major dates, persons, and events.

1850 Robert Lewis Balfour Stevenson is born in Edinburgh to Thomas Stevenson, of a family of engineers renowned for its lighthouses, and Margaret Isabella (Balfour) Stevenson, a daughter of the manse. He is a small child, soon nursed by Alison Cunningham ("Cummy"), a Calvinist. His name is subsequently changed to Louis, and he is nicknamed Smout, which means "small fry."

1866 *The Pentland Rising* is published anonymously at his father's expense.

1867 Stevenson matriculates at Edinburgh University, having studied Latin, philosophy, mathematics, and engineering.

1868 He begins to study lighthouse engineering with his father.

1870 He spends three months on the island of Earraid watching lighthouse construction.

1871 He begins to study law at Edinburgh and publishes essays in the *Edinburgh University Magazine*.

1873 He declares himself an agnostic and quarrels with his father. He publishes "On the Thermal Influence of Forests" in *Proceedings of the Royal*

Society of Edinburgh and "Roads," his first paid publication, in the *Portfolio*. He goes to London to take the English bar but instead travels on to Mentone for a rest cure.

1874 He begins to publish in the *Cornhill*.

1875 He meets W. E. Henley, who is undergoing treatment by Lister at the Royal Infirmary, Edinburgh. The two collaborate on plays like *Deacon Brodie* (perf. 1882). Stevenson is called to the Scottish bar.

1876 He travels by canoe through France with Walter Simpson. Afterward he meets Fanny Osbourne in Grez and starts essays that are later included in *Virginibus Puerisque*.

1878 He takes a walking tour in the Cévennes with a donkey as a pack animal. His *An Inland Voyage* and *Edinburgh: Picturesque Notes* are published.

1879 *Travels with a Donkey in the Cevennes* is published. Against the advice of friends and without the knowledge of his parents, he sets off for the United States, traveling one level above steerage both to save money and to acquire good material. His account of this voyage will be suppressed by his father. He takes the emigrant train to Monterey in quest of Fanny, who is not yet divorced. He writes articles for the *Monterey Californian*.

1880 He marries Fanny in May and honeymoons in an abandoned cabin at Silverado. They return to Britain, then head to Davos for Stevenson's health.

1881 *Virginibus Puerisque* is published. Stevenson writes Scottish stories and begins *Treasure Island* in the highlands. He agrees to the novel's advance serialization in *Young Folks*.

1882 "The Foreigner at Home" appears in the *Cornhill*. He publishes *New Arabian Nights* and *Familiar Studies of Men and Books*. He visits France for his health.

1883 His account of traveling across the United States begins to appear in *Longman's*—it later takes book form as *Across the Plains* (1892). *Treasure Island* is published.

1884 *The Silverado Squatters* is published. Still ill, Stevenson takes up residence at Bournemouth. He writes "A Humble Remonstrance" in response to Henry James's "The Art of Fiction." The writers begin a fast friendship. Stevenson begins to collaborate with Fanny on *The Dynamiter*.

1885 *A Child's Garden of Verses*, *More New Arabian Nights* (*The Dynamiter*), and *Prince Otto* (a complex tale of gender and politics) are published. The Stevensons move in Bournemouth to Skerryvore, bought for them by Thomas Stevenson. Stevenson writes *Strange Case of Dr Jekyll and Mr Hyde*—after a nightmare, he claims.

1886 *Jekyll and Hyde* is published. In May, *Kidnapped* begins serialization in *Young Folks* and is then published as a book. Stevenson plans a sequel.

1887 He writes on international copyright to the *Times* and publishes *The Merry Men*, *Memories and Portraits*, and *Underwoods*. His father dies. Stevenson signs a contract for *David Balfour* (which will not appear for some years). He and his family (including his mother) set out for the United States, where he is feted as the author of *Jekyll and Hyde*. They go to Saranac Lake for his health. Lloyd begins *A Game of Bluff*, on which, as *The Wrong Box*, Stevenson will collaborate. He begins *The Master of Ballantrae*.

1888 *The Black Arrow* is published. He embarks for the Pacific islands, planning a seven-month trip and supported with a contract from the American publisher S. S. McClure to publish the resultant essays. He travels through the Marquesas to Tahiti.

1889 He settles at Waikiki and studies Hawaiian. He publishes a letter on colonial politics in the islands. He visits the leper colony at Molokai. *The Master of Ballantrae* and *The Wrong Box* are published, and he begins another collaboration with Lloyd, *The Wrecker*. The family travels on to the Gilbert Islands, then Samoa.

1890 He settles on Upolu and buys land that will be Vailima. He visits Australia (Sydney) then New Zealand (Auckland). A second tour takes him to the Gilbert and Ellis Islands and the Marshall Islands. His pamphlet defending Father Damien, a missionary to the lepers, is published. After another tour to Sydney, Lloyd returns to Britain to sell Skerryvore. *In the South Seas* is published. Stevenson will continue trips around the South Seas.

1891 *In the South Seas* is serialized in Australia, the United States, and Britain. Stevenson's South Sea stories appear—"The Bottle Imp" in the *New York Herald*. He negotiates with Tauchnitz for publication of his works.

1892 He returns to the *Kidnapped* sequel, named *David Balfour*. *The Beach of Falesá* begins serialization in *Illustrated London News* and is promptly published as a book. *The Wrecker* is published. All year, he writes letters to the *Times* on Samoan politics. He publishes *A Footnote to History* on the subject.

1893 *David Balfour* (*Catriona* in the United Kingdom) is published. *The Ebb-Tide* is serialized in *Today*. He publishes *Island Nights Entertainments*, which includes *The Beach of Falesá*, "The Isle of Voices," and "The Bottle Imp."

1894 He plans the Edinburgh edition of his works with Charles Baxter; Sidney Colvin will edit. *The Amateur Emigrant*, Stevenson's realist account of his emigrant voyage, once suppressed by his father, now heads toward print (1895). Stevenson publishes "My First Book: *Treasure Island*" in the *Idler*. *The Ebb-Tide* is published as a book. He is writing *Weir of Hermiston*. He dies of a cerebral hemorrhage on 3 December, having exclaimed, "Has my face changed?"

Part Two

APPROACHES

Introduction

"Read more books, kids—but not this one." So ran the headline in the Edinburgh *Scotsman* newspaper when *Strange Case of Dr Jekyll and Mr Hyde* was handed out free in schools and libraries in celebration of Edinburgh as UNESCO City of Literature (Cornwell). The motto of this MLA Approaches volume is precisely the reverse: read *these* books—especially the ones your parents told you not to, and while you're at it, take a second look at the ones they *did* allow you to read! The problem for an editor of approaches to Stevenson is that he poses so many and varied challenges to literary and cultural norms that it is difficult to exclude anything but impossible to include everything. Equally, there are numerous ways to arrange the materials, each way emphasizing different aspects of Stevenson, allowing different creative uses of his work in class, encouraging different recombinations of ideas by faculty members and students, and putting forward different critical assumptions.

The survey process that accompanies every MLA volume here provided guidance. Respondents to the Stevenson survey foregrounded different (if predictable) texts in class according to their research preferences and the curricular requirements of their institutions. *Jekyll and Hyde*, *Kidnapped*, *The Master of Ballantrae*, *A Child's Garden of Verses*, and the short stories (e.g., "Thrawn Janet," "Markheim") led the way. *Travels with a Donkey*, *New Arabian Nights*, *Virginibus Puerisque*, and the debate with Henry James over the art of fiction were much taught too. At the same time, respondents clearly acknowledged ongoing shifts in Stevenson's classroom relevance and interest: the South Seas writings, both essays and tales, were fascinating to students and essential in class, but needed support from volumes such as this one. Stevenson's travel writing in general was seen as increasingly important in our age of nonfiction prose.

The survey also showed that Stevenson looms large outside the literary studies classroom across the United States. His prose challenges in the composition classroom; his collaborative writing raises issues for creative writing; his children's writing poses questions about rhetorical triangles for young children and teenagers and thus for elementary and English education teachers in training.

Even as respondents felt that Stevenson's versatility invited them to pursue his works well beyond the classroom canon, they agreed that his works are inviting because of their challenges to established norms but also difficult to teach for that reason. What is one to make of an author whose children's books "fascinated a Prime Minister" (according to the *Pall Mall Gazette*'s advertisement for "The Body Snatcher" ["Christmas Extra," 5 Dec. 1884: 16]) but whose adult volumes were more provocative than Thomas Hardy's—and who yet found Hardy's *Tess of the D'Urbervilles* reprehensible (*Letters* 7: 450)? How is one to categorize an author who lived in so many places that he belongs to all or none and who experimented in so many genres that in effect he critiques many of them? This Approaches volume argues that our teaching and research prove most meaningful when knowledge is both established and contested—when conclusions challenge themselves. Stevenson encourages us to move beyond the generic and biographical pigeonholes that criticism visits on any author. His wide-ranging, porous, and abbreviated oeuvre (he died at forty-four) welcomes narrow attention in fields where he excels and expansive thinking across texts, times, places, genres, and lives.

The essays of this volume address a variety of pedagogical needs from this perspective. Its authors range from the doyens of Stevenson studies, with all their thoughtful experience, to faculty members seeing the classroom for the first time and Stevenson with fresh eyes. "Background" provides information that underpins our current understanding of Stevenson but complicates the clichés of Stevenson study—as more than one respondent pointed out, an author so widely remembered and so beloved is wound about with myth. This section tracks the progress of an author claimed by Scotland, England, the United States, and Samoa but examines the complex motivations that drove him—motivations not necessarily Romantic, pathetic, or politically correct. The "Scottish" Stevenson contrasts with a Stevenson arguably American in literary sensibility. Stevenson's Scots turns out to be a matter of strategy and negotiation in the political and cultural marketplace. The romance of his image is carefully constructed in art and photography, not least by the author himself as part of his ongoing debate about identity.

In the second section, "Theoretical Contexts," contributors locate Stevenson in the major debates of his time—to which he was a substantial contributor. Stevenson and James together broke free of criticism's reductive investment in binary thinking (realism/romance). This Stevenson challenges narrow definitions of the modern and postmodern. Indeed, close attention to such troubling texts as *The Ebb-Tide* and *The New Arabian Nights* suggests that he may belong within today's shifting fields of theory, which he often prefigured and which he helped develop through, for instance, his complex narrative strategies (narratology), his writings on South Seas exploration (the postcolonial), or on the indeterminacies of gender (queer theory).

"Literary Contexts" pursues Stevenson's role in four major areas: genre fiction, travel literature, children's literature, and the essay. Colleagues will find both the sources that shaped Stevenson's writing and information and argument about how he directed and energized these genres—and subgenres like detective or gothic fiction—for subsequent writers.

All the essays in this volume keep to the fore our shared commitment to the classroom and offer careful advice. Surveyed instructors wanted reliable background information and a clearer sense of Stevenson's role in the traditions of theory and literature; they also asked for specifics about how to bring Stevenson's texts into the classroom and how to activate their complexities to disturb what we all take for granted. They pointed out that there is more to Stevenson than is easily reached in the standard texts and usual courses. Luckily, our many and various respondents together made clear that Stevenson already is taught in unexpected places and with important results. So in this next section, colleagues share their own experiences, difficulties, and successes.

"Classroom Conventions and Challenges" takes on student expectations and gives them a new pedagogical fillip. Here we find Stevenson the Scot, with all the problems history and language can pose for today's classroom. But from difficulty comes opportunity: Scottish Stevenson turns transatlantic. Then romance challenges as a disturbing discourse of power. The South Seas, no warmer bohemia, snap to life through photography. Jekyll and Hyde pose a problem of duality that requires a second look. Victorian science problematizes science fiction. Stevenson the collaborator questions the whole notion of literary authority.

"Course Contexts" considers particular texts in specific classrooms. Even as readers turn to the text, the question, or the course level of their particular interest, they can at the same time gain a detailed understanding of Stevenson's role in the wider curriculum. Teachers of *A Child's Garden* can exploit students' vague childhood familiarity with the verses in the literary survey. Survey courses can use Stevenson's American travel writings to break down the binaries of English/American, high/low culture, and author/editor. English education majors must tangle with the author's young adult literature; students of elementary education must grapple with Stevenson's remarkable, encouraging, but sometimes troubling persistence into twenty-first-century childhood lore. Students in diversity classes can benefit from observing how the author attempts to adopt a South Seas perspective. His essays model in the composition classroom; the short stories challenge creative writers. The theory classroom can be illuminated by asking what theory derives from a "children's" author and how it thus derives. With Stevenson's insistent variability in text and consistent questioning of literary traditions and personal identities, no one is better at generating or tying together loose ends. This author, Matthew Wickman concludes, is thus "an exemplar for anybody teaching—or hoping that his or her students will generate—serious ideas."

And here is the lesson about how to use this book. On the one hand, colleagues who read from the top will work their way from biographical backgrounds down through theoretical and literary contexts to the specific texts of their interest. Such reading layers in background information in preparation for teaching. Others may prefer to focus on a particular theme. Given that Stevenson's oeuvre challenges literary theories and cultural norms even as it presents itself for popular consumption, readers may find it useful to weave back and forth between texts and contexts as they construct their classes. And equally, this book should support the gadfly approach. Stevenson's multiplicity should allow us to drop down anywhere within this volume and land on issues and texts that challenge and engage. Each of these approaches, with the lively and different perspectives brought by each of us as readers, can only increase the opportunities for our students.

BACKGROUND

Stevenson in His Place: Scotland, England, the United States, and Samoa

Jenni Calder

> There is a sense, of course, in which all true books are books of travel.
>
> —Robert Louis Stevenson, "Walt Whitman"

Four places claim Robert Louis Stevenson to the extent of having a Stevenson museum (California has two, plus a state park named for him). Four distinct passages of the author's life were lived out in Edinburgh, California, Saranac, and Samoa. Mentone, Barbizon, Davos, Bournemouth, and a host of other places might also claim him as resident and writer. For faculty members teaching Stevenson and for students reading him, these diverse geographic contexts inform his work. But it is important to realize that although his writing conveys a strong sense of place, he often was far from a given locality when he wrote about it, producing in France *Edinburgh: Picturesque Notes*; in Monterey "The Pavilion on the Links," set in Scotland; in Bournemouth *Kidnapped*; and in the South Seas *The Wreckers*, with its San Francisco vignettes, and much of *The Master of Ballantrae*, with its upstate New York conclusion. Classes benefit from considering the productive tension generated by location as a place of origins, site of story, subject for romance, and problem posed to authorial identity. This essay lays out Stevenson's topographical biography and suggests emphases and problems that might usefully be pursued by professor and student.

Stevenson was born in Edinburgh, capital of Scotland, in 1850 and died in Upolu, Samoa, in the South Pacific, in 1894. Wherever he went, his identity as a Scot infused everything he wrote without limiting his vision or his openness to experience, while his acceptance of exile and empathetic response to new places and new people enriched and illuminated his writing. Few Europeans writing in the second half of the nineteenth century shared his diversity of interest in and clarity of comment about other countries.

An only child, Stevenson grew up in a peculiarly Scottish environment of professional aspiration and religious conviction: his middle-class, Presbyterian parents and devoted nurse instilled in him an awareness of sin and an acceptance of responsibility. Frequently ill, he used his imagination to compensate for his constrained activities and in his sickbed entertained himself with fantasies of travel and adventure. These fantasies were enriched by his immersion in Scotland's history. He was growing up in a city reverberating with past exploits and personalities, which fed his appetite for storytelling. His earliest travels were in the city itself, first on walks with Alison Cunningham, his nurse, then as a young man exploring Edinburgh's underworld, a literal and metaphoric labyrinth of dark wynds (alleyways), ancient buildings, and sudden vistas of hills and water. Family holidays and later his own independent travels embedded him in the Scottish landscape and its history, particularly in the Borders and the Highlands. Perhaps above all, his father's profession as lighthouse and harbor engineer introduced Stevenson to Scotland's extensive coastline and its cliffs, islands, and skerries. He accompanied his father on inspections of the many lighthouses constructed by the Stevensons. Thus he grew up with the knowledge that the sea played a key role in Scotland's past as well as in Stevenson family history and understood that for the seafarer the land could be as dangerous as the sea—as demonstrated in *Kidnapped*.

By the time Stevenson was a student at Edinburgh University, the narrow outlook of his parents' milieu had become a burden that he longed to throw off. The urge to broaden his experience went hand in hand with an urge to write, which grew into a determination to make writing his career rather than enter his father's profession. In the 1870s, Edinburgh had lost its edge as a creative center of writing and publishing, and London was seen as the cultural capital of Scotland as well as of England. It was to London that Stevenson looked both for publishing opportunities and for like-minded writers. It had a magnetic pull, and most of his literary friendships were London-based.

Thus travel, imagined and actual, became a driving force in Stevenson's literary development. His first step as a professional writer, the publication in *Macmillan's Magazine* of his essay "Ordered South" (May 1874; *Works* 25: 61–72), was the product of a stay in Mentone in the south of France but also about the act of travel itself. France was a favored destination. Through his artist cousin Bob (R. A. M.) Stevenson, he was introduced to artists' colonies at Barbizon and Grez-sur-Loing, both near Fontainebleau, and to bohemian life in Paris. His first book, *An Inland Voyage* (1878; *Works* 17: 3–124), described a river-and-canal canoeing trip from Belgium into France with his friend Walter Simpson. Stevenson relished being on the move, whether on foot or on the water, both for its own sake and because it was an unending source of new experience and fresh incentive. Moreover his travels as a reader in French literature influenced both his response to France and his development as a writer.

Along with *An Inland Voyage*, Stevenson's next two books laid the foundation on which his career was built. *Edinburgh: Picturesque Notes* (1879; *Works* 26: 133–97) revealed his ambivalent love for his native city and the depth of its emotional and intellectual imprint, while *Travels with a Donkey in the Cevennes* (1879; *Works* 17: 131–253) transported Stevenson to an environment that was unfamiliar yet at the same time connected him to his roots: he recognized parallels in both landscape and history. In all three books we can see emerging a talent for blending the personal with history and topography, a talent strikingly present in his Scottish fiction and continuing to develop when he reached the South Seas.

It was at Grez-sur-Loing that Stevenson met his future wife, Fanny Osbourne. An American raised on the American frontier, she too was a wanderer, having escaped an unhappy marriage to study as an artist in Paris. Here was an unconventional woman, exotic in looks, background, and personality and sharing his appetite for adventure. Journeys would become an integral feature of their personal and literary relationship. Stevenson's tramp in the Cévennes was followed by the journey that was probably the most momentous of his life, when in August 1879 he precipitately set off for California to join Fanny, who had returned there. He was leaving Europe for the first time—and of course his experiences became a book.

Students should be reminded that Stevenson was making a journey that thousands of Scots had made before him, as there had been heavy emigration from Scotland to North America for over a century. Indeed he had witnessed the distressing departure of emigrant ships from the West Highlands—described in *Kidnapped*—and understood its impact in the form of abandoned communities. *The Amateur Emigrant* (1880) recounts leaving the River Clyde on the SS *Devonia*. Both "anxious to see the worst of emigrant life" and lacking money, Stevenson traveled second-class, which afforded only a little more privacy than steerage (*Works* 18: 1). He was profoundly affected by the experience of crossing the Atlantic in the company of men and women "unable to prevail against circumstances in the one land . . . fleeing pitifully to another" (10). He was aware that although separated from most of his fellow passengers by class and background, he shared elements of their sense of failure and their hopes for something better. He was now in his twenty-ninth year and a long way from self-sufficiency. Without the financial support of his parents, he would have had to give up his attempts to make his way as a writer.

Stevenson's transcontinental train journey from New York to California, described in *Across the Plains* (1883, 1895; *Works* 18: 1–123 [J. D. Hart's is the preferred edition]), was both traumatic and illuminating. Stevenson had always been drawn to the world of the underprivileged, but now he had no choice but to engage with the experience of the disadvantaged and to witness at first hand discrimination and abuse. In the chapter on "despised races," he examines the treatment of Native Americans and of the Chinese who on the emigrant train were segregated from the Europeans. He comments with humor and sadness on the nature of prejudice and the tendency of those who are themselves oppressed to identify, however illogically, a group they can in turn oppress. He is appalled at the emigrants' mockery of destitute Indians "over whose own hereditary continent we had been steaming all these days" (118). Such writing calls for comparison with contemporary emigrant tales and myths.

Weakened by ill health and the emotional complications of his relationship with Fanny, who was still married to a wayward husband, Stevenson in Monterey and then in San Francisco was troubled and penniless. But the situation was eventually resolved, and Stevenson and Fanny Osbourne were married in San Francisco in May 1880. They immediately set off on an adventure, heading north to honeymoon in a deserted mining camp on Mount Saint Helena, an experience exuberantly recounted in *The Silverado Squatters* (1883; *Works* 18: 151–247).

This first visit to the United States changed his life and his writing. He returned to Scotland later that year with an increased commitment to authorship, but his health was still fragile, and he would remain financially dependent on his parents for several more years. The hostile Scottish climate drove him to seek environments more suited to his vulnerable physical state, a search that took him to Davos in Switzerland, the south of France, and Bournemouth on England's south coast, with only summer visits to Scotland. This nomadic existence suited him and his talent for connecting with place and people wherever he found himself. Although the search for health was the overt reason for this peripatetic life, it is clear that it was also driven by restlessness and curiosity. When for the first time he and Fanny settled into a house of their own, in Bournemouth, he was ambivalent about the bourgeois implications of becoming a householder. Conventional domesticity was part of what he had escaped in the city of his birth. The very name of the house, Skerryvore, after one of the Stevensons' most remote and dramatic Hebridean lighthouses, only accentuated the incompatibility.

This vein of ambivalence permeates Stevenson's writing. Students can track how, again and again, he releases his characters from a conventional, limited environment and explores how they fare in unusual circumstances—at sea, stranded on an island, in a wild landscape. But their experience is measured against the stability, however distanced or imagined, of a settled existence. *Kidnapped*'s David Balfour will become a solid, professional man (1886); Wiltshire in *The Beach of Falesá* will never leave the South Seas but dreams of running a country pub in England (1892; *Works* 13: 1–75 [Menikoff's *Beach* is the preferred edition]).

Stevenson inherited this tension, not only growing up in a city where respectability cohabited with an insalubrious underworld that it tried to ignore but also absorbing from his father's profession a heightened sense of contrast. The family of Thomas Stevenson lived in the heart of Edinburgh's relatively safe New Town, but his work exposed him, and on occasion his son, to the dangers of Scotland's treacherous coast and volatile weather (see Bathurst). His son's acute awareness of the heroism of those who worked to make Scotland's coastal waters safe is best expressed in Stevenson's *Records of a Family of Engineers* (1896; *Works* 19: 155–330) but is also reflected in letters and poems. Although many Victorian writers, Charles Dickens preeminently, dealt with the threats that lay beyond the domestic front door, Stevenson took himself and his characters to new frontiers of experience.

After the death of his father, Stevenson again embarked for the United States, this time with Fanny, his mother, and his stepson, Lloyd. By 1887 Stevenson was an established author, well known in London literary circles and to the public. His arrival in the United States this time brought a clash of incongruities. He was lionized by the press and propelled into celebrity status as a result of the huge success of *Strange Case of Dr Jekyll and Mr Hyde*, published the previous year. It was very different from his arrival eight years earlier, when he was unknown, penniless, and struggling. He prepared to spend the winter in the Adirondacks, to attend the clinic that the eminent lung physician E. L. Trudeau had established at Saranac Lake. Stevenson relished the pioneering spirit there: the challenging environment, the winter temperatures way below zero. The Stevensons' rented house and their life in it were fairly basic. Saranac was frontier territory, and the Adirondacks reminded Stevenson of the Highlands.

Stevenson's new celebrity meant that he was much in demand, and here lay the incongruity at the heart of his life at Saranac. In this rugged environment he was, he wrote to the critic William Archer, "a salaried party . . . a *bourgeois*," as he had been signed up to write regularly for *Scribner's Magazine*; "I am like to be a millionaire if this goes on, and be publicly hanged at the social revolution: well, I would prefer that to dying in my bed; and it would be a godsend to my biographer, if ever I have one" (*Letters* 6: 32). In Bournemouth, Stevenson was uneasy at having lapsed into respectable domesticity; in Saranac he was apologizing for having a regular income. At the same time he rejoiced in it. "[Times] are changed since the Lothian Road," he wrote to his Edinburgh friend Charles Baxter, referring to one of the city's main thoroughfares. "[Well] the Lothian Road was grand fun too: I could take an afternoon of it with great delight. But I'm awfü grand, noo, and lang may it last!" (58). "Awfü grand," maybe, but he was reminding his Edinburgh friend, as he often did, that his Scots identity was as strong as ever.

Money enabled Stevenson to revive a long-held dream of sailing in the South Seas, tales of which had entranced him since childhood. Now there was a realistic prospect of spending time at sea in a kind climate with the promise of new and invigorating experiences. June 1889 found RLS (as he was always known) and Fanny Stevenson in San Francisco completing arrangements for hiring the yacht *Casco*, and on 28 June, with RLS, Fanny, Lloyd, and RLS's mother on board, the *Casco* slipped out of San Francisco harbor on the start of a Pacific voyage from which the writer would never return to the United States or to Scotland.

At sea, Stevenson felt at home, in good health, and energized. A month of voyaging brought the first landfall: Nukahiva in the Marquesas Islands. He was on deck at daybreak to watch the mountains loom out of the diminishing darkness, mountains that reminded him of Scottish Highland landscapes at the same time as being tantalizingly exotic. This blend of familiar and alien challenged and delighted him. The next port of call was Fakarava in the Dangerous Archipelago, whose name indicated the treacherous nature of this collection of atolls and half-submerged reefs. During this leg of the voyage, on deck at night observing the stars and the steersman by the binnacle lamp, Stevenson had a sudden vision of Edinburgh's Drummond Street, a favorite haunt as a student. "It came on me like a flash of lightning," he wrote; "I simply returned thither, and into the past" (*Letters* 6: 207). This memory triggered a reflection on how far he had come since that time, personally and professionally as well as in miles. He thought of his youth, when he "feared I should make a mere shipwreck" (207), and now here he was, on a ship threading its way through dangerous waters, a family man and successful author but with a prospect of shipwreck that was not at all metaphoric. Poems like his "The Tropics Vanish" can allow students in class to work through this closeness of past and present experience.

Such a vision, suddenly present and vividly described, underlines how Scotland remained in the consciousness of Stevenson even as he immersed himself in new surroundings and experiences. This dual awareness informed all his writing in his Pacific years and spurred him to look for similarities and make connections at the same time as he was embracing difference. This gift characterized his response to the islands and the island peoples he encountered. *In the South Seas* (1896; *Works* 20) links Gaelic and Kanaka, both barbaric languages to many late Victorians, and laments the passing of island cultures eroded by the incursions of colonialist activity. Stevenson makes analogies between the disappearing traditions of Polynesia and Melanesia and the erosion of Scotland's clan society; his understanding of Scotland's history enabled him to identify parallels and establish a rapport with the islanders he encountered. In Tahiti, he developed a friendship with a local chief, Ori a Ori, and his sister, Princess Moe, who provided wonderful hospitality and care—Stevenson was ill for some of the time he was there. He had the opportunity to observe Polynesian life at close quarters, to note island customs and hear island stories. He reciprocated with traditional stories from Scotland. This was, he believed, the most rewarding kind of cultural exchange, the mutual confirmation of identity with stories organic to place and history. It highlighted, yet again, the shared territory of human experience, and it translated into stories like "The Isle of Voices" and "The Bottle Imp," with their understanding of indigenous voices and the problems of colonialism.

The voyage of the *Casco* came to an end in Honolulu, but it wasn't the end of Stevenson's Pacific journeys. During his five-month stay in Hawai'i, Stevenson drew *The Master of Ballantrae* to a close in distant New York State and visited the leper island of Molokai, which resulted in his championing in print the much criticized Father Damien, who ran the colony. In late June 1889, the

Stevensons left Honolulu on the *Equator*, a trading ship that plied among the islands collecting copra, the staple of South Sea commerce. This voyage took them to the Gilbert Islands (Kiribati), where they had prolonged stays at Butaritari and Apemama and gained an insight into the commercial life of the islands and its effect on the native populations, an insight that would be put to good use in his writing—most notably, in *The Beach of Falesá* and *The Ebb-Tide*. The Stevensons arrived at Apia in Samoa with no intention to linger, as they were bound for Australia, but in a few weeks Stevenson became the owner of four hundred acres of land and was excitedly planning the house he would build on it. He continued on to Sydney, extended his experience of Pacific voyaging on a grubby, cramped little steamer, the *Janet Nichol*, and returned to Apia in October 1890. There Stevenson and his family took up residence in the home they called Vailima, where he would spend the rest of his life.

There was no plan to settle in Samoa, no decision not to return to the United States or the United Kingdom, but there were good reasons to stay in the Pacific. The climate suited Stevenson. Despite bouts of illness, he was in consistently better health than ever in his life. He was writing energetically: magazine articles, fiction, poetry, history, and of course the letters that contain his most vivid and immediate descriptions of life ten thousand miles from Scotland. He was now chief breadwinner for a considerably extended family, and it made sense to settle them somewhere. Fanny had had her fill of life at sea. Vailima was an accident: there happened to be land available and a persuasive agent keen to sell. But having made the decision to purchase, Stevenson threw himself enthusiastically into his multiple roles as paterfamilias, provider, land improver, author, and advocate and adviser to both family and the wider clan he had gathered around him.

During his Edinburgh youth, the South Seas nourished dreams of escape from the restraints and pressures of middle-class Edinburgh life and its unkind climate. But he had no wish to abandon Scotland or the city of his birth, and in effect he took both with him. They continued to imprint his life, his thinking, and his writing. In the Pacific islands he could abandon the requirements of polite Victorian society, wander barefoot, adopt an eccentric style of dress, participate in native customs, and live in the eye of constant new experiences. But Victorian society hovered at his elbow, just as Scotland directed much of his creative energy even when he was writing about people and places on the other side of the world. For the laird of Vailima, life was beset with hazards—practical, personal, and professional. There were tensions, but there was also an inspiring fusion of cultural disparities, of past and present, of the exotic and the quotidian, which kept him alert to new horizons and which make his later works unique classroom reading.

In his four years in Samoa he engaged with island life, culture, and politics and wrote about them directly and indirectly. At the same time he produced some of his most rigorous Scottish fiction and was planning more when he died. Two of his last works, *The Ebb-Tide* (1894; *Works* 14: 1–140) and *Weir of Her-*

miston (1896; *Works* 16: 1–124), powerfully express features that were organic to his writing from the start: his passion for vagabondage, his sensitivity to place, and the depth and ambivalence of his Scottish identity. Faculty members and students alike, whether they study *Jekyll and Hyde*, *The Amateur Emigrant*, or Stevenson's letters on Samoan politics to the *Times* and whether they focus on realism or romance, must keep in mind the problems and potentials of the author in place.

Scotland: Politics, Religion, Literature

Penny Fielding

To read Stevenson in terms of Scottish literature may require adjustment of literary contours that many students take for granted. If students have a sense of the history of the nineteenth-century novel before Stevenson, it usually comprises Jane Austen, the Brontës, Charles Dickens, and George Eliot and hovers around ideas of social and psychological realism in the presentation of close-knit, localized, contemporaneous societies. To understand Stevenson we need to add both the romance mode and the temporal sweep of Walter Scott to that lineage (parts of a tradition inherited by Dickens and Eliot too in their historical novels).

Scottish history may be unfamiliar to classes or else familiar in the wrong way. The year 1745 represents a largely Scottish Jacobite (Stuart and Catholic) rebellion against the House of Hanover—installed as the British monarchy in 1714 following the 1707 parliamentary Act of Union between England and Scotland. It is a much more important date for Scottish literature than for other anglophone literatures. Its survival in popular culture—which tends to be how most undergraduates receive it—is in images of the romanticization of the Highlands and "Bonnie Prince Charlie" (sometimes anachronistically fighting alongside a swashbuckling and nationalist version of Rob Roy from the earlier Jacobite uprising of 1715). Most students, then, will need help with the historical context as well as with the historical novel, but the two can usefully be taught in relation with each other: we can use the development of the novel as a form to explore how historicism is important for national autoethnographies and sensibilities, a historicism in this case understood not only through Scottish but also through British forms of national identity.

One way of approaching this question is to introduce students to the contours of the national tale, in which the protagonist sets off from England, or sometimes Lowland Scotland, to encounter the wild, peripheral, Celtic, Gaelic-speaking people of Ireland or the Scottish Highlands. (It is a good idea to make clear to students that three languages were spoken in nineteenth-century Scotland: English, Scots, and Gaelic.) Through the romance space of improbable adventure, the hero learns about cultural difference and forges alliances (usually marriage) that result in a greater British unity. A course designed on this model could include Sydney Owenson's (Lady Morgan's) *The Wild Irish Girl* (1806) and Christian Isobel Johnstone's *Clan-Albin* (1815), but the most important point of comparison for Stevenson is Walter Scott. In tracing with undergraduates a line between Scott, or the national tale as a genre, and Stevenson, there will be a danger of oversimplification, as the historical novel itself directs the focus to large structures of history. The best way forward is to use specific examples, and the most obvious suggestion is to pair clearly contrasting novels such as Scott's *Waverley* (1814) and Stevenson's *The Master of Ballan-*

trae (1888), both set during and after the Jacobite rebellion of 1745. Here students could trace two radically different trajectories of historical plotting: one in which national divisions are viewed through the eyes of Edward Waverley, a protagonist only partly aware of historical process moving toward the possibility of national union, and one in which the violent disruptions of civil war fragment the historical context so that neither a historical overview nor a political resolution is possible.

Waverley moves its readers through distant but recognizable history (we see the effects, not the action, of the Jacobite rebellion); escorts us through the Highlands, where we witness the different cultural practices of the Gaelic-speaking people; offers a complex but clearly nuanced reading of the politics of late-eighteenth-century Britain; and suggests a resolution through the marriage of the English Waverley and Rose, daughter of the Jacobite Baron Bradwardine. *The Master of Ballantrae*, on the other hand, follows the division of the Durie family between Jacobite and Hanoverian factions on expedient rather than ideological grounds (a coin toss decides allegiance in order to hedge the family's political bets), an array of partial narrators and different narrative forms, and the geographic dispersal of characters without any sense (as in the national tale) of tracing a space that could be understood through a unifying principle like Enlightenment or progress.

If a class is using the comparison between Scott and Stevenson, more advanced students might be introduced to the theory of the historical novel with a seminal text like Georg Lukács's *The Historical Novel*. Lukács, taking Scott as his most important example, argues that what happens in a novel, the individual actions and experiences of its characters, can be understood only in relation to the totality of historical process (for Lukács, a Marxist interpretation of history; for Scott, the inevitable movement of stadial history from primitive tribes to commercial modernity). Set against this model, Stevenson's novel represents a modern denial of these forms of historical process and totality. The novel works to fragment and obfuscate historical structures in a world of national and global confusion: readers often cannot tell which side characters are on, the novel shifts so restlessly between causes, political positions, personal attractions, and places. An insistently peripatetic novel (I often ask students simply to list the localities that figure in the plot, which range from Scotland to India to America), *Master* addresses not national identity but global fluidity and fractured national identities. Where Scott's novels seem to lead to the historical future of progress and improvement in Scotland, critics see in Stevenson the end of a distinct Highland culture without hope of assimilation (see Calder, "Figures," esp. 127–29; J. Reid, *Robert Louis Stevenson* 130–31).

Another strategy, one that doesn't call on students to read a whole Scott novel before beginning to compare him with Stevenson, is to contrast *Master* with chapter 2 of *The Bride of Lammermoor* (1819): a broad historical panorama where the aristocratic, doomed Ravenswood family gives way to the new, legalistic, professional order in the form of the Ashtons, a move that can be tracked clearly in the landscape (the decayed Ravenswood property), political forces (the Ravenswoods' ruinous support for James II), and the social order (Sir William Ashton's professional success through the law). Whereas Scott lays these patterns down from the outset, Stevenson's novel gives no clear sense of the structuring forces of history. Edgar, the master of Ravenswood, might usefully be compared with James, the master of Ballantrae: it is impossible to tell whose side (other than his own) James is on. Whereas *Bride* tells the story of a single, contained locality in the southeast of Scotland as it moves through the determining forces and social structures of history, *Master* is about emigration and dissipation. Far from being shaped by history, social identities become disguises or acted positions that enable the characters to cope with the demands of a new global order. Students can work through the number of disguises, poses, or caricatures the characters adopt in place of an authentic social identity: the Irish Jacobite Burke assumes the role of a stage Irishman on the pirate ship; the pirate captain is a pantomime villain masquerading under the name of William Teach (the original Blackbeard); James dresses in native clothing in India.

When students go on to read the whole of *Bride*, they can then trace ways in which Stevenson can be read in the same tradition as Scott and can see that anxieties about Scottish history were not born with modernism. Both novels drive their central characters into dead ends: Edgar vanishes into the morass of the "Kelpie's flow" (*Bride* 267–68), and the Durie brothers into graves in the American wilderness. Both novels begin with a somewhat cryptic frame narrator—Scott's antiquarian schoolmaster Peter Pattieson and Stevenson's version of himself as fictional editor, neither of whom comes upon the story entire. Peter is given "a parcel of loose scraps" from the artist Dick Tinto, "where outlines of caricatures, sketches of turrets, mills, old gables, and dove-cotes disputed the ground with his written memoranda" (14). Stevenson as editor finds the bundle of papers left by *Master*'s principal narrator, Ephraim Mackellar, consisting of Mackellar's own narrative patched up with the accounts of other characters. These prefaces throw into relief the function of novels and their sense of historical purpose. I invite students to consider the temporal synecdoche that Mackellar's edict produces: that his narrative not be read for one hundred years. Mackellar wants his account to be a story about the Durie family in the eighteenth century, yet we read it against the historical framework of the opening of his papers in the late nineteenth. This can engage students in contexts with which they may be more familiar: the fin de siècle and the decline of empire, or, in the specific case of Scotland, the Highland clearances and movement of the population to North America, Australia, and New Zealand. In its temporal disjunction this historical novel offers a form of estrangement: how can a text set in one period comment on another? I ask students to compare that staple of the imperial adventure story, the treasure-hunting, colonizing romance into the interior of a nation (the African adventures of Rider Haggard are an example), with the fate of the Durie brothers in the wilderness of upstate New York in a colony moving rapidly toward national self-determination. What is unearthed here are not the riches of empire; rather, we find the body, artificially preserved and soon to expire, of a corrupt representative of the colonizing country. Parallels can be drawn with Stevenson's explicitly anti-imperial novel *The Ebb-Tide* or with Joseph Conrad's *Heart of Darkness*.

When comparing Stevenson and Scott, we should be careful not to reduce Scott to a cheerful Unionist who offers a straightforward historical vision of the inevitable unity of Great Britain founded on the principles of the Enlightenment. As Alison Lumsden points out, both writers share a fascination with historicizing as an act of commemoration (78–85). Students might consider theories of history that address trauma in the act of memorializing and take account of the civil unrest of the late seventeenth century, the 1745 Jacobite rebellion and the ensuing disassembling of Highland culture, the depopulation of the land as a wound in history that can be only partly closed through acts of representation. A helpful focus of comparison might be the use of gravestones by both novelists. The opening of *Weir of Hermiston* (left unfinished on Stevenson's death and published in 1896; *Works* 16: 1–124) shadows that of Scott's *Tale of Old Mortality* (1816): in both novels, the historical record seems to depend on the almost obsessive activities of an old man maintaining the graves of Covenanters who died in the "Killing Time" of the 1680s. Most strikingly, the end of *The Master of Ballantrae* reproduces the gravestone of the two brothers whose career has narrowed, from their initial roles as representatives of the Jacobite and Hanoverian factions in 1745, to a deadly mutual dependency in the wilderness of America, where according to the cryptic and ambiguous inscription on their graves they lie "forgotten" (*Works* 10: 233). There are other ways in which Stevenson can be seen in the same line of development as Scott. Both cast a wary eye on the romanticization of the Highlands even as they acknowledge the attraction of such a cultural process. Both create Jacobite characters who perform rather than fully embody the political stance of Jacobitism. Scott's Fergus McIvor, from *Waverley* (1814), is a French-educated aristocrat who likes to put on a show, while Stevenson's Alan Breck, from *Kidnapped* (1886), is equally attached to his French clothes and Highland ceremonial.

It is hard to avoid Calvinism in the history of Scottish literature—witness the Covenanting graves of *Old Mortality* and *Weir* that recall the struggles in Scotland between Episcopalian and Presbyterian forms of government in the seventeenth century. But for Stevenson it is more a context than a subject. Unlike James Hogg, whose *The Private Memoirs and Confessions of a Justified Sinner* (1824) influenced him in other ways (for instance, through its dualities), Stevenson does not tend to address directly the strict theology of Calvinism. By the 1880s, questions of the relation between election and sin had already been subsumed in a more general cultural mythology, into which Presbyterianism and the Covenanting tradition had become mixed, so it is just as important (and possibly more fun for students) to discuss how the Calvinism of past generations became intertwined with gothic motifs of evil as a deterministic and physical presence and how it implied repressive moral and religious strictures.

The question of Calvinism might be approached in two ways. Glenda Norquay uses Calvinism as a trope to configure Stevenson's anxieties about writing. She argues that Stevenson inherited a pervasive distrust of art as verbal iconography founded in the Calvinist belief that the imaginative engagement with the world through fiction was a snare and a delusion, that the only Word one should pursue was that of God, and that the world was given, not interpreted or—worse—imaginatively re-created. Students interested in the debates about realism and romance in the 1880s might think about Stevenson in this way. His reluctance, as Norquay puts it, "to present himself as authoritative interpreter" combines with "a defiant rejection of Calvinist opprobrium towards the seductions of art" in essays like "A Gossip on Romance," so that his mixed feelings about his Calvinist inheritance can be read as a theory of reading (*Robert Louis Stevenson* 52, 92).

We might also take a Calvinist route into the novels via *Weir of Hermiston*, a novel on which a number of Scottish themes converge. The stern, authoritarian figure of Lord Hermiston terrorizes his sensitive and poetic son, Archie, through an absolute claim to be right and an equally absolute dismissal of fiction. Lord Hermiston's more articulate colleague, Lord Glenalmond, explains to Archie after one unfilial but graphic outburst: "[Y]ou will find some of these expressions rise on you like a remorse. They are merely literary and decorative; they do not aptly express your thought, nor is your thought clearly apprehended" (*Works* 16: 20). Archie's language, the language of fiction, is dangerous both because it is iconographic ("merely literary and decorative") and because it cannot be a direct expression of the world. Only Archie's remorseless father—a judge and, to his son, image of the Calvinist God—can claim language as an unmediated expression of truth. The fear of being judged—or, even more powerfully, of having been already judged in the terms of predestination—lies at the heart of Stevenson's concept of the ferocious psychology of Calvinism. As a child, he wrote in *Memoirs*, he would lie awake, fearing to sleep "lest I was not accepted and should slip, ere I awoke, into eternal ruin" (*Works* 29: 154). Cairns Craig identifies one of the sources of the modern Scottish novel in the "fearful self" bred by Calvinism and rightly points out that Archie is one of its victims (*Modern Scottish Novel* 37–74).

But Calvinism is not always a set of discrete theological tenets. Scottish religion has a long literary history of encounters with a popular, rural tradition of belief and storytelling in which representatives of Kirk authority do not always get their way. Stevenson's "Thrawn Janet" tells of the encounter between the Reverend Soulis and a local woman, Janet, whom her neighbors claim to be possessed by the devil. The book-learned Soulis dismisses these superstitions, but then, during the course of the story, encounters Janet as a terrifyingly animated corpse—and he is never the same again. After this encounter, the story passes into the local community to be circulated and handed on: "Now and again . . . one of the older folk would warm into courage over his third tumbler, and recount the cause of the minister's strange looks and solitary life" (*Works* 8: 110).

The story is part of a tradition of Scottish writing in which the supernatural account is associated with traditional forms of memory and explanation (often in dialect) and is set against an official or rational account. "Thrawn Janet" is another way of giving students an entry point into some longer Scottish novels that often contain interpolated tales in which supernatural explanations of events are given an airing within the greater architectonics of history. "Wandering Willie's Tale," from Scott's *Redgauntlet* (1824), and the Auchtermuchty preacher's tale in Hogg's *Confessions of a Justified Sinner* are examples of such a tale, as is "The Tale of Tod Lapraik," from Stevenson's *David Balfour* (*Catriona* in Britain). Students might also compare "Thrawn Janet" with Robert Burns's poem "Address to the Deil" (1785), in which Milton's Satan is taken down a peg or two. Here the official theological version of evil is corrected by the opinions and experiences of Burns and his "rev'rend *Graunie,*" who has heard a folklore devil droning and crooning in lonely lanes (136).

A final aspect of Scottish literature against which Stevenson may be evaluated is one with which he provides a marked contrast: the kailyard. Kailyard fiction (named after the homely cabbage patches featured in its rustic settings) was a short-lived but immensely popular genre that flourished first in periodical stories from 1886 in *The British Weekly*, then was expanded into novels from 1888 to the end of the century, though it can be traced back to Burns's "The Cotter's Saturday Night" (116–21). Kailyard stories typically embrace village characters and values, especially in the schoolmaster and the lad o' pairts (an able, self-sufficient young man, well educated in the parish school), and they exemplify the decent, kindly ideals of the Scottish countryside, sometimes opposed to the alienating forces of the city. Students need read only a short sample, perhaps one of the stories from *Beside the Bonnie Brier Bush* (1894), by Ian Maclaren, to get a flavor of kailyard values. Recent studies of the kailyard school have cautioned against oversimplifying its authors, and although there are plenty of contrasts to be made, students might avoid an overly Manichaean approach by thinking about ways in which both Stevenson and the kailyard provide ways of negotiating Scottish humble, rural life amid increasing urban wealth and a revolution in global technology (Nash). In this context, it is worth noting that Stevenson himself contributed to the *British Weekly*.

Kidnapped's David Balfour looks like a lad o' pairts. But we find out nothing about his education: the novel explicitly rejects any description of his early life in its opening sentence, when the teenage Davie announces that he will begin his adventure "with a certain morning early in the month of June, the year of grace 1751, when [he] took the key for the last time out of the door of [his] father's house" (*Works* 6: 1). There is no nostalgia for home, and Davie profits from his rootlessness. What he discovers on his adventure is, in part, social and economic realism. His solitary journey before meeting Alan includes an inn that is "the most beggarly vile place that ever pigs were styed in" (109), a scene of emigration on a beach (107–08), and "plenty of people, grubbing in little miserable fields that would not keep a cat" (100). These people are not made more kindly by rural poverty. By the early 1890s, as the kailyard school took root, Stevenson was in Samoa writing his dark, ironic tales of the failure of colonization, of anthropology, of trade, and finally, in *The Ebb-Tide*, of the self. Both the kailyard and Stevenson are part of Scottish modernity, but Stevenson is a modernist who looks forward.

American Literary Contexts

Glenda Norquay

One of the fascinations of Robert Louis Stevenson for students is the diversity of cultural contexts in and about which he wrote. Students are surprised to discover that key episodes in his writing career were played out in the United States: his journey across the country to Monterey in 1879, reading George Bancroft's *History of the United* States as he traveled; his feted arrival in New York in 1887, after the publication of *Jekyll and Hyde*, where he learned what it meant to be a celebrity author; his stay in the Adirondacks, where he produced *The Master of Ballantrae* and essays for *Scribner's Magazine*. Some of his most compelling travel writing arises from his voyages to and trips in the United States: *The Amateur Emigrant*, *Across the Plains*, *The Silverado Squatters*. As critics have noted, his American experiences had a profound effect on him and on his writing (Furnas; Katz; Noble, *From the Clyde*). Stevenson's engagement with American thinkers, novelists, and critics was likewise prolonged, wide-ranging, and significant. Drawing on his fiction, literary criticism, essays, and letters, this essay shows three routes to classroom engagement with Stevenson in the United States: it analyzes his writing in the context of transatlantic literary debate over the novel form; discusses his direct commentaries on Walt Whitman and Henry David Thoreau and less explicit dialogues with Herman Melville, Nathaniel Hawthorne, and Mark Twain; and outlines his influence on subsequent American writers. Stevenson emerges as a writer active in a transatlantic tradition—as a figure who demonstrates the complicated network of literary relations that surround an author and his work.

Stevenson was a theorist as well as a practitioner of fiction at a time when the future of the novel form was hotly contested. Students exploring theories of the novel can get an important transatlantic perspective by considering that some of his liveliest contributions to this debate came through engagement with American critics. A short 1890 satire by J. M. Barrie sets the context: a "romancist," a realist, a stylist, and an Elsmerian (from Mrs. Humphry Ward's religious novel *Robert Elsmere*), meeting in the library of a club in Piccadilly, are joined by "an American novelist" whose "methods" they all dislike. They converse with the ghosts of great writers from the past, each striking a pose appropriate to their literary outlook: the American sees the earlier writers are "antiquated, played out"; he espouses newness, declaiming, "The story in a novel is of as little importance as the stone in a cherry" ("Brought Back" 847, 849). He dismisses all great writers, from Walter Scott to Charles Dickens, but the scene ends with a rebuke from William Makepeace Thackeray: "[P]erhaps if you thought and wrote less about your styles and methods and the aim of fiction, and, in short, forgot yourselves now and again in your stories, you might get on better with your work" (854). This caricature of the American analyst illustrates the intensity of theoretical debates in American literary culture as well as the increasingly polarized positions taken by European scientific realists, American moralists, English aesthetes, and masculine romancers. Stevenson's own interventions on fiction confound schematic stances; often anecdotal, his essays are inspired by an incident or thought rather than by a theory. Exchanges with two position-taking American novelists, however, reveal his interest in literary debate.

Stevenson's most important contribution to transatlantic theorizing was his correspondence with Henry James (recorded in J. Smith). James published "The Art of Fiction" in *Longman's* in September 1884, as a response to a published lecture on that topic given by Walter Besant, a British novelist. Stevenson responded in December with "A Humble Remonstrance," an essay that prompted ongoing correspondence on the subject and established a warm friendship between the two men. These exchanges encapsulate the literary debate that Barrie later mocked, but students will find that the conversation between James and Stevenson transcends rigid position taking; it presents a sophisticated discussion of the nature and role of fiction. Besant had advised the modern novelist never to go beyond personal experience, arguing that in fiction human interest comes before everything else. James welcomed Besant's piece, because it attempted to theorize the novel form. Until then there had been little literary self-awareness in England: "[T]here was a comfortable, good-humoured feeling abroad that a novel is a novel, as a pudding is a pudding" (54). Disliking, however, the catalog of rules articulated by Besant, James redefined the argument, suggesting that experience is what most engages a reader and that experience cannot be easily categorized: "[I]t is an immense sensibility, a kind of huge spider-web, of the finest silken threads, suspended in the chamber of consciousness and catching every air-borne particle in its tissue" (66). A novel, James argued, is organic; character can be understood only in relation to incident and vice versa. Stevenson, well versed in debates on art through correspondence with his cousin, R. A. M. [Bob] Stevenson, an art critic, questioned the terms used by both Besant and James, suggesting that both were discussing "the art of narrative," not fiction, and he argued that narrative shapes all kinds of writing, not just the novel. He was also uneasy with the ways in which James (and Besant) used the word *truth*. Literature, according to Stevenson, should be seen as a reorganization and shaping of life. A novel, he asserted, exists by virtue of its differences from life: "And as the root of the whole matter, let him bear in mind that his novel is not a transcript of life, to be judged by its exactitude; but a simplification of some side or point of life, to stand or fall by its significant simplicity" (*Works* 29: 142). Stevenson's interest lay in patterning out the "significant" instead of offering a faithful representation of the everyday world. His essay offers a suggestive model for thinking about his own fiction and narrative in general.

Students will find that the courteous and admiring tone of the James-Stevenson correspondence is very different from Stevenson's response to another American novelist, William Dean Howells. In his second version of the essay, published in *Memories and Portraits* in 1887, Stevenson addressed comments made on the "art of fiction" debate by Howells, who, unlike James, had a difficult personal encounter with Stevenson. On reading Howells's novel *A Modern Instance* (1882), which he saw as condemning divorce, Stevenson declined further acquaintance: "I desire to know no-one who considers himself holier than my wife" (*Letters* 4: 35). Howells was a moralist and a firm believer in literary realism—although, as Stevenson noted, Howells's fiction showed an inclination toward romance. Mounting a sustained attack on romance in *Harpers New Monthly Magazine* between 1886 and 1892, Howells named as the criterion for a novel's success the question, "Is it true?—true to the motives, the impulses, the principles that shape the life of actual men and women?" (826). This emphasis on what is true set Howells at odds, aesthetically and morally, with Stevenson, who warned in his "Remonstrance": "[T]he danger is lest, in seeking to draw the normal, a man should draw the null, and write the novel of society instead of the romance of man" (*Works* 29: 143). Subtle differences in ideas about the role of fiction and the nature of the reading experience in the James-Stevenson exchange, and the rather cruder positions taken by Besant and Howells, offer useful starting points for examining meanings assigned to the novel near the end of the nineteenth century and discussing more generally the relation between art and life.

Stevenson does not operate with as fully articulated an artistic agenda as his American fellow writers, but students reading through this debate will see that he is more a theorist than many of his British contemporaries. Through his questioning of realism, his emphasis on the value of incident, and his view of action and adventure as significant, they may wonder if he does not have more connection with American literature than with the English tradition of the novel. They may explore how far that connection derives from a deeper, religious and aesthetic, parallelism. The product of a Calvinist upbringing, Stevenson shares a conflicted attitude to fiction with American writers working in a strongly Protestant belief system. In the prologue to *The Scarlet Letter*, Hawthorne expresses uneasiness with the whole business of fiction making: "'What is he,' murmurs one grey shadow of my forefathers to the other. 'A writer of storybooks! What kind of business in life—what mode of glorifying God, or being serviceable to mankind in his day and generation—may that be?'" (16). The latitude that Hawthorne gained by calling his work a "romance" also appealed to Stevenson (see Warren; Bunge; Mulholland; Norquay, *Robert Louis Stevenson*). In essays and correspondence, Stevenson, often deprecating his own work, shows an anxiety about the relation between the profession of storyteller and more obvious ways of being "serviceable" to the world and shows a resultant concern with tensions between a writer's popularity and his seriousness (Ambrosini; Norquay, *Robert Louis Stevenson*). Hawthorne, a novelist whom Stevenson explicitly imitated, addresses similar questions about the relation between a Protestant worldview in which God is the ultimate author and the business of fiction making. Melville's assessment of "this great power of blackness" in Hawthorne, which "derives its force from its appeals to that Calvinistic sense of Innate Depravity and Original Sin, from whose visitations, in some shape or other, no deeply thinking mind is always and wholly free" ("Hawthorne"; see also Levin), might well be used as a frame for assessing some of Stevenson's work, in terms of both thematic concerns and anxieties about fiction making—from *The Master of Ballantrae*, with its explorations of guilt and sin, good and evil, to short stories such as "Markheim," "Thrawn Janet," and "The Merry Men" as well as the more obvious example of *Jekyll and Hyde*.

Tracing specific literary influences is, of course, a complicated business. Luckily, when Stevenson was at a distance from literary friends in England (which was often), he corresponded enthusiastically about books he had read. So the fully indexed *Letters* are a great resource. After the author's death, his books from Samoa were auctioned, so there is evidence about his library too (*Autograph Letters*). Because he was not a great annotator of books, specific engagement and influence are difficult to determine. Still, his relation to Melville allows students to unravel some of these intricacies of influence. Basic research reveals that the writers shared literary antecedents: both owed a debt to Hawthorne, and both liked Captain Marryat's seafaring fiction. Stevenson admired Melville and read *Omoo* (1847) before embarking on his South Seas adventures. Travel for Stevenson, a leisured and relatively free explorer, carrying with him family and dependents, was very different from travel for the single, indentured, hardworking young American, but this difference may have been part of the attraction. In his preface to *Typee* (1846), Melville notes, "Sailors are the only class of men who now-a-days see anything like stirring adventure; and many things which to fire-side people appear strange and romantic, to them seem as common-place as a jacket out at elbows" (9). Stevenson, although always excited by the strange and romantic, was aware, through youthful experience of his father's lighthouse work, from steerage passage to America, and from encounters in the South Seas, that a sailor's life was one of hardship and demanded confrontation of difficult cultural and moral questions. Another adventurous American, Charles Warren Stoddard, had given Stevenson *Typee* and *Omoo*. Both books can be seen as forerunners of Stevenson's accounts of the South Seas, not only in location but also in the crafting of apparently autobiographical travel narratives that explore colonial cultural encounters (Hillier 10; R. L. Stevenson, *Works* 20 [*In the South Seas*]). As he traveled, Stevenson wrote corrections of Polynesian spelling and vocabulary in Melville's text and took this work so seriously that his wife felt that he, unlike Melville, became too involved in the subject of and opinions on the South Seas (Hillier 38–39). Stevenson's late novels *The Wrecker* (1892) and *The Ebb-Tide* (1894) and the short story "The Beach of Falesá" (1892) represent complex engagements with character types and colonial contexts recognizable from Melville (see Buckton; Colley, *Robert Louis Stevenson*; Hillier; Jolly, *Robert Louis Stevenson*; J. Smith; Menikoff, "'These Problematic Shores'"; Rennie 211–18).

Tracking Stevenson's physical journeys can support such literary comparisons, showing contrast and adding nuance. If Stevenson followed in Melville's actual footsteps, he also followed the route of Twain, who had lived in the Sandwich

Islands and possibly talked to Stevenson about the Pacific when they met in New York in 1888 (Harman, *Robert Louis Stevenson* 358). Twain's fiction had accompanied Stevenson and his family on much of their travels. Writing from Saranac Lake in 1888, he describes to Twain how he had first "got *Huckleberry* when I was pretty ill at Bournemouth, my first winter there; read it straight through, began again at the beginning and read it straight through again without a break" (*Letters* 6: 161). He had since read it four times. *Tom Sawyer's Comrade*, *Roughing It*, and *The Innocents at Home* were all in Stevenson's library in Samoa, as well as a copy of *Tom Sawyer Abroad* bearing the signature of Stevenson's step-grandson. Stevenson wrote, "We have . . . had . . . a boy on the premises who would consent to read nothing at all except *Tom Sawyer*, *Huck Finn* and (from family partiality) *Treasure Island*" (8: 57). A letter from 1885 notes that *Huckleberry Finn* "contains many excellent things; above all, the whole story of a healthy boy's dealings with his conscience, incredibly well done" (5: 80). This description applies equally well to Jim Hawkins in *Treasure Island* (1883). Twain and Stevenson are drawn to the figure of a boy as the point of entry into exploring moral psychology; together they set the convention for boy's novels and the construction of the adolescent male. *Huckleberry Finn* and *Treasure Island* might be compared as fiction that produces a deep—and possibly uncritical—affection in young readerships yet challenges the division drawn between childhood and adult reading.

Tracking relationships between Stevenson and American authors shows how literature shapes culture in a broader sense. American writers stimulated Stevenson's outlook on life. As Wendy Katz suggests, Whitman and Thoreau, in *Leaves of Grass* and *Walden*, shaped "the imagination that created the American travel books"; they were Stevenson's "literary stowaways," lodged in his memory and helping articulate his experiences (328, 329). Stevenson wrote "The Gospel according to Walt Whitman" (1878) before he visited America. Even then, Katz argues, he found in Whitman a democratizing approach that allowed for tolerance and engagement with the commonplace and ordinary people, an approach that influenced his responses to the United States and extended to his South Seas writing. Katz concludes, "From Whitman and Thoreau, Stevenson learned much about how to 'write' American. [In] them he encountered a forward-looking optimism, an appreciative regard for the variegated spirit of democracy, and the responsibility to speak critically of the developing society" (335). Stevenson's essays on Whitman and Thoreau therefore provide useful starting points for students interested in the development of his thinking and of his attraction to American viewpoints. Stevenson viewed both writers as inspirational social critics, but while Thoreau's emphasis on individuality, his delight in work, and the appreciation of being out of doors all appealed, it was Whitman's writing style and response to life that particularly drew him: "[I]t is what Thoreau clearly whispered that Whitman so uproariously bawls" (*Works* 27: 103 ["Henry David Thoreau"]). Stevenson admired the richness of Whitman's language, his exuberant use of nomenclature in particular, and his project to create "a

Literature which was to inhere in the life of the present" (58 ["Walt Whitman"]). The American prompts a key question for Stevenson, one that had long concerned him: "[H]ow is the poet to convince like nature, and not like books?" (61). He sees Whitman as reasoning that to draw "at first hand from himself and his neighbours, accepting without shame the inconsistencies and brutalities that go to make up man, and yet treating the whole in a highly magnanimous spirit, he would make sure of belief, and at the same time encourage people forward by means of praise" (62). This positivity, Whitman's emphasis on how good we are, not how good we should be, was a refreshing change from Stevenson's moral upbringing and suggested the potential for new philosophies emerging from the United States.

Just as Whitman, Thoreau, Hawthorne, Melville, and Twain spoke to Stevenson, so subsequent American writers have looked to Stevenson for transatlantic inspiration. Tracing his influence to the present is a never-ending and productive research task, fascinating to students. Those working on travel or the idea of America might consider how Stevenson's travel writings contributed to the construction of an American landscape. If his idea of the American West was shaped by his boyhood reading—Ohio, as he notes on his first journey through America in 1879, "had early been a favourite home of my imagination; I have played at being in Ohio by the week, and enjoyed some capital sport there with a dummy gun, my person being still unbreeched" (*Works* 18: 88 [*Across the Plains*])—so his deepening sense of a distance between the promise of newness and the realities of life in the developing country contributes to the construction of national identity.

The question of Stevenson's influence can arise in courses on United States adventure fiction. Two near contemporaries in particular—Stephen Crane and Owen Wister—reflect his combination of swashbuckling action and an emphasis on the ordinariness of the hero, as found in *Kidnapped* and *Treasure Island*. Wister was a great admirer; although his attempts to meet Stevenson came to nothing, his character of the cowpuncher in *The Virginian* (1902) has been read as an amalgam of the Western figures created by Howells and those of Stevenson (Vorpahl). Crane also engages with heroes who retain their ordinariness throughout their adventures and encounters with extremes: like David Balfour in *Kidnapped* (1886), "the youth" at the centre of *The Red Badge of Courage* (1895) is caught up in and learns from events he does not fully comprehend. Wister and Crane, like Stevenson, were writers who crossed popular and literary divides, using the adventure form to raise questions of identity and agency.

Stevenson's precision and power in language caught the imagination of many authors; his writing was admired by John Steinbeck, Ernest Hemingway, and Italo Calvino (Borges was also a fan). Students are especially impressed by Vladimir Nabokov's response to *Jekyll and Hyde*. Teaching the course Masters of European Fiction at Cornell in the 1950s, the novelist selected four works for his students to study: *Jekyll and Hyde* was included alongside *Ulysses*, *Bleak House*, and *Mansfield Park*. Nabokov was attracted to Stevenson's text as a "phenomenon of style," an aspect that, Andrew Jefford argues, brings the writers together in their "enormous emphasis on the craft and business of writing" (49). Alert not only to the style but also to the spatial dynamics of the tale, Nabokov's essay in *Lectures on Literature*, paying close attention to the interiors of Dr. Jekyll's house and diagrammatically sketching the relationship between Jekyll and Hyde, illuminates Stevenson's tale but also offers an insight into Nabokov's own approach to fiction.

Jekyll and Hyde presents a particularly traceable and fascinating case study of Stevenson's influence in America (Veeder and Hirsch; Danahay and Chisholm). Published in 1886, the novella made Stevenson a celebrity in America when he arrived for his second visit in 1887. It captured the public imagination on both sides of the Atlantic—Twain talked about Jekyll and Hyde and dual personality as he was dying (Kaplan 388). In the twentieth century, novelists were still reworking the theme of dual personality. Stephen King's *The Dark Half* (1989), written in response to the outing of the author's pseudonymous and darker literary self, Richard Bachman, projects the splitting of identity onto literary production as well as morality through the tale of a writer who had a fetal twin removed from his brain and is later pursued by the grown and grotesque manifestation of that dark other. *A Scanner Darkly* (1977), by Philip K. Dick, operates in a claustrophobic atmosphere of dysfunctional male characters focused on the drug-induced splitting of the self. An undercover narcotics agent in a futuristic world is searching for the source of Substance D, a drug that causes the two hemispheres of the brain to function separately. Taking the drug to penetrate the users' world, he finds himself spying, through scanner technology, on his own undercover character, from whose activities he feels an increasing disassociation. *Fight Club*, by Chuck Palahniuk (1996), inhabits a masculine world of double identity. In contrast, *Mary Reilly*, by Valerie Martin, (1990) challenges the masculine domain of Stevenson's tale by viewing events from the perspective of a serving maid in Dr. Jekyll's household, thus rewriting and interrogating the closed world of nineteenth-century class privilege. If Stevenson's imagination and narratives still have resonance and the power to stimulate in a modern United States, they invite our students into an unusually engaged and implicated relationship with a distant author.

Stevenson and Scots

J. Derrick McClure

Stevenson is one of the most accomplished writers ever to exploit the literary potential of the Scots language, but the precise extent to which he used it in any given passage may be difficult to quantify. Sometimes the Scots is unmistakable: in "Thrawn Janet," for example, the vocabulary, grammar, and pronunciation (as represented orthographically) make no compromise for the uninitiated reader. A sentence like "he would threep it doun their thrapples that thir days were a' gane by" (*Works* 8: 111–12) will present difficulties to non-Scottish readers (and nowadays even to some Scots). Even the question of how to pronounce the words, let alone what they mean, can be daunting. There are also many cases where the "Scotsness" of Stevenson's language is more subtle and elusive, inhering in Scottish idioms or turns of phrase that outsiders might fail to appreciate or even to recognize. And though Stevenson was a careful stylist, skilled in adjusting his language not only for realism of presentation but also to accommodate the needs of his intended audience, editors have at times watered down his Scots for the benefit of the English market: debate rages, for example, over the extent to which *Kidnapped* originally had more Scots in its language than appears in published editions (Menikoff, Introduction; McCracken-Flesher, "Mapping"). This essay gives a review of some distinctive features of Scots for the assistance of English-language classes where students may be unfamiliar with dialects other than standard literary English. It should be of use, too, to teachers wishing to introduce their students to the diversity of "English literature." Perhaps most importantly, it suggests ways for literature students to overcome the difficulty of Stevenson's Scots and to access the complex meanings and cultural challenges that he poses by its use. To address specific classroom needs and approaches with regard to language, this essay should be read along with Alan Riach's contribution to this volume, which considers how a close reading of Stevenson can be applied in creative writing classes.

By the time Stevenson appeared on the Scottish literary scene, the Scots tongue had a long and brilliant history as a literary medium. Scots originated in the Northumbrian dialect of Anglo-Saxon, as standard literary English originated in the Mercian, and the differences between the two forms of English are the result of centuries of mutual divergence. The distinctive characteristics of Scots are visible at all linguistic levels. In pronunciation many sets of words illustrate different sound developments from the ancestral Old English: Scots *toun*, *doun*, *hous* (*ou* pronounced as in French) compared with English *town*, *down*, *house*; Scots *hame*, *bane*, *stane* with English *home*, *bone*, *stone*; Scots *guid*, *muin*, *tuith* with English *good*, *moon*, *tooth*. (The *ui* is variously sounded in different dialects of Scots, but the most common pronunciation is like *i* in *bit* or, when lengthened as in *puir* ["poor"], like *ay* in *say*. Stevenson's occasional use of an umlaut in words of this class [*müne*, *shüne*] suggests a lip-rounding that gives a vowel almost like the French *eu*, still heard in those words in some Border dialects.) *Gress*, *efter*, *gether* are cognate with *grass*, *after*, *gather*; *fairm*, *hairt*, *pairt* with *farm*, *heart*, *part*; *aff*, *saft*, *drap* with *off*, *soft*, *drop*. Consonants as well as vowels have developed differently in Scots and English: perhaps the most striking contrast is the retention of the velar fricative in *nicht*, *licht*, *bricht*. The loss of the *d* in the medial and final cluster *–nd* in *finn*, *enn*, *haun*, *hunner* (*find*, *end*, *hand*, *hundred*), of *l* after a back vowel in *faa*, *caa*, *howe*, *gowd*, *fou*, *ou* (*fall*, *call*, *hole*, *gold*, *full*, *wool*), and of *v* in *gie*, *hae*, *loe*, *ower*, *hairst* (*give*, *have*, *love*, *over*, *harvest*) are also conspicuous divergences. This list could be greatly lengthened by citing examples of sound features that separate one dialect of Scots from another. An elementary fallacy would be to regard these Scots words as variants (or, still worse, corruptions) of their present-day English cognates: the differences long predate the emergence of the standard literary English of modern times, and in some cases (the diphthongization of the original long *u* in the "town" set or the loss of the fricative *ch*) it is English that has diverged further from the ancestral form.

Even more striking in its distinctiveness is the Scots vocabulary. Many words for everyday things or concepts are different from those of standard literary English. These may be simply native Anglo-Saxon words that have survived in Scots but not in English—Scots by default, as it were—such as *bairn* ("child"), *bide* ("stay, live"), *dwine* ("dwindle, fade away"), *gloaming* ("twilight"), *thrawn* ("obstinate, perverse, sullen"), *smeddum* (a popular word among modern writers, originally meaning "fine flour" or "powder" but having come to mean something like "resourcefulness, courage in adversity, strength of character"). Some words are borrowed from other languages: Gaelic gives, among others, *sonsie* ("prosperous" or "comfortable" or, by a later semantic development, "plump"), *ingle* ("domestic fire" or "hearth"), *clachan* ("village" or "ale house"), *tocher* ("dowry"), *caur* ("left," as in *caurie-cloukit*, "left-handed"), *crummock* ("crooked stick"); French gives *braw* (from *brave*: "fine, handsome"), *dour* ("grim, stern"), *fash* ("irritate, annoy"), *cummer* ("female friend or gossip"), *houlet* ("owl"), *Hogmanay* ("New Year's Eve," from *aguillaneuf*: "a New Year gift"); Dutch gives *craig* ("neck"), *callant* ("fellow"), *doit* ("small coin"), *geck* ("scornful gesture"), *howff* ("inn"), and *scone*; Scandinavian gives *lass* ("girl"), *lug* ("ear"), *brae* ("hill"), *gowk* ("cuckoo"), *lowp* ("jump"), *meikle* ("big")—and even *kilt*!

Much more important than such relatively commonplace vocabulary items in their contribution to the literary potential of Scots are the colorful and phonaesthetically expressive words, some apparently having their origin in nonce concoctions, which abound in Scots. A random selection among hundreds yields *bambaizit* ("astounded"), *stamagastert* (the same, but still more extreme), *disjaskit* ("downcast, depressed"), *forfochen* ("exhausted"), *fusionless* ("spineless, lacking in strength"), *scunner* ("a source of disgust or vexation"), *stramash* ("uproar"), *ugsome* ("repulsive"). More fanciful examples are *cattiewurrie* ("a noisy dispute"), *clamihewit* ("a heavy blow"), *curryborum* ("a noisy crowd in a small space"), *flichtmafletheries* ("useless or excessive ornamentation"), *fliskmahago* ("a frivolous woman"), *hallyrackit* ("harebrained," "boisterous"), *heelstergowdie* ("head over heels"), and *tappietourie* ("pile" or "peak"). Some of these, especially the last group, are and probably always have been rare in both speech and writing, but they testify to the scope that the Scots tongue affords for imaginative and inventive expression.

A fallacy regarding the lexis of Scots, and a more subtle and insidious one than the obvious error already mentioned regarding the phonology of Scots words, would be to imagine that a text was Scots only to the extent that its vocabulary was different from that of Standard English. This would be wholly misguided, for the simple reason that since Scots and English have a common ancestor in Anglo-Saxon, an enormous number of words from the parent language are necessarily shared: some, as we have seen, have taken different forms in the two languages because of independent sound changes, but many remain identical. Those words are not "English" in the exclusive sense but common to both languages. In the same way, though Scots contains many French borrowings that either do not survive or never existed in English, the two languages share numerous French words adopted in a period preceding the emergence of Scots as a distinctive form among the Anglo-Saxon dialects. These words too belong to Scots as fully as to standard literary English. The vocabulary in a poem or passage of dialogue may be as densely Scots as the author chooses, but it is a mistake to imagine that "Scotsness" as a property of a literary text is a simple function of the number of words in it that a monolingual Anglophone would not understand. Scots grammatical usages, idioms, and the characteristic Scots use of proverbial and aphoristic expressions can unmistakably proclaim a text to be Scots even if exclusively Scots lexemes are sparse.

To understand Stevenson's literary context, it is important to appreciate the diminished and endangered state of Scots in his time. The gradual but inexorable decline of the rural communities and the 1872 Education Act (which imposed a uniform school system on Scotland) were two of the most important in a complex of factors leading to a diminution in both the actual use and the perceived desirability of the language. Stevenson confronted the problem in the thought-provoking introduction to his poem collection *Underwoods* (1887), noting regretfully, "The day draws near when this illustrious and malleable tongue shall be quite forgotten; and Burns's Ayrshire, and Dr Macdonald's Aberdeen-awa', and Scott's brave, metropolitan utterance will be all equally the ghosts of speech" (*Collected Poems* 71). Indeed, the recent history of poetry in Scots had been marked by a conspicuous failure among writers to maintain the standards set by their predecessors. In the late medieval and Renaissance periods, Scots was one of the richest and best developed literary languages in Europe, not least because of the enthusiastic patronage of literature and the other arts pursued as a matter of policy by the Stewart kings. The strife-torn seventeenth century was, comparatively at least, a barren period in Scottish literature; but the early eighteenth saw a successful revival, fueled at first by the Edinburgh printer James

Watson's publication of an anthology of earlier Scottish poetry and promoted by the vigorous efforts of Allan Ramsay, whose command of a rich vernacular Scots and ability to use it in poetry of many styles and genres set the language on a new course of literary development, which was maintained throughout the century and well beyond. Ramsay was followed by Robert Fergusson and he by Robert Burns, each learning from and improving on the achievements of his predecessor. Many lesser poets participated in the exuberant literary culture that had emerged: Burns's Ayrshire in particular was a hive of poetic activity. Somewhat later, Scots found a use in another field: as dialogue in prose fiction. Sir Walter Scott was not the first to adopt the practice of making fictional characters speak Scots as representatives of their class would do in actual life, but he developed it with a greater degree of realism, expressiveness, and literary vitality than anyone had done previously, and many novelists proceeded to make their own individual use of the technique. John Galt, James Hogg, and George Macdonald were among the finest of Scott's immediate successors, MacDonald using the highly distinctive dialect of Aberdeen and the Northeast (what Stevenson referred to as "Dr Macdonald's Aberdeen-awa'").

By 1887, however, the great literary impetus of the eighteenth century and much of the nineteenth century appeared to have been spent. In poetry, standards had declined sadly since the death of Burns, who before his death himself had ruefully observed a disappointing lack of initiative among younger poets. Stevenson was far from the only writer to predict the imminent demise of the Scots tongue. It is salutary to note that this had been predicted since over a century before Stevenson's preface and has not come true over a century after it, but the decline in the literary and social status of Scots that prompted him to make the prediction was real enough. A contemporary poet, J. Logie Robertson, had written a long and dreary poem titled "On the Decadence of the Scots Language, Manners and Customs," ending:

> Oh, Ichabod!—the better plan
> Were just to end as I began—
> To note the waefu' change, an' cry
> The guid auld times are a' gaun by! (62)

In contrast to Robertson's lachrymose defeatism, Stevenson's response, as students will readily see from his preface to *Underwoods*, was far more dynamic. Arguing that, as Scots would soon be extinct, dialectal accuracy was of no moment, he cheerfully acknowledged that he had not tried to make his written Scots an accurate representation of any specific dialect: "I simply wrote my Scots as well as I was able, not caring if it hailed from Lauderdale or Angus, from the Mearns or Galloway; if I had ever heard a good word, I used it without shame; and when Scots was lacking, or the rhyme jibbed, I was glad (like my betters) to fall back on English" (*Collected Poems* 71). That is, the doomed state of Scots, though a sad fact in itself, was also in some sense a liberation of the tongue's creative potential, since he could now exploit the combined lexical treasures of all the dialects, unhampered by the consideration of whether words used together in a poem could ever have been used together in any individual's actual speech.

The poems of *Underwoods* are divided into "Book I: *In English*," and "Book II: *In Scots*." In the first Scots poem, "The Maker [poet] to Posterity," Stevenson envisages a future reader puzzled by the language of his poems. To help students sharpen their linguistic skills, only the uniquely Scots vocabulary items are glossed here: the task of identifying the words that have phonological cognates in English is left as an exercise for the students.

> *"What tongue does your auld bookie speak?"*
> He'll **spier**; an' I, his mou to **steik**: [ask, shut]
> *"No bein' fit to write in Greek,*
> *I wrote in* ***Lallan****,* [Lowland—Scots, not Gaelic]
> *Dear to my heart as the peat* ***reek****,* [smoke]
> *Auld as Tantallon.*
>
> *"Few spak it than, an' noo there's nane.*
> *My puir auld sangs lie a' their lane,*
> *Their sense, that aince was* ***braw*** *an' plain,* [fine]
> ***Tint*** *a'thegether,* [lost]
> *Like runes upon a standin' stane*
> *Amang the heather.* (99–100)

From this example, students can acquire the ability to appreciate the complexity of Stevenson's language, recognizing that despite what is often assumed, the difference between English and Scots is not a simple two-way choice. Like many Scots writers, Stevenson often uses a Standard English spelling when the pronunciation he has in mind is actually Scots: *to my heart*, for example, is pronounced [te mʌ hɛrt]. Furthermore, the precise nuance of a Scots word or feature can vary with its context. The characteristic Scots diminutive in "bookie" can express affection or (as here) suggest a dismissive tone, appropriately answered by the pugnacious "his mou to steik" and the ironic suggestion that his Scots is, or was, a language for the unlearned ("no bein' fit to write in Greek"). Tantallon is a castle on the southeast Scottish coast and proverbially invincible—the simile has greater depth of meaning than at first appears, that is, by its suggested counter to the assumed imminent disappearance of Scots. And in the simile in the next verse ("like runes upon a standin' stane"), Stevenson likens the language of his poems to something mysterious, potent, and indestructible.

Elsewhere in the collection, the author makes still more exuberant use of Scots vocabulary: a notable example is the evocation of a stormy night and the fearful thoughts it aroused in "Late in the nicht in bed I lay":

Late in the nicht in bed I lay,
The winds were at their weary play,
An' **tirlin'** wa's an' **skirlin'** wae [shaking, screaming]
        Through Heev'n they battered;—
On-ding o' hail, **on-blaff** o' spray, [downpour, battering]
        The tempest **blattered**. [beat violently]

The masoned house it **dinled** through; [resounded]
It **dung** the ship, it **cowped** the coo. [struck, upended]
The rankit aiks it overthrew,
        Had braved a' weathers;
The strang **sea-gleds** it took an' blew [sea eagles]
        Awa' like feathers. . . .

To hear in the **pit-mirk** on hie [pitch dark]
The **brangled collieshangie** flie, [confused uproar]
The warl', they thocht, wi' land an' sea,
        Itsel' **wad cowpit**; [would have overturned]
An' for auld airn, the smashed debris
        By God be **rowpit**. [auctioned]
(118–20)

As well as the expressive force of the words themselves (treated with creative freedom: *on-blaff* is a nonce elaboration of *blaff* ["blast"] to match the common *on-ding* ["downpour"]), Stevenson's poetic skill is here seen in his use of alliteration, internal rhyme, and carefully balanced clauses.

Relatively little of Stevenson's substantial poetic output is in Scots, but what there is suffices to establish him as the most accomplished practitioner in the language since Burns. As students will learn, his intimate knowledge of Scots is applied with the skill of a master rhetorician: his choice of Scots as a medium is merely a preliminary to his masterly exploitation of it. Indeed, the example of Robert Louis Stevenson, with his stylistic mastery of both English and Scots and ability to modulate freely from one to the other as befits his tone or subject matter, can lead students to a finer appreciation not only of the linguistic aspect of Scottish literary identity but also of the expressive potential within their own language and the standard dialect that they take for granted.

The Visual Culture of Robert Louis Stevenson: Face to Face

Dennis Denisoff

> For some time Macfarlane stood motionless, holding up the lamp. A nameless dread was swathed, like a wet sheet, about the body, and tightened the white skin upon the face of Fettes. . . . "Hold that lamp," said [Macfarlane]. "I must see her face."
>
> —"The Body Snatcher"

> The eager and hurrying man of affairs I hate,
> Because he bears his intolerance writ on his face
> And every movement and word of him tells me how
> much he hates me.
>
> —"My brain swims empty and light . . ."

> And still the figure had no face by which he might know it; even in his dreams, it had no face, or one that baffled him and melted before his eyes; and thus it was that there sprang up and grew apace in the lawyer's mind a singularly strong, almost an inordinate, curiosity to behold the features of the real Mr. Hyde.
>
> —*Strange Case of Dr Jekyll and Mr Hyde*

Robert Louis Stevenson, himself a much painted and photographed author, displayed a keen interest in the relations among visuality, the human face, and the psychology of individual identity. For over a century, readers have registered and been fascinated by the emotional tension manifested in moments and phrasings of face-to-face encounters such as those above (resp., *Works* 11: 203, *Collected Poems* 260; *Works* 5: 11). As students become less familiar with Stevenson as author or velvet-coated icon of aestheticism but more adept in today's burgeoning visual culture, these encounters can provide a link to Victorian ideas of the visual and its meanings and allow a modern reappreciation of an always edgy author.

Even today, some students have been raised on Stevenson's *Child's Garden of Verses*, and many—before taking a college or university course—have read one or more of his most popular novels and stories. Whether they did so out of interest or because they were assigned the reading in class, they generally have fond memories of the man's writing. In the last few years, however, the assumption that any significant portion of students in an undergraduate class has already read some Stevenson has become less feasible. Students are more likely to have accessed the author through visual media. One thinks of the numerous graphic novels and comic books of novels such as *Kidnapped* (available in English and Scots) and of short stories such as "The Bottle Imp" and "The Suicide Club," not to mention the Treasure Island Casinos in Las Vegas, Nevada, and Saint Paul, Minnesota.

Film, comics, and graphic novels are, many students argue, easier to consume. If pressed to explain why, they often begin by noting the immediacy, vividness, and familiarity of these visual genres. In my teaching, I have found that this shift in media is a useful entry point into a discussion of the place of visuality, immediacy, and emotion in Stevenson's own aesthetics and views on the role of culture in the formation of human identity. Students are drawn into the discussion because many of them are at home with visual technologies. It is a relatively short step from the well-worn discussion of the current era as a uniquely visual age to the subject of the human face as a site of philosophical and cultural contestation and to Stevenson's powerful contribution to that subject.

This essay offers a few approaches I have found effective for using students' general preference for visual culture to explore the visuality of Stevenson's literary works. It is not that I use subterfuge to get students to enjoy the author's writing, coating the bitter pill of literary analysis in a sweet shell of working with the visual arts. Rather, the premise I put before students is that, despite the many changes in media and culture over the past century, the interests and excitements that drive our current penchant for visual popular culture are not that different from those that drew Victorians to Stevenson's writing. I emphasize the author's conception of visuality's relation to identity and the act of writing. The sickly son, the bohemian, the high seas adventurer—these are only a few of the many faces of the man explored in this volume. Instead of using the concept of face simply as a metaphor for identity, I suggest ways of encouraging students to recognize Stevenson's visualist theories of self-fashioning as they inform his relation to stories, paintings, and other works.

The demand for a quick fix of entertaining sensation was well established by the time Stevenson became a popular author. Wilkie Collins, in his 1858 essay "The Unknown Public," had depicted pulp periodicals as aggressively attacking unsuspecting consumers: "Buy me, borrow me, stare at me, steal me," this populist material demanded, "do anything, O inattentive stranger, except contemptuously pass me by!" (217). Writing twenty years later, the journalist and author Alexander Innes Shand observed that "[t]he ferment of thought, the restless craving for intellectual excitement of some kind, have been stimulated; till now, in the last quarter of the nineteenth century, we are being driven along at high-pressure pace; and it is impossible for any one who is recalcitrant to stop himself" (238–39). Collins and Shand were addressing the public's increased reading habit derived from the growth of cheap periodicals since 1855, when Britain removed the duty on newspapers. Both men were especially interested in the resultant ubiquity of periodicals of varying quality. Shand, for instance, found them strewn across train carriages, scattered over tables in pubs (the lower cost of newspapers was supposed to increase reading and reduce drinking among the lower classes), and being read aloud by one to many, adding sound pollution to pollution by paper. The barrage of lowbrow pulp had, Shand suggested, changed Victorian society: no one could avoid either the sensational materials proffered or the buzz of stimulation they exuded.

Collins's and Shand's concern regarding the multimedia onslaught on British society has, of course, been echoed in Western society to the present day, and that concern, then as now, was less about the means of transmission than about the material being transmitted. Similarly, the subject that I address in my lectures on Stevenson's face is less about the effect of mass media or popular culture than about the visual interests and needs that arise for students as they read Stevenson and the emotions that percolate up through the historical layers of media, ideology, and cultural packaging surrounding the author's work.

The conventional distinction between the emotional and the cultural, the private and the social, also offers the opportunity for an extended consideration of whether anything precedes or, more accurately, can be known to precede ideology. However, when Stevenson's writing is approached through the subject of the face, aesthetics and psychology become the main fields of inquiry, and the personal and the uncanny lead students to question their own confidence in their understanding of the media that consume them. As Collins's panicky response to the onslaught of popular entertainment suggests, the realization that one is being consumed by modern media instead of consuming them can make anybody uncomfortable. The loss of humanist coherence and of the power to construct one's own identity is disconcerting, but the assumption of such coherence also complicates the attraction of many modern readers to the notion of themselves as some sort of mediated, posthumanist avatar. There is pleasure in the loss of self in gaming and Internet environments—an entertaining titillation that comes from retaining the security of humanist individualism while temporarily releasing oneself into another realm of being. This exciting escapism through visual technology is, I argue, an extension of the uncanny thrill readers in Stevenson's time got, and readers in our own time get, from entering his works.

Issues of ideology and identity can be addressed through a number of Stevenson's works. I have found it particularly engaging to develop this thread of analysis through a short tale that few students know, "Markheim" (1885; *Works* 8: 87–106). Its gothic and existentialist qualities, as well as its brooding Dostoevskian tone, draw readers into the philosophical angst that it activates. The character Markheim enters a pawnbroker's shop intending to murder and rob the owner, whom he knows. He asks for a gift for his girlfriend, but when the pawnbroker offers him a hand mirror, the would-be murderer feels "a sudden leap of many tumultuous passions to the face," a series of physical reactions that readily expose his diabolical thoughts (90). It is the mirror—the face confronting the face—that prompts a visualized confession onto which Stevenson appends the verbal:

> Why, look here—look in it—look at yourself! Do you like to see it? No! nor I—nor any man. . . .—this damned reminder of years, and sins and follies—this hand-conscience! Did you mean it? Had you a thought in your mind? Tell me. It will be better for you if you do. Come, tell me about yourself. (90–91)

As Michela Vanon Alliata notes, in one sense the mirror "becomes an extension of Markheim's haunted soul, making him painfully aware of his past, his mistakes, and finally of his mortality" (303). But even before this moment of self-recognition and repulsion, Markeim appears to recognize himself in the shopkeeper. As the pawnbroker looks at his would-be assassin, waiting to hear what he wants, Markheim "return[s] his gaze with one of infinite pity, and a touch of horror." The mix of pity and horror connotes the complex psychological realization that this "little pale, round-shouldered dealer" is not simply his double but an externalized manifestation of his inner thoughts and values (89).

The act of facing oneself, this opening confessional scene suggests, creates the desire to tell one's story. Students will quickly observe that the desire for confession and self-exposure has made its way to the front page of modern culture through reality television shows, tabloid magazines, and *Twitter*. But what broader cultural movement has spurred this impulse to confess? Michel Foucault argues that, since the Middle Ages, Western society has developed a culture of the confession, where interrogation and inquest supersede other processes of reaching what is seen to be the truth: "Western man has become a confessing animal" (*History* 59). By the nineteenth century, he argues, the confession "lost its ritualistic and exclusive localization; it spread; it has been employed in a whole series of relationships: children and parents, students and educators, patients and psychiatrists, delinquents and experts" (63). "Markheim" suggests that Foucault's list can be extended to customers and shopkeepers, victims and their murderers.

Curiously, in Stevenson's text it is the potential criminal who demands the confession. Moreover, in the light of the fact that Markheim recognizes himself in the store owner, he is in more than a metaphoric sense asking for a confession from himself. Foucault's analysis of self-surveillance in *Discipline and Punish* offers one explanation for this convoluted self-interrogation. The logic of cultural constructionism to which Foucault contributed in this work was apparent in mid-Victorian society, even if the terminology was different. As Karl Marx put it:

> In the social production of their existence, men inevitably enter into definite relations, which are independent of their will, namely relations of

> production appropriate to a given stage in the development of their material forces of production. . . . It is not the consciousness of men that determines their existence, but their social existence that determines their consciousness. (3)

Stevenson was fully aware of the influence of production and consumer culture on his society's self-analysis and self-identification, but his writing is more than an acknowledgment or critique of them; it is a sustained effort to foreground forces beyond the realm of labor, industry, production, and consumption that contribute to these processes. Foucault's theories of confession and discipline do not adequately address the psychological issues that interested Stevenson even before he read about the subconscious in a French scientific journal. The concept of the subconscious was in part responsible for his writing "Markheim" as well as *Jekyll and Hyde* (see Fanny Stevenson's prefatory note to *Jekyll and Hyde* in *Works* 5: xvi).

Instead of proposing a macrostructural or constructionist interpretation of Stevenson's text, my emphasis on the face takes a more personalized approach; it allows students to practice developing modified analyses instead of casting everything they read, view, and listen to into the first general theoretical model that fits. The passage from "Markheim" discussed here encapsulates the intricate association in Stevenson's work among visuality, self-identification, and writing as an act of confession. At some point in the discussion of Foucault and confession, I ask the class what Markheim means when he declares that the hand mirror is a "hand-conscience." Students explain how looking at one's own face in a mirror, portrait, or close relative results in emotions that reveal more about one's thoughts than about one's face or the face of the subject being observed.

Stevenson's own face appears to have confessed its fair share of mystery and emotion. "He was an odd fellow to look at," noted Stephen Chalmers in 1916. "Eagle-beaked and eagle-eyed, his face was ever touched with a Pan-like humor, 'a deal of Ariel, just a streak of Puck.' Whimsical, purposeful, quick-tempered, generous, selfish, lovable, fierce, forgiving—a human paradox" (4). John Singer Sargent is the visual artist most famous for capturing the author's image, but a comparison of two of Sargent's portraits demonstrates the crucial space for viewers' transposition of their own emotions or inner turmoil. In the mid-Victorian era, when Sargent created the paintings, portraiture was going through an aesthetic revolution. The genre had been a conservative marker of propriety, tradition, and steadfastness. Because it was affordable only to the wealthy, simply having one's portrait painted or owning paintings of one's ancestors marked a person as part of the establishment. According to Pierre Bourdieu, family heirlooms such as painted portraits

> not only bear material witness to the age and continuity of the lineage and so consecrate its social identity . . . they also contribute in a practical way to its spiritual reproduction, that is, to transmitting the values, virtues and

> competences which are the basis of legitimate membership in bourgeois dynasties. (76–77)

The portrait as an object in itself—regardless of its subject—was a marker of cultural value, but it was also more than this. Society had been habituated to see this visual genre as signifying human character traits such as refined taste, tradition, and resolve.

At the same time, however, the rise of aestheticism, impressionism, and symbolism moved immediacy and emotion to the foreground of aesthetic theory. Long seen as a marker of constancy and lineage, portraiture was now asked to capture the fleeting, momentary essence of a person's character as well. Writing on portraiture in his notebook, Edgar Degas advised himself:

> Above all give to their faces the same choice of expression that one gives to their bodies. Thus if laughter is the hallmark of a person, make him laugh. Of course, there are feelings that one can't render, from considerations of propriety; portraits not being just for us, painters. (566)

As Degas notes, a portrait is not painted for the artist alone but is a negotiation among artist, subject, and buyer. He also recognizes that facial expressions in portraits are habitually read as signs of a person's character. Yet Degas's impressionist aesthetics come through in his conclusion that the most important aspect of the early modern painting *Belle Feronnière* (attributed to the school of Leonardo da Vinci) was not a character trait but the mystery arising from the subject's expression. The portrait exposes an unarticulated truth about the sitter but only by encouraging repeated attempts, which fail, to unlock the mystery.

The attention to personal expression and hidden emotion is central to Sargent's portraits of Stevenson (the portraits can be found on the Web site www.johnsingersargent.org). In a portrait titled *Robert Louis Stevenson* (1887), the author is depicted seated in a whirlpool of illuminated movement. The carpet, the rattan chair, the subject's trousers, even the wainscoting all swirl in flashes of light. The bend of his legs makes them seem almost to be swept up in the action without Stevenson's permission. But his face, severed from the rest of his body by an inky jacket, floats in a pool of calm. His visage is warm, inviting, and, as Chalmers recalls in a different context, "touched with a Pan-like humor, . . . a human paradox." The enigmatic smile leads one to interpret the dazzling movement surrounding the subject as an external manifestation of the playful machinations of the man's mind.

In Sargent's *Robert Louis Stevenson and His Wife* (1885), the equation is very different. Students should not make too much of the fact that this portrait was painted in the same year that Stevenson published "Markheim," but the convergence does offer an opportunity to help them develop skills in interartistic analysis. Some students will be drawn to investigate other artworks and writings that came from Stevenson's community. They might also consider what portraits the author sat for when writing *Jekyll and Hyde*. Interestingly, he wrote the first draft of the novella in the autumn of 1885, having just sat for Sargent's *Robert Louis Stevenson and His Wife* earlier that August. The proximity in time of the creation of these two works encourages students to consider the relation of the characters Jekyll and Hyde, on one hand, to the representations of Stevenson and his wife, Fanny, on the other. Just as Hyde is an obscure and shrouded figure throughout the novel, Sargent presents Fanny in a flowing garment that hides most of her from the viewer, while he situates a considerable portion of her figure outside the frame of the painting entirely. Moreover, Sargent's impressionist brushstrokes capture the garment's exoticism and splendor, while creating a sense of energy and movement reinforced by the angles of the slouching female sitter's torso and limbs. Thus Hyde and Fanny are both characterized by energy, movement, and the breaking of boundaries. The echo gets even more interesting when one notes that Sargent repeats Fanny's energy and posture in his 1887 depiction of her husband in the portrait *Robert Louis Stevenson*. Through a consideration of this repeated doubling, students are drawn beyond discussing the binary of the double to consider the infinite multiplicity of the self that Stevenson explores in so much of his writing.

Stevenson wrote at a time when one of the most popular forms of mass entertainment in England was the music hall, which originated in public houses and consisted of a combination of music, dance, sketches, and other forms of performance. Dioramas, panoramas, and photography had also become standard fare of popular culture, and film began in the 1890s. These various modes of visual media fit with the impressionist emphasis on capturing the blur of time and with the symbolist and decadent attention to the hallucinogenic, illusionary, and otherworldly. People used cameras to capture images of ghosts and fairy folk (as Arthur Conan Doyle and others asserted). Stevenson threw himself into this cultural context, but, as Markheim's "hand-conscience" attests, he did so with a particular interest in the relation of visual culture to what we often keep hidden—our self-identities and our personal hopes and fears. Students might today proclaim that with such things as surveillance and cell phone cameras it is harder to hide oneself from society. But through Stevenson they may see that it has always been hard to hide oneself. When his victim is dead, Markheim proceeds to stuff his pockets with loot, but already he can see his fate has been sealed:

> [H]is face repeated and repeated, as it were an army of spies; his own eyes met and detected him; and the sound of his own steps, lightly as they fell, vexed the surrounding quiet. . . . Meanwhile, and behind all this activity, brute terrors, like the scurrying of rats in a deserted attic, filled the more remote chambers of his brain with riot. (93)

THEORETICAL CONTEXTS

Realism and Romance

Scott Hames

> Beware of realism; it is the devil: it is one of the means of art, and now they make it the end!
>
> —Robert Louis Stevenson

Stevenson was the outstanding romancer of his age but also a crucial participant in the 1880s debate that first consolidated a theory of novelistic realism in English-language criticism. This essay documents his role in that "art of fiction" debate with a particular interest in denaturalizing *realism* for undergraduates, both formally and historically. Revisiting Stevenson's dialogue with Henry James and appreciating the strength of his arguments against realism (he calls it "the devil" in *Letters* 4: 141) can enrich and complicate monolithic notions of the novel's essential trueness to life. This episode also illuminates the reductive literary history that makes Stevenson's defense of romance sound so "late" and his antirealism sound so "early."

Restored to its original context as a debate, the Stevenson-James correspondence is a vivid way of showing students that our default setting as commonsensical readers—interpreting the text as referential, mimetic, and containing truths about recognizable experience—has a contested history. To this end, it is often easier to convey that realism is a constructed, conventionalized way of reading by first showing how it is a constructed, conventionalized way of writing, with its own (particularist) aesthetic agenda, (post-Romantic) history, and (materialist, empirical) epistemology. By showing how these factors, as contested by Stevenson and James, constitute the novel's claim to artistic legitimacy, we see the crystallization of both a self-conscious technique and a critical rubric for describing fictional practice.

This is not, of course, the rubric most students bring to class, and the schoolroom commonplace "realism versus romance" is admittedly a limited (and limiting) basis for discussion. As a classificatory device it is crude verging on puerile, and as a definitional schema it merely codifies the self-evident. Despite or perhaps because of these limitations, realism versus romance is likely to remain an attractive framework for beginning English students. For them, its apparent lack of ambiguity provides a sturdy conceptual support to be clung to while taking the first tentative steps in formal and generic description. Stevenson can be used to combat what is gauche and misleading about the opposition between realism and romance while retaining these familiar terms in a more sophisticated critical and literary-historical repertoire.

One of the main problems with realism versus romance is that it is intrinsically weighted toward the first term; we could as easily say that realism tends to place "romance" under erasure. This reflects the dominance of realism in the fictive experience and critical vocabulary most students bring to the classroom and in the handbooks on which they often rely. Take the following gloss from a standard primer, the most recent (ninth) edition of M. H. Abrams's *Glossary of Literary Terms*, under the entry "Realism and Naturalism":

> Realistic fiction is often opposed to romantic fiction. The *romance* is said to present life as we would have it be—more picturesque, fantastic, adventurous, or heroic than actuality; realism, on the other hand, is said to represent life as it really is. This distinction in terms solely of subject matter, while relevant, is clearly inadequate. . . . It is more useful to identify realism in terms of the intended effect on the reader: realistic fiction is written to give the effect that it represents life and the social world as it seems to the common reader, evoking the sense that its characters might in fact exist, and that such things might well happen. (303)

This gloss is a small performance of the realist sensibility in itself, privileging tangible, self-evident "effects" (confirmed by untutored experience of how the world "seems") over a conceptual opposition between actual and ideal that is "ideal" by its very nature. By a subtle tautology realism is defined as writing that successfully presses the reader's realist buttons.

Situating this opposition in literary history is only a partial remedy, since the familiar narrative makes the "realism versus romance" binary largely illegible. Consigned firmly to the prehistory of the novel by critical authorities, for our students romance can signal a kind of childish phoniness antecedent to everything worth reading. On the first pages of Ian Watt's *The Rise of the Novel* we learn that the earliest English novelists "viewed their work as involving a break with the old-fashioned romances" (9–10). If romance was obsolete for figures as antique as Samuel Richardson and Henry Fielding, it quickly declines into the quaintly ancient for most students.

In fact, this debate in English criticism is relatively recent. In 1884, James wrote "The Art of Fiction" in response to the pamphlet publication of a lecture given by Walter Besant. James opens by welcoming Besant's attempt to supply a "theory" for novelistic practice that will bolster the seriousness of fiction and render it "what the French call *discutable*" (53–54). James's attempt to formulate a principle for the artfulness of fiction, largely by analogy with the other fine arts of painting and music, is consciously provisional and open-ended but moves swiftly to first principles—principles Stevenson felt confident, only a few months later, he had demolished.

James begins by rebutting the "old superstition about fiction being 'wicked,'" insofar as it peddles illusions and fosters idolatry, and insists "the only reason for the existence of a novel is that it *does* compete with life" (55–56). Pace the schoolmen and moralists, the fundamental character of the novel is its scorn of rules and formulas. James's emphasis on the novel's freedom and openness is pragmatic and impressionistic:

> [T]he good health of an art which undertakes so immediately to reproduce life must demand that it be perfectly free. . . . A novel is in its broadest definition a personal impression of life; that, to begin with, constitutes its value, which is greater or less according to the intensity of the impression. But there will be no intensity at all, and therefore no value, unless there is freedom to feel and say. (61–62)

The first rule of the novel is that there are no rules; we look to fiction for precisely those personal, experiential truths that evade codification and preconception. Authentically reproducing the intensity and disorder of experience preserves the novel's revelatory character; rearranging life to fit artificial conventions or patterns is fatal to its truth.

By this account, experience (actual or imaginative) is both the raw material of fiction and the basis of its own "reality." A special kind of sensitive and imaginative person can amplify and concentrate even the most partial experience, distilling and extrapolating it into artworks that compete with actuality:

> The power to guess the unseen from the seen, to trace the implication of things, to judge the whole piece by the pattern, the condition of feeling life, in general, so completely that you are well on your way to knowing any particular corner of it—this cluster of gifts may almost be said to constitute experience, and they occur in country and in town, and in the most differing stages of education. . . . "Try to be one of the people on whom nothing is lost!" (67)

This noticing novelistic sensibility is an acute sensitivity and imaginative responsiveness to the particulars of experience. Transmuting such impressions into art hinges on "exactness" or "truth of detail" (67). (Stevenson would later write to another correspondent, "Have you observed that the famous problem of realism and idealism, is one purely of detail?" [*Letters* 5: 203]). For James, the concretion of the fictive illusion is paramount: "[T]he air of reality (solidity of specification) seems to me to be the supreme virtue of a novel—the merit on which all its other merits . . . depend" (67). Any further attempt to delineate the "essentials" of the novel—say, narrative, character, dramatic embodiment—seems to James "to bring the novel back to the hapless little *rôle* of being an artificial, ingenious thing—bring it down from its large, free character of an immense and exquisite correspondence with life" (79).

Stevenson's rejoinder came four months later (December 1884), also in *Longman's*, under the title "A Humble Remonstrance." Stevenson was initially rather cocky about besting James's theory, describing "The Art of Fiction" to friends as "dreadful nonsense admirably said" and exulting in holding "the whip hand of the argument" (*Letters* 5: 9, 88). In his "charming, most friendly, most genial" letter acknowledging "A Humble Remonstrance," Stevenson wrote, James "seemed to struggle under a combined sense of having been thrashed and feeling that if all were as it ought to be, he should have been the thrasher. We shall see" (5: 52).

In essence, "A Humble Remonstrance" argues that the art of fiction is defined by its distance from and simplification of experience, not by its correspondence to or competition with life. This difference is partly a matter of taste but mainly a matter of necessity. The thrust of Stevenson's critique concerns the benign, readily containable sense of life and experience James's theory seems to presuppose.

> No art—to use the daring phrase of Mr. James—can successfully "compete with life"; and the art that seeks to do so is condemned to perish *montibus aviis* ["in the pathless mountains"]. Life goes before us, infinite in complication. . . . To "compete with life," whose sun we cannot look upon, whose passions and diseases waste and slay us—to compete with the flavour of wine . . . here are, indeed, labours for a Hercules in a dress coat, armed with a pen and a dictionary to depict the passions, armed with a tube of superior flake-white to paint the portrait of the insufferable sun. . . . No art is true in this sense; none can "compete with life."
>
> (*Works* 29: 134–35)

What little art can do, Stevenson continues, is a consequence of design, of the deliberate filtering and planned evasion of life's chaos and brutal intensity. A conscious awareness of artifice is therefore necessary in any mature discussion of fictive technique; after all, "phantom reproductions of experience, even at their most acute, convey decided pleasure; while experience itself, in the cockpit of life, can torture and slay" (135).

Art is ruthlessly and defensively selective, subsuming the particular impression under a general and abstract pattern instead of amplifying gross nature. This selectivity applies especially to the narrative arts, whose temporal dimension requires the careful omission and orchestration of reality in order to issue in the designed significance of story. Pattern governs matter:

> Man's one method, whether he reasons or creates, is to half-shut his eyes against the dazzle and confusion of reality. The arts, like arithmetic and geometry, turn away their eyes from the gross, coloured, and mobile nature at our feet, and regard instead a certain figmentary abstraction. . . . Painting, ruefully comparing sunshine and flake-white, gives up truth of colour, as it had already given up relief and movement; and instead of vying with nature, arranges a scheme of harmonious tints. Literature, above all in its most typical mood, the mood of narrative, similarly flees the direct challenge and pursues instead an independent and creative aim. (135–36)

If modernist writing, according to Georg Lukács, replaces the "concrete typicality" of the realist novel with a distorted "abstract particularity" (*Meaning* 43), Stevenson rejects the bad faith of mimetic particularism *tout court*, pressing for a recognition that abstract typicality is all the representative artwork can honestly aspire to.

> Our art is occupied, and bound to be occupied, not so much in making stories true as in making them typical; not so much in capturing the lineaments of each fact, as in marshalling all of them towards a common end. For the welter of impressions, all forcible but all discrete, which life presents, it substitutes a certain artificial series of impressions, all indeed most feebly represented, but all aiming at the same effect, all eloquent of the same ideas, all chiming together like consonant notes in music or like the graduated tints in a good picture. (*Works* 29: 136)

The fault of James's realism is not stylistic but constitutive: it presupposes a domesticated sense of life and then pretends to boldly, intrepidly reproduce it. The truth is that art cannot avoid reducing life to its own scope and technical limitations:

> Life is monstrous, infinite, illogical, abrupt, and poignant; a work of art, in comparison, is neat, finite, self-contained, rational, flowing and emasculate. Life imposes by brute energy, like inarticulate thunder; art catches the ear, among the far louder noises of experience, like an air artificially made by a discreet musician. A proposition of geometry does not compete with life; and a proposition of geometry is a fair and luminous parallel for

> a work of art. Both are reasonable, both untrue to the crude fact; both inhere in nature, neither represents it. The novel which is a work of art exists, not by its resemblances to life, which are forced and material, as a shoe must still consist of leather, but by its immeasurable difference from life, which is designed and significant, and is both the method and the meaning of the work. (136–37)

James suggested in his initial letter to Stevenson that "we agree, I think, much more than we disagree . . . no one can assent more than I to your proposition that all art is a simplification" (qtd. in J. Smith 101). Yet a crucial disagreement remains. For Stevenson, the literary artist's duty is "not simply to convince, but to enchant" (*Works* 29: 117 ["A Gossip on a Novel of Dumas's"]).

Students may usefully debate Stevenson's position piece on the relation among romance, the childish imagination, and the adult reader—which puts them, as readers, at the crux of realism and romance as a critical problem. Stevenson's "A Gossip on Romance" (1882) makes the appetites of the youthful imagination the touchstone of literary art: "we read story-books in childhood, not for eloquence or character or thought, but for some quality of the brute incident" (120). Precisely the intense vividness of experience James sniffs in "the air of reality" Stevenson traces to imaginative pleasure and desire: "[T]he great creative writer shows us the realisation and the apotheosis of the day-dreams of common men. His stories may be nourished with the realities of life, but their true mark is to satisfy the nameless longings of the reader, and to obey the ideal laws of the day-dream" (123). The novelist's role is not to reproduce impressions of actual life but to create a textual experience that makes fantasy real. The fictive impressions so designed and executed have a lasting power that goes far beyond the petty, empirical correspondences of realism, satisfying a "capacity for sympathetic pleasure" that compels us to "adopt into the very bosom of our mind that neither time nor tide can efface or weaken the impression. This, then, is the plastic part of literature: to embody character, thought, or emotion in some act or attitude that shall be remarkably striking to the mind's eye" (123). Stevenson observes that works of the greatest imaginative transport and appeal, such as the *Arabian Nights* or the novels of Alexandre Dumas, are almost wholly free of realism in James's (and Abrams's) sense. "No human face or voice greets us among that wooden crowd of kings and genies, sorcerers and beggarmen . . . the characters are no more than puppets. The bony fist of the showman visibly propels them" (126).

Developing this antirealist point, students can see how Stevenson anticipates later modernist critiques of passive and immersive ways of consuming realist fictions, insisting:

> No art produces illusion; in the theatre we never forget that we are in the theatre; and while we read a story, we sit wavering between two minds, now merely clapping our hands at the merit of the performance, now con-

> descending to take an active part in fancy with the characters. This last is the triumph of romantic story-telling: when the reader consciously plays at being the hero, the scene is a good scene. . . . But the characters are still themselves, they are not us; the more clearly they are depicted, the more widely do they stand away from us, the more imperiously do they thrust us back into our place as a spectator. (128)

This, I would argue, is a much healthier disposition to the literary text to recommend to undergraduates than Jamesian immediacy, and its conflation of artificial "impressions" and actual "experience." In the words of Stephen Arata, "Stevenson defines good reading as an ever more refined and sophisticated attention to the surface elements of the text. One is not trying to read through the text to get at something else" ("Stevenson" 199). Stevenson's critical attitude toward realism—dating from the mid-1880s—has been so thoroughly sidelined that his words may strike us as ahead of their time. In class, students might usefully consider Stevenson's affinity with Barthesian debunkings of the reality effect or with Brechtian explorations of theatrical identification.

Unfortunately for our students, bluffer's guides to literary form, and simplistic narratives of literary history, continually reinforce the naturalization of realism as the essential fictive mode. Of course, that serious and modern writers did not regard realism versus romance as a one-way bet and had compelling arguments for going "in quest of the ideal" (Stevenson, *Works* 28: 74 ["A Note on Realism"]) is hardly news to the professional scholar. Ian Duncan's *Modern Romance and Transformations of the Novel* (1992) is an excellent tonic to familiar Whiggish histories of the realist novel, and Matthew Beaumont's collection *Adventures in Realism* (2007) signals a revisionist trend in accounting for the sheer variety and historical dispersion of realist practice. Still, undergraduates are far more likely to resort to shortcuts and handbooks, and here the reification of realism as the sine qua non of literary fiction is actually deepening. Stevenson is included alongside James in Walter Allen's account of the realism debate in *The English Novel* (1954) and likewise in Stephen Coote's *Penguin Short History of English Literature* (1993). But James Wood's otherwise brilliant *How Fiction Works* (2008), which seems destined to become a standard primer for years to come, omits Stevenson's side of the debate entirely. The book is lucid, winningly accessible, and brims with insights into novelistic technique; it is notably strong on the conventionality of realism; but it is committed to a realist metaphysics of fiction, going out of its way to dismiss as "more or less nonsense" the notion that "realism is a genre (rather than, say, a central impulse in fiction-making)" (169). The peroration of the book declares that

> realism, seen broadly as truthfulness to the way things are, cannot be mere verisimilitude, cannot be mere lifelikeness, or lifesameness, but what I must call *lifeness*; life on the page, life brought to different life by the highest artistry. . . . The true writer, that free servant of life, is one who

> must always be acting as if life were a category beyond anything the novel had yet grasped; as if life itself were always on the verge of becoming conventional. (186–87)

This statement is little more than a repackaging of James's argument in "The Art of Fiction." You would never guess, from Wood's book, that this vision of the novel's "lifeness" had been challenged in the intervening century and a quarter; in fact, Stevenson had—at the very least—seriously dented James's central thesis within months of its publication. How perverse that James's generous *essai* should have the last word, that the very arguments employed to render fictional technique *discutable* should now be used to shut down debate. Here is a final reason to attend to Stevenson's occluded role in the formation of realism as a critical paradigm. Simply showing that this argument had two sides demonstrates to students that literary history, like the novel, is profoundly shaped by omissions and suppressions. It may even energize them to doubt categories, perform their own critiques, and embrace different possibilities for experience as romance.

Modernism

Roderick Watson

Robert Louis Stevenson's location between Victorianism and modernism has long been a subject of debate. This essay reviews the range of modernist concerns refracted through his works that might be pursued in a range of classes but that particularly show his value for courses considering the time and terms of modernism.

Recent critical approaches to Stevenson have come to consider him in the context of early modernism and even as a writer who prefigures aspects of postmodernism. In his magisterial 1996 study *Robert Louis Stevenson and the Appearance of Modernism*, Alan Sandison signaled Stevenson's "intense artistic self-consciousness," especially in "matters of form and metafictional structures," as well as his interest in psychological complexity and his destabilization of moral, social, and textual authority, leading the reader to a very modern awareness of contingency and indeterminacy (4–5). My aim here is not to claim Stevenson as a modernist or postmodernist per se but to explore the structural and thematic aspects of his writing that undoubtedly anticipate some of the critical and creative insights that characterize modernist and postmodern preoccupations. The first such aspect I offer is what he did with genre fiction.

Nineteenth-century literary critics were dismissive of genre or adventure fiction, and Stevenson's critical reputation suffered accordingly. Today's scholars have fewer prejudices, and significant revaluations have been made, for example, of *Treasure Island*, which began as a weekly serial for a boy's paper called *Young Folks*. The novel offers rousing adventure as a rite of passage to the adult world for Jim Hawkins, yet modern readers have been struck by the ambiguity of the world he enters. Long John Silver is one of literature's most memorable, morally slippery, and fascinating antiheroes, yet he is the character closest to the young protagonist and the one whose tutelage makes the deepest mark. So when Jim has been tested and proved sound and become the author of the very tale we have just finished reading, he is nevertheless left haunted by the sound of that "accursed" island's booming surf and the idiotic repetitive cries of an ancient parrot—both of which are darkly evocative but ultimately meaningless sounds (*Works* 2: 220). By such open-ended, symbolic devices Stevenson often gives a powerful undertone of meaning and a psychological complexity to his narratives. He was equally alert to the peculiar and paradoxical nature of the narrative act itself. Students can explore this self-consciousness through "The Persons of the Tale," where before returning to the last chapter of *Treasure Island*, Silver and Captain Smollett take time out to discuss which one of them the author prefers and which is more central to the book. It is a jeu d'esprit, but its metafictional playfulness also makes a serious and prophetically postmodern point. Popular adventure fiction rarely complicates the narrative line or the tale's final resolution, much less its ultimate meaning. Stevenson's fiction does.

Stevenson's art frequently recognizes and even undermines the very processes by which narratives are brought to us in the first place, which is to say that Stevenson offers his readers competing narratives, with no clear indication as to which of them, if any, is to be privileged. Students might consider how the "strange case" of Dr. Jekyll and Mr. Hyde comes to us through a succession of "incidents," reports, and "cases" from several sources, not the least of which are the two documents that conclude the tale—namely, "Dr Lanyon's Narrative" and "Henry Jekyll's Full Statement of the Case." The strategy slows the release of information, leading us from puzzlement to hideous revelation as we retrace the suspicions of Jekyll's friends. This is the very stuff of mystery fiction, after all, delivered in an appropriately sensational style. (Note that the original title from January 1886, having no definite article ["Strange Case of Dr Jekyll and Mr Hyde"], imitated tabloid journalism, as do the novella's numerous subsections, which adopt the style of subheadings in a popular journal.) Stevenson is entirely conscious of the generic implications of this approach, and in fact the book was originally presented as a "shilling shocker" for the Christmas market. The final effect is more subtle, however, and similar to postmodern criticism's fascination with unreliable narrators and the innate instability and ambiguity of all texts. Indeed the final truth of this strange case may be that there is no final truth.

Jekyll is made free to embrace pleasure and liberation in the body of Hyde, but the specifics of this liberation are curiously opaque. The trampling of the girl and the murder of Sir Danvers Carew are deplorable, but Hyde's snug little room in one of the worst parts of town seems curiously at odds with this vision of monstrosity. Critics recognize the influence on the text of the nineteenth century's theories about physical and moral degeneration: the pseudoscience of the time created anxieties about criminal types, racial dilution, genetic decline, and the possibly apelike reversal of Darwinian evolution. Some readers see contemporary anxieties about alcoholism or drug addiction. The unspoken (and unspeakable) specter of sexual exploitation hovers over this story, just as it hovered over Victorian society. Critics identify, too, a homosexual or homosocial subtext in the respectable bachelors' anxiety about the good doctor's peculiar relationship with his younger, smaller, and less sophisticated protégé. Yet these narrative strands, representing different perspectives, and the fragmented way in which the story is put together cannot be said to privilege any single reading. All are possible, and none go against the grain of a text that leaves so much in shadow.

In psychological terms, *Jekyll and Hyde* is a landmark text in the popular perception of the duality of human beings, which was a significant theme in nineteenth-century literature. "Man is not truly one, but truly two," says Jekyll, nor it is it a question of one or the other (or of one and then the other, as the story seems to imply), for Jekyll eventually recognizes that he is, as a deconstructionist might put it, always already "radically both." He goes on to propose that "man will be ultimately known for a mere polity of multifarious, incongruous and independent denizens" (*Works* 5: 58). This vision of multiplicity and unknowability goes far beyond the simple dualism of the nineteenth century. In fact, the true monstrosity of Hyde's condition is his monological singleness. For a shilling shocker, this is a strikingly modern insight. The unalloyed purity of Hyde's condition is as addictive and seductive as the most powerful drug, and Stevenson enjoys the irony that it was available only because of an unrepeatable impurity in the original composition of Jekyll's potion. Our true condition, Stevenson says, is to be found only in our plural, mixed, and hidden natures.

The unconscious was much discussed by philosophers and thinkers in the later nineteenth century, but it was Sigmund Freud who proposed the material study of that part of us that is forever unknowable, the brute id of our unconscious selves hidden by the shame of the superego. Jekyll discovers Hyde, but he still cannot know "the brute that slept within me," a state perfectly expressed in Jekyll's semantic confusion when he talks of Hyde: "He, I say—I cannot say, I" (71).

One of Stevenson's claims to modernity is his skillful use of duality and narrative methods to generate ambiguity and uncertainty. (Recent critics have argued that textual instability is a feature of Scotland's literary tradition [Randall Stevenson; Craig, "Beyond Reason"].) Students can discuss this engagement with duality further through the story "Markheim" (1885) and consider how Stevenson uses structural pairings in his plots in *Kidnapped* (1886), pairings that contrast the sturdy pragmatism of David Balfour with the romantic energy of Alan Breck. The playing of similarities and differences against each other in this way is akin to Fyodor Dostoevsky's use of doubling—for example, with Raskolnikov and Svidrigaylov in *Crime and Punishment*—to generate structural and psychological complexity out of simple narrative elements.

Students reading *The Master of Ballantrae* (1889) will see that Stevenson made good use of the pairing method when he revisited Jacobite history and Highland romance. This novel also rethinks adventure fiction, not least *Treasure Island* and *Kidnapped*, and I have argued elsewhere that the absurdly ineffective pirates and the sour account of how the Durie family came to support the Jacobite rising (one brother supported each side as a matter of political expediency, the decision made on the spin of a coin) are a dark commentary on those sunnier, earlier books (Watson, "'You Cannot Fight Me'"). Stevenson subtitled *Master* "A Winter's Tale," and early readers were much struck by what Andrew Lang called an "elaborate, melancholy, and almost hopeless book" with a "very modern gloom" (qtd. in Maixner 346).

Master is told by Ephraim Mackellar, faithful servant and steward of the Durie estate, as he remembers his involvement with the family more than forty years ago. The narrative encourages us to favor Henry Durie, the straitlaced Mackellar's favorite, as opposed to James, the master, whom Mackellar sees in increasingly devilish terms. But as the tale of the brothers' rivalry unfolds, we come to doubt this version, and the simple dualism of the structure is complicated and ultimately confounded as we come to see the unhealthiness of Henry's obsession with his fraternal rival and other and to recognize that the religiose Mackellar has confused James's cynicism and his disregard for social hypocrisy with something satanic. The text has other unreliable narrators, such as John Mountain and Chevalier Burke, while the tragic heroism of the Jacobite rising and the adventure of life as a pirate or of the search for gold in the wilderness are reenvisioned as a series of shabby, absurd, bloody, and inconsequential shams.

At key points in the story James surrenders to contingency by deciding his course of action on the spin of a coin—first to join Prince Charlie, then when lost in the North American wilderness. "I know no better way," he replies when charged with the childishness of this strategy, "to express my scorn of human reason" (*Works* 10: 57). Stevenson was fascinated with the Master's "causeless duplicity," which was "all I know of the devil" (*Letters* 6: 87). The origin of the brothers' murderous rivalry is shown to be equally closed to human reason by repeated passing references to the biblical tale of the twins Jacob and Esau, who left the womb at war with each other, without cause yet according to the will of God.

In the last analysis, the universe of *Master* is as bleak and meaningless as the wilderness of swamps and rotten wood that James Durie finds himself in, through which "we must cut our way like mites in a cheese" (55). Students will find that this bleakness is completely in keeping with the Darwinian sermon of Stevenson's essay "Pulvis et Umbra," written while Stevenson was working on *Master*, in which he confronted the possibility that all matter "rots uncleanly into something we call life" and that human beings are "a disease of the agglutinated dust" on a planet "more drenched with blood . . . than ever mutinied ship, [scudding] through space with unimaginable speed, and [turning] alternate cheeks to the reverberation of a blazing world, ninety million miles away" (*Letters* 6: 60; *Works* 26: 61, 62). This vision of contingency and existential disaffection, prefiguring Jean-Paul Sartre's philosophical nausea, lies at the heart of *The Master of Ballantrae*, even up to the sensational double death at the end of the tale, in a conclusion whose absurdity, like the chiseled boulder to one who "lies here forgotten" in the wilderness, speaks in its own way with a bleak eloquence (*Works* 10: 234).

The same vision can be found in the later fiction set in modern times—perhaps more easily for today's students—especially in *The Wrecker* (1892) and *The Ebb-Tide* (1894), both cowritten with Lloyd Osbourne but largely Stevenson's work. *The Wrecker* is a long, picaresque novel of financial speculation, disastrous reversals, fraud, double identities, and horrifically brutal murders. Yet the book is curiously lighthearted, as a black comedy about capitalism, American optimism, and the entrepreneurial ethic. In this respect it reads in the same irreverent, extended, but piercing style as Tom Wolfe's *Bonfire of the Vanities* (Watson, "Unrest"). Unfortunately, *The Wrecker* is difficult to find for teaching purposes. *The Ebb-Tide*, however, is both available and teachable throughout the curriculum.

The Ebb-Tide is undoubtedly Stevenson's modernist masterpiece, and students might read it alongside *Heart of Darkness* (written six years later). In what it says about the modern world and what little we can ever know about that world and about ourselves, it offers a worthy comparison with Joseph Conrad's work, as does *The Beach of Falesá*. Stevenson himself wrote:

> [*The Beach*] is the first realistic South Seas story; I mean with real South Sea character and details of life; everybody else who has tried, that I have seen, got carried away by the romance and ended in a kind of sugar candy sham epic, and the whole effect was lost—there was no etching, no human grin, consequently no conviction. Now I have got the smell and look of the thing a good deal. (*Letters* 7: 161)

Developing a vision of colonial decay, *The Ebb-Tide* starts with three men down on their luck and washed up on the beach of Papeete. Robert Herrick, having the name of an English poet (also known as "Hay"), is an educated failure, close to suicide, hanging out with a vicious cockney clerk and petty thief called Huish (also known as "Hay" and "Tomkins") and John Davis (also known as "Brown"), a disgraced alcoholic American skipper in a raging fever. "Everyone has a false nyme in the Pacific," says Huish (*Works* 14: 20), and indeed identities are curiously fluid in this world, for the novel, like *Heart of Darkness*, proves to be a symbolic fable as well as a postcolonial critique.

The trio see a chance to escape their predicament by agreeing to sail a smallpox-infected schooner, the *Farallone*, to deliver a cargo of champagne to Sydney, Australia. They plan to hijack the ship and change its name for their own profit, only to discover that most of the champagne is in fact water, for the ship and its cargo are part of an insurance fraud. The three men are caught in a web of duplicity, their own and others', where nothing is as it seems. Drunk, squabbling, and incompetent, they lose track of where they are and make landfall at an uncharted island, which turns out to be a secret pearl fishery run by a tall, brilliant, strikingly aristocratic, Cambridge-educated Englishman called Attwater. The Englishman rules the island alone, deeply suspicious of his unsavory visitors as he waits for a ship to collect his treasury of pearls. The group has now become a quartet ("Trio" and "Quartette" are Stevenson's ironically musical headings for the two halves of the novel), and an uneasy game of cat and mouse ensues, which ends with the death of Huish; the hysterical Christian conversion of Davis, who becomes Attwater's creature; and Herrick's attending the arrival of the pearl schooner *Trinity Hall*, named after Attwater's old college.

The book is a powerful critique of colonial reality, as its opening lines make clear: "Throughout the island world of the Pacific, scattered men of many European races and from almost every grade of society carry activity and disseminate disease" (1). It is also haunted by Stevenson's sense of our mislocated place in a much larger universe, on our own island world, as it were, rather as he imagined the earth itself as a blood-stained "mutinied ship" scudding through space in "Pulvis et Umbra."

Students can sense the enduring protomodernist power of *Ebb-Tide* from the symbolic and metaphysical unease that it generates through Stevenson's use of images and details from the setting and through the war of nerves between the three feckless adventurers and the patriarchal, godlike Attwater. Attwater is practically a deity in his little kingdom, and he believes in what amounts to an insane version of Calvinist predestination as a justification for his brutal exploitation of the natives and the island's wealth of pearls. Possessing a Nietzschean will to power, Attwater—one of Stevenson's most memorable characters—explains to his visitors why he is not alone. "Empty houses, empty sea, solitary beaches!" he says. "And yet God hears the bell!" (100–01). Looking at the diving suits he uses for pearl fishing, he offers a parable:

> "I saw these machines come up dripping and go down again, and come up dripping and go down again, and all the while the fellow inside as dry as toast!" said Attwater, "and I thought we all wanted a dress to go down into the world in, and come up scatheless. What do you think the name was?" he inquired. . . .
>
> "Why not the grace of your Maker and Redeemer, he who died for you, he who upholds you, he whom you daily crucify afresh? There is nothing here,"—striking on his bosom—"nothing there"—smiting the wall—"and nothing there"—stamping—"nothing but God's grace!" (87–88)

His assertion of universal nothingness without God's grace comes across instead as a vision of utter nihilism and suggests a terrible hollowness at the heart of things. "[R]eligion is a savage thing, like the universe it illuminates," says Attwater, "savage, cold, and bare, but infinitely strong" (89). This vision is what he has given himself to, as Kurtz will in his jungle.

Attwater shoots Huish, who tries to attack him with vitriol, while Davis chooses to stay on the island worshipping—in effect—Attwater. Herrick, however, having contemplated suicide more than once in the novel, decides to wait for passage on the *Trinity Hall* when it eventually appears. To seal this decision, he sets fire to the *Farallone*, and that is how the novel closes. It is as if the extraordinary confrontation with universal hollowness and an insane deity, in a microcosm of our own island universe, has steadied his nerves. Yet the novel's last words are given to the blubbering Davis, crying, "[W]hy not be one of us? . . . just say Lord, I believe, help thou mine unbelief! And He'll fold you in His arms. You see, I know! I been a sinner myself!" (140).

The strangely metaphysical burden of this work—a heart of emptiness rather than of darkness—is reinforced throughout the novel by Stevenson's use of symbols that seem to offer meaning only to end up curiously blank. Almost every image in *Ebb-Tide* rewards closer reading in this way. The ship's figurehead, which dominates the island, is mislocated on the shore; it has the shape of a huge woman beached and bleached "white as snow . . . beckoning with uplifted arm" (74). In another passage, it is "hurling something" (85). That ambiguous gesture, her size, and her eerie whiteness become very modernist indexes of blankness, of an unfathomable or even an entirely absent meaning. The island itself is not on any chart and looks as if it might sink beneath the waves at any point. Its strange beauty, low, delicate, and spectral, has a curious effect on Herrick, who "forgot the past and the present; forgot that he was menaced by a prison on the one hand and starvation on the other; forgot that he was come to that island, desperately foraging, clutching at expedients" (73).

Herrick's voyage, like that of Aeneas (the tale makes several references to Vergil), is more than literal. Like Aeneas, Herrick might even be contemplating a return to duty at the end. Yet the story does not offer closure of any sort. He has burned the *Farallone*, but he is still on the island, and the last words are given to Davis. If there are epic echoes in the text, they are fragmented or ironized like those in T. S. Eliot's *The Waste Land* or James Joyce's *Ulysses*. On the other hand, if Herrick has no clear future aim, at least he has decided—like Samuel Beckett's Vladimir and Estragon—not to commit suicide.

With insights such as these, and in its confrontation with human shame, failure, and existential absurdity, caught between the prospect of an empty universe and one presided over by an insane god, *Ebb-Tide* offers a compelling vision of modernity against which students can test their assumptions of the modernist canon.

Colonialism and Postcolonialism

Graham Tulloch

When one teaches Stevenson in a colonial and postcolonial context, his literary journey from Edinburgh to Samoa can be viewed in several different ways. From the perspective of national identity we can see this journey, if we accept the frequently held but contestable view of Scotland as a colony of England, as one from an old, established colonial context close to the imperial center to a new, precolonial or incipient colonial context on the edges of empire. One can compare Stevenson's writing about Scotland with his writing on the South Pacific, using both fictional and nonfictional texts, in terms of its treatment of the colonial subject and that subject's relation to the imperial center. From a literary perspective, Stevenson's journey can be seen as moving from a world that possessed long-established means, both literary and linguistic, of negotiating its relation to the dominant English culture to a world in which the colonial voice was still in the process of being formed and in which traditional European literary negotiations no longer operated. In this scenario, Stevenson's use of many new and different English voices he discovered in the South Seas may be compared with the interplay of Scots and English in his Scottish fiction. Moving beyond the dominant English-speaking voices, we can also consider whether Stevenson's introduction of occasional words from South Pacific languages, of longer passages of pidgin, or even of whole stories told from an indigenous perspective allows any effective voice to the indigenous people of the area (see Hill in this volume). Further, we can consider how far Stevenson succeeds in giving the colonized Gael a voice in his Scottish writing.

There is another, entirely different interpretation of Stevenson's journey: Stevenson is from the beginning allied with empire; to use his own terms, he has an English side along with his Scottish side. The notion of "Scotland's empire" (to borrow the title of Tom Devine's 2003 book) is helpful here: the Scots were subjects of the empire yet prominent among its leaders. But is this not a false dichotomy? Is not the colonial subject always partly complicit with the colonizer, if only because of the need to use the colonizer's language to write back to the metropole or even to describe the subject's colonial status? The most fruitful and illuminating colonial and postcolonial interpretations are often those that accept the conflicted position of the colonial who is simultaneously attracted to the colonizing power and rejects it.

A great deal of Stevenson's work, whether set in Scotland, the South Pacific, or elsewhere, is amenable to consideration in a colonial and postcolonial context. It can be considered in the context of other colonial and postcolonial writing, by writers of empire, like Joseph Conrad and Rudyard Kipling; by indigenous writers who use the colonial language (in Samoa, for example, Albert Wendt); and by Scottish people writing in Gaelic and South Pacific people writing in indigenous languages. But the most practical classroom strategy is to start with

Stevenson's most obviously colonial or postcolonial text, *The Beach of Falesá*, and work out from there.

We do not know the colonial status of the fictional island on which *Beach* is set, but the conditions, with Europeans challenging nominal independence, seem similar to those in Samoa, the place that particularly molded Stevenson's perceptions of colonial power. (Samoa was not a colony when Stevenson wrote, its legal status as an independent country having been confirmed by the Treaty of Berlin of 1889, but the imperial powers had encroached so far on the supposed independence of the Samoan archipelago as to render the island a quasi-colony ten years before its legal reduction to colonial status.) This quasi-colonial status enables us to consider *Beach* in the context of colonialism and also permits an interesting comparison with the perceived colonial status of Scotland. *Beach* presents key issues for a colonial or postcolonial reading: voice, standpoint, subject matter, and genre and their ability, together and separately, to disturb and challenge the metropolitan discourse.

Nowhere does Stevenson's Scottishness show itself so clearly, in this text devoid of Scottish references, than in his concern with voice. The narrator, Wiltshire, is the voice of "the beach," a term referring to the community of traders occupying the liminal space between the wider imperial world and the indigenous interior (*Works* 13: 2). His racist voice of imperial economic expansion, so brilliantly maintained by Stevenson throughout the narrative, can be challenging for today's audience, so sensitive to and condemning of racist language, but confronting this challenge in class provides a good entry point to the story. If Wiltshire remains unrepentantly racist in language to the end, his last sentences nevertheless offer a perfect example of how his voice undercuts itself:

> But what bothers me is the girls. They're only half-castes, of course; I know that as well as you do, and there's nobody thinks less of half-castes than I do; but they're mine, and about all I've got. I can't reconcile my mind to their taking up with Kanakas, and I'd like to know where I'm to find the whites? (75)

His typically understated expression of love for his daughters undermines his description of them as "half-castes," just as the erotically charged scene of his reconciliation with Uma after their quarrel shows the intensity of his connection with the indigenous world that he believes he despises. Thus the content and the language convey different messages. As Roslyn Jolly neatly expresses it, "Wiltshire's thinking remains trapped within a racial ideology from which his emotions have been liberated" ("Stevenson's 'Sterling Domestic Fiction'" 481). Similarly his frank admission that he intends to exploit the indigenous population in his trade disrupts the high moral claims of the imperialist endeavor, while his determinedly demotic tone unsettles the formal discourse of an imperial ruling class.

Students can recognize that in the dialogue Wiltshire shows his command of another, quite different voice, the South Pacific pidgin known as Beach-la-Mar (or "Beach de Mar," as he calls it [*Works* 13: 30]). By its very nature a hybrid, Beach-la-Mar both supports imperial power and resists it. The group of pidgins to which it belongs spread with European imperial power, and its adoption by indigenous people gave them power to communicate with the colonizer and with people speaking other languages. As expert speakers of Beach-la-Mar they could outdo their colonial masters, whose native European language often stood in the way of complete command of the pidgin. At the same time, pidgins could be denigrated as inferior forms of the metropolitan language. Stevenson shows himself aware of this complexity when he has Wiltshire take over the telling of Uma's life story, "all which would be very tedious, and fill sheets if I set it down in Beach de Mar, but which I must give a hint of in plain English" (30). Wiltshire's retelling of Uma's story of the devil women in his own words ensures that her tale is treated with respect (nowhere in the story is its validity called into question), but is also an act of cultural appropriation. This act raises a question well worth pursuing in teaching the text: if Stevenson gives a voice to Wiltshire, the partially colonized Englishman, does he give one to the indigenous colonial subject, Uma? It might also be helpful to consider how far in a story like "The Isle of Voices" Stevenson was able to write from an indigenous perspective.

Wiltshire's relation to the metropolitan culture is closely connected to his voice. His name, that of an English county, suggests an identification with the imperial center, yet he casually mentions that he is "mostly called Welsher" (36). Does he welsh on imperialism? Is he like the Welsh, England's first other? In any case it is clear that, although he represents a trading company and is an agent of economic imperialism, he speaks from the margins of empire, not from the center. Indeed his cultural associations with England have become attentuated almost to breaking point. He realizes that his dream of returning to live in an English pub is a fantasy, that his real point of reference is now much closer: he has time to "fix up [his] store regular Sydney style" (16). Christianity, so often an agent of imperialism, has ceased to have much meaning for him; he tells us that his "stove was alight, the smoke going up in a Christian manner" (14). Although he takes Uma's Bible with him when he ventures into Case's supposed devil's home, he does this to placate her; his only reference to the Bible is not to its content but to its illustrations when he describes the inhabitants of the island as "wrapped in their many-coloured sleeping clothes, like Bedouins in Bible pictures" (13). Cut adrift from his original cultural moorings, he has become so deeply connected with the people among whom he lives that he is a cultural hybrid, the typical product of colonialism. Whatever he says, his actions reveal him as both a trader, an agent of economic imperialism, and a supporter of indigenous life. He truly belongs to that meeting place of cultures, the Beach, and his commitment at the end to his hybrid daughters tells us more of the man than any of his protestations that he is a white man who despises the Kanakas.

Wiltshire's hybrid voice and perspective continue in the subject matter of his story, which is hybridity in its most basic sense: miscegenation. Generically too the story is a hybrid, combining the domestic novel with the adventure novel but providing transgressive versions of each (see Jolly, "Stevenson's 'Sterling Domestic Fiction'" 470–82). The domestic novel sometimes ends in a symbolic marriage of different cultural forces, but a mixed-race marriage exceeds the generic conventions. The incursion of the domestic space into the adventure space (emotionally for Wiltshire, literally for Uma) ensures that this story cannot be the boys' own adventure of imperialism. Stevenson's presentation of hybridity reminds us of Homi Bhabha's notion that hybridity "unsettles the mimetic or narcissistic demands of Colonial power" (112), as Ann Colley notes ("Robert Louis Stevenson's South Seas Crossings" 877). Hybridity can thus provide a useful starting point for the discussion of Stevenson's tale in a colonial-postcolonial context.

The unsettling of colonial power continues in Stevenson's other overtly colonial text, *The Ebb-Tide*. That two of the imperial powers then contending in the South Pacific, Britain and the United States, should be represented by the English Herrick and Huish and the American Davis is itself a commentary on imperial pretensions. First presented to us on the beach of Papeete, they are in their different ways offscourings of empire. These three disreputable characters embark on a parody of the imperial adventure story in one of its classics forms, Europeans landing on an unknown island in an exotic location. Stevenson handles the challenge to the discourse of colonialism quite differently in *Ebb-Tide*, but voice remains central to his technique. For Stevenson the South Pacific was a place of many voices, more complex even than the triple-voiced (English, Scots, and Gaelic) country in which he was born. In *The Beach of Falesá*, a single narrative voice undercuts itself; in *Ebb-Tide*, a trio of contending colonialist voices undercut one another. Neither the educated English voice of Herrick nor the cockney voice of Huish nor the American voice of Davis establishes dominance. Their ineffectuality calls into question the effectiveness of imperialism, and their failure to achieve a unified voice calls into question the unified imperial discourse. Even Herrick, a university-educated man and therefore closest to the class that directed the imperial enterprise, cannot speak for empire. His education has alienated him from his roots: what most powerfully recalls England for him is Vergil's *Aeneid* (*Works* 14: 3).

Students can experience a quite different approach to the critique of colonialism in Attwater's miniature colony. Attwater's ruthless determination to impose his will on the indigenous population, whom he has brought to the island to live completely under his control, and his single-minded exploitation of the natural resources mimic the grand enterprise of the colonial powers. Where Wiltshire accepts mixed-race marriage (with his heart if not with his head), Attwater forces his two workers to marry against their will so as to preserve his own sexual purity for his return to the imperial center, thus exposing the inhumanity of colonialism's suppression of hybridity (95–96). Attwater is not only the self-appointed ruler of the island but also its missionary. He is extreme in both roles. As missionary he imposes his version of Christianity on his colonial subjects, demanding that they adopt his beliefs without question; he demands the same of Herrick.

Students often view Wiltshire as the simple mouthpiece of the author's views and accuse Stevenson of racism. In fact, the perspective of Wiltshire, and of Herrick, is not totally alien to Stevenson: he too belonged to the colonizing power, brought cultural attitudes with him from home even if he jettisoned some of them along the way, and spoke the colonizing language. Stevenson did not endorse everything said or thought by Wiltshire and Herrick, but they expressed some of his own attitudes. In his South Pacific writing, attitudes to missionaries provide an interesting example of partial concurrence between Stevenson and the narrative perspective of his stories. Wiltshire remarks that missionaries are "partly Kanakaised, and suck up with natives instead of with other white men like themselves" (*Works* 13: 35). He speaks as a trader and in racist language, and it would be a mistake to accept this remark as an unmediated representation of Stevenson's views. Nevertheless Stevenson did have reservations about the activities of missionaries. Students can review his caution to Adelaide Boodle about the effects of missionary activity ("[R]emember that *you cannot change ancestral feelings of right and wrong without what is practically soul-murder*" [*Letters* 8: 326]) or his defense of Father Damien's work with lepers (*Works* 21: 27–42 ["Father Damien"]). These statements suggest that Herrick's revulsion for the missionary Attwater is aligned with Stevenson's attitude toward missionaries.

The question is how far Stevenson shared the racism embedded in colonial discourse. If Wiltshire's story endorses mixed-race marriage, does it also endorse his view of his wife as a child (*Works* 13: 5, 11, 29)? Perhaps not, since Wiltshire tells us that Uma treated him like a child and that they cooked together, "making a play of it like children" (28, 30). The question of the author's racism can be fully explored only by considering *The Wrecker*, *In the South Seas*, *A Footnote to History*, Stevenson's letters to the *Times*, and his personal letters. For classroom purposes, carefully selected extracts and photographs taken during the Stevensons' travels in the South Pacific will serve (see www.robert-louis-stevenson.org; F. Stevenson). The many images of the Stevensons with indigenous people can be read as commentary on their interracial relationships. Turning to these extra sources of information will not resolve the question — note that Stevenson's attitudes concerning race shifted over time — but it will deepen the discussion.

A further step to understand Stevenson in colonial and postcolonial context is to consider his British writings. *Treasure Island*, for example, provides an illuminating counterpart to *Ebb-Tide* (see Veeser in this volume). When we look at his Scottish writing for evidence of a colonial consciousness, several caveats might be borne in mind. First, Stevenson regularly set his Scottish fiction in the past, when Scottish identity was less compromised. Second, his Scottish world is largely self-contained; he does not use Walter Scott's ploy of bringing an Englishman to Scotland in order to introduce an English consciousness in opposition to a Scottish one. Third, Stevenson wrote at a time when Scotland had succeeded in negotiating for itself a secure and comfortable position in the

Union, in which its separate identity was acknowledged, and it could even claim a kind of preeminence over England, as symbolized by Queen Victoria's preference for her Scottish castle, Balmoral. During Stevenson's lifetime, the Scots could plausibly consider themselves to be making an even bigger contribution to the British imperial venture than the English. At all levels they were the agents of empire. Thus their colonial consciousness was often that of colonizer rather than colonized.

All that said, there is a colonial or quasi-colonial dimension in Scottish literature, if only because the dominant language is English and not Scots or Gaelic. Scots in particular is almost always enclosed within an English context. Even when the English voice has a distinctively Scottish color to it, as in David Balfour's narrative (*Kidnapped*) and seems entirely self-confident in its Scottishness, it is in fact a self-consciously created literary voice: David does not write like an actual eighteenth-century Scot writing English. The Scottish elements in this voice act as a submerged form of resistance to English linguistic dominance. There are relatively few texts written in Scots, like Stevenson's "Thrawn Janet." Even in these texts, where the assertion of Scottishness is at first sight complete and unassailed, the Scottish writer is actually involved in a complex act of resistance to English dominance, as Caroline McCracken-Flesher has shown ("Thinking Nationally" 312–18). Scottish literature also confronts internal colonization; if the English colonized Scotland, the Lowland Scots colonized the Highlands. David Balfour encounters this internal colonization in *Kidnapped* and *Catriona*. In regard to the comparison of it with the colonization of the South Pacific, Jolly provides a useful reading of *Catriona*, which was written in the South Pacific: colonial power's subversion of the rule of law is read in conjunction with Stevenson's letters to the *Times* about contemporary Samoa (*Robert Louis Stevenson* 113–56).

Finally we might consider an even broader comparison. One obvious text for this comparison is Conrad's *Heart of Darkness*. Although very different, it provides suggestive parallels to both *Beach* and *Ebb-Tide*. In each work, a European man travels to the remote edges of empire and finds another European man who is implicated in the secular and religious domination of indigenous people and with whom the first man has an ambivalent relationship. Furthermore, Conrad's Congo shared with Samoa and Scotland the position of being not quite a colony. There are other, minor parallels: Herrick finds salvation in caring for the steering of the boat, just as Marlow remains sane by concentrating on the mechanics of keeping his boat functional. But there are substantial differences. Wiltshire is both, as narrator, the Marlow and, because of his sexual involvement with an indigenous woman, the Kurtz of Conrad's story, although in other respects it is Case who fills Kurtz's role. Attwater, by preserving his sexual purity for marriage back in the imperial center, is both unlike Kurtz, who does involve himself with an indigenous woman, and like Kurtz, who plans to return to his Intended at home. The existential horror in Conrad has no counterpart in either of Stevenson's stories—Wiltshire exposes the apparent devilry as mere trickery. Whether in the end Stevenson's stories are less effective because they lack this dark center is a question worth pursuing, but there are more fruitful ways of making the comparison illuminate all three texts. Still, students can find rich enough material for comparative postcolonial analysis without moving outside Stevenson's work.

Narrative and Narratology: The Ebb Tide of Action

Robert L. Caserio

"He told himself no stories."
—Robert Louis Stevenson, *The Ebb-Tide*

Robert Louis Stevenson is a master novelist whose work is essential reading for students of narrative fiction. But what is a narrative? Is *narrative* a term whose definition students can take for granted? If a classroom is to foster lively discussion, students must thoughtfully engage the key terms it relies on. Stevenson's *The Ebb-Tide* (1894), cowritten with Lloyd Osbourne, uses its tale to represent narrative itself—and simultaneously to challenge expectations about it. *The Ebb-Tide* gives students an opportunity to define narrative and to grapple with its complexity.

This story is remarkable for its vision of human failure. Its trio of protagonists are losers, desperate to succeed but unable to. Robert Herrick stays aloof from religious conversion but will not be saved from his history of unachieved purposes. In fact he acknowledges that the condition of failure is his permanent fate. Stevenson startlingly suggests that Herrick's undergoing of failure, which includes loss of willpower, can be more valuable than self-assertive activity. Attwater, representing resolute will and activity, makes both look repulsive. Herrick, Attwater's opposite, is estranged from action yet is the object of the narrative's sympathy and hence of the reader's. That Stevenson in effect asks readers to see Herrick's failure as a good thing makes *The Ebb-Tide* unusual and gives students the opportunity to discuss Stevenson's challenge to their expectations about narrative—above all, about action's role in narrative.

But this opportunity depends on responding to more than *The Ebb-Tide*. Characterizing the uniqueness of any literary text is essential to interpretation, but while every text is unique, each shares characteristics with others of its genre. Students can too easily overlook the influence of a genre on one of its instances. To grasp the uniqueness of *The Ebb-Tide* it is necessary to consider the work's generic relation to narrative.

Theorizing and describing what constitutes the genre of narrative are the province of narratology. According to the narratologist Mieke Bal, narrative requires a teller who recites a sequence of actions and events that are initiated or undergone by actors (actors in a narrative include characters but are not necessarily persons) (*Narratology* 5–6). The narrator might be one of the actors but can also be external to the events recounted. Narrators see in some ways rather than others the actions and events that they tell. To understand how a narrator sees, we must hypothesize a difference between the matter-of-fact events of a story and the way they are seen, which is an essential part of the way they are told. We can better understand the multiple meanings and perspectives at play in a story by becoming conscious of how narratives differentiate the telling and seeing of actions from the actions themselves.

Students can easily recognize that the narrator of *The Ebb-Tide* is external, although he sees what he narrates more in conjunction with Herrick's perspective than with the perspectives of the other characters. What constitutes the actions and events undergirding the narration? Actions and events are identifiable as changes in the conflicts and fortunes of the actors. What change achieves the aims or resolves the conflicts of the actors in *The Ebb-Tide*? Classroom discussion can become complex, because the novel is a series of deadlocks, and every attempt by the trio to improve their existence reverses itself. One might call the reversal a change, an event; but the reversal is illusory, because the result of it is stasis. Huish destroys himself but is unchangingly self-destructive and malicious; Attwater converts Davis, but Davis's conversion looks like a variant of his alcoholism and does not help Davis to get home. Perhaps Herrick provides the narrative's pivotal, defining event. At a climactic moment he attempts suicide. Students might think of the attempt as an act of ultimate volition: at last Herrick will master his fate and transform it by taking it into his own hands. But Stevenson presents this act in a perplexing way. It fails, in line with Herrick's talent for failure, in a way that negates or at least compromises his volition. The suicide attempt suggests that Herrick's actions are inseparable from inaction and that this inseparability, amounting to a negation of action and its powers, turns out to be a saving grace—albeit not in any religious sense. Herrick is saved to the extent that he is permitted to go on, not enacting a life but enduring one.

But Herrick's saving grace is death for narrative. This problem provides an opportunity to discuss narrative's apparently irreducible characteristics. Without action, does story devolve into description or argument? Description, narratologists have thought, is at odds with narrative, inasmuch as description requires no action or event as its object. Neither does argumentation. Narrative would die, then, if it collapsed the difference between action and inaction, valued the inability to differentiate them, or altogether derogated action's importance. Students see this derogation in *The Ebb-Tide*. Stevenson's first paragraph declares that "European races . . . carry activity and disseminate disease" wherever they go (*Works* 14: 1). The "and" suggests synonymy between action and disease. The novel's title derives from a speech in Shakespeare's *Julius Caesar* that proclaims humanity's ability to control fate by mastering events when they are at high tide (4.3.218–24). Emphasizing the ebbing of that tide, Stevenson uses Herrick to interest us in the ebbing of human mastery and in the loss of personal possibilities of action. Herrick, always unable to do what he aims to, recalls another Shakespeare hero: Hamlet, a figure notorious for his inability to act.

The word *drama* derives from the Greek word for "action." Hamlet's inaction, and the drama in which he appears have long been considered surprising, because both character and play are at odds with their generic matrix. *The Ebb-Tide*, I suggest to students, has a relation to its narrative genre that is analagous to *Hamlet*'s relation to drama. The ebbing of the importance of action in it makes it a remarkably antinarrative narrative.

Evidence for this approach to *The Ebb-Tide* might begin with the prominence that Stevenson gives to Herrick's learning. Herrick's education provides a clue to meanings for narrative and action that Stevenson wants his readers to consider. Herrick's learned quotations evoke both the possibilities and impossibilities of coping with failure by means of opportune activity. They also introduce a sequence of types of narrative, subgenres, each of which expresses the importance of action and for which Stevenson invites comparison with action's perplexed status in Herrick's story.

The topic of opportune action is introduced by quotations from Vergil, whose *Aeneid* tells of Aeneas's effort to found a new fatherland for refugees from the Trojan War. In epic narrative, a hero's powers of choice and action are harshly tested but pass the test. Aeneas is tested by his passion for a Carthaginian queen, because it stands in the way of his achieving his national mission. By crushing that passion, he fulfills his goal, even though his abandonment of Dido drives her to suicide. The heightened power of action, raising mortal ability to a quasi-divine level, is one of epic narrative's generic hallmarks.

Herrick's knowledge of the epic enables readers to assess *The Ebb-Tide*'s narrative in comparison with Vergil's. Herrick opens Vergil at random, hoping to find a passage that will inspire him to renewed activity. When he arrives at Attwater's island, he learns that Attwater has named it Zacynthos, after a place in the *Aeneid*. Does this mean that Herrick has become a heroic actor in an epic narrative? That is unlikely. Students will see Attwater as a more suitable candidate for that role. Certainly Attwater thinks of himself in grand terms. He tells Herrick that he has been "making a new people here" (*Works* 14: 89). He declares that everything he does interests God, in the same way that the deeds of heroes in epic narratives interest divinities: "[W]e sit in this verandah on a lighted stage with all heaven for spectators! . . . the least beat of my heart and the least thought in my mind echo . . . into eternity for ever" (100–01).

Attwater's epic ambition is interwoven with religious evangelism. Attwater might remind students of the Acts of the Apostles, where Paul's conversion and his conversion of others drive the narrative. Attwater's boast and history suggest a fusion of epic with another subgenre, the adventure story. The original adventure story is Homer's *Odyssey*. Adventure stories pile unexpected event upon event, making action even more prominent. Herrick's history doesn't measure up to Attwater's identification with epic and adventure. Nor does it measure up to another narrative subgenre that emphasizes human action, romance, though Herrick favors it.

Students can move from comparing subgenres to considering narratology. Does narratology's soldering of narrative to actions and events result from an underexamined reliance on epic, adventure, and romance as models of storytelling? We see that Herrick relies on romance when he invents an encounter with a magician from the *Arabian Nights* (7). The magician gives him a flying carpet so that he can return to his abandoned family and sweetheart in England. The magic carpet is a metaphor for the ability of action to overcome the constraints of time and circumstance. One might argue that romance narrative, by ignoring those constraints, lies. Captain Davis also is a romancer. His magic carpet is the fantasy that his daughter, Ada, will save him from alcoholism. But Ada is dead. Stevenson implies that romance too is dead, along with the redemptive power of action it represents.

Stevenson's narration calls Herrick's romance tale a parable (56–57). *Parable* is another term students will want to consider. A parable encapsulates a thought or lesson by translating it into actions and events; it speaks in words, yet its action speaks louder than words. Contributions to narratology from the field of cognitive psychology tell us that parable-like projections are the origin and medium of all language, thought, and knowledge (Turner). Attwater, the man of action, is quick to turn thoughts and events into parables. Showing Herrick the diving equipment that Attwater's "people" wear to harvest pearls, Attwater insists that Herrick read the equipment as a parable of God's gracious ability to buoy up swimmers (and sinners) in life's troubled waters (87–88). Herrick prefers to see the diving suits, true to keeping his distance from resolved action, in terms of what he calls "impression[s]" (86). Impressions are states of feeling or sensation, passively received. They are amenable to description more than to parable or other types of narration.

Students will see that if Attwater is a success—unlike Herrick, who is a failure—he is no poster boy for action. His resistance to impressions is evident in the narrative that he makes out of the action he has taken against two of his native servants. He drove one to suicide and killed the other in cold blood. He presents what he did as an allegory, which is an extended parable. One servant is named Sullens, the other Obsequiousness. By thus elevating his account, Attwater stereotypes the natives and dramatizes himself as a heroic opponent battling their personifications. His allegorical projection magnifies his stature as an actor in an action-packed universe, but it erases humane intimacy and covers up colonialist and racist exploitation.

Thus *The Ebb-Tide* bundles together a spectrum of narrative types to which action is essential. Herrick does not fit in that spectrum. It is a great irony of literary history that Stevenson is identified only as a master of the adventure tale and of romance, genres that he defended, yet *The Ebb-Tide* is a criticism, expressed through Herrick, of what adventure and romance, and narrative itself, cannot do without. Immediately before Attwater's story of "my activity in the South Pacific," Stevenson focuses on tropical crabs, which have "an air of imperfect wooden things inspired with wicked activity" (90, 89). Echoing its initial identification of activity with disease, the narrative likens the crabs to Attwater, Davis, and Huish. The narrative suggests that all activity is wicked but goes a step further: it suggests that activity is an illusion. Huish aims to blind Attwater. His name, which can be pronounced "You wish," conveys the idea that action is indeed a process of projection, as the cognitive theorists claim. Yet the name simultaneously transmits the idea that action is a destructive projection of wishful thinking about our abilities. Perhaps our cherished ideas of action are a mirage we have derived from fiction.

Students can be encouraged to think about how we ordinarily recognize actions and events in terms of the intentions that shape them and by the way they stand out against an indefinite medium or context (Caserio). Students can then think about how Stevenson shapes Herrick's suicide attempt to be neither a voluntary action nor a definite event. At the moment Herrick means to drown, he becomes will-less, even though he feels he is grasped by a "fixed resolve." It is unclear whose resolve it is: "[A]t once he and not he . . . an external fate ineluctable as gravity" (115). The ineluctable force sets him swimming again, loaning him courageous purpose. But Herrick hopes a shark will stop him. Does he intend to die or not? When by chance he reaches the beach, the description of his state implies a defeat of action: "With the consequences of his acts he saw himself implacably confronted for the duration of life: stretched upon a cross, and nailed there with . . . his own cowardice. . . . [He] told himself no stories . . . even the process of apologetic mythology [i.e., self-justification] had ceased. . . . [He] did not attempt to rise" (117). Parodying scriptural narrative, he lies down on the cross but not in order to rise from it. He experiences no triumph of exertion, no resurrection of an active will, only the "incredible simplicity of submission to ascertained fact" (116).

Counterarguments are essential to the process of analytic reading, so at this point students should consider them. One perspective might argue that Herrick's "submission" is his resolved choice after all, therefore a definite action or event. Another argument is that if Stevenson uses Herrick's failed suicide to subvert the importance of action in narrative, he does so not absolutely but only to redefine action's role.

The first counterargument might claim that Herrick acts with deliberation not only when he resists suicide but also when he saves the ship by demanding that Captain Davis sober up and take charge, when he defends the native crew against Davis's threats, when he joins the murder plot, and when he refuses conversion. Five events, instancing change, would thus define the profile of his action and make it as prominent in him as in Attwater and Huish. The novel's action and events would then be in line with narratological and parable-centered assumptions, and Stevenson's narrative would not appear so startlingly at odds with its genre.

But Stevenson has outflanked this counterargument by presenting Herrick's response to the squall and his surrender to the murder plot with equivocations about their character as acts. "The passion of anger" moves Herrick in the squall, so we see not his action but his submission to something beyond his control (53). When the squall temporarily triumphs, Stevenson tells us that Herrick "exult[ed]; he was done with life, and he gloried in the release" (54). His resolute lifesaving turns suddenly into its opposite, leaving his action indeterminate. Meanwhile, not Davis but the squall is in charge: by chance it blows the ship over, by chance it rights it. The role of human action in the scene is more illusory than actual. It is no illusion when Herrick stands up for the crew—throwing down "his gage," like a knight in a romance, as a preface to battle with Huish

(66). But again Stevenson takes the wind out of the sails of action. Herrick's purpose is instantly undone by the discovery of Zacynthos. When the discovery is characterized by Herrick as "rather in the conditional mood"—that is, as a possibility rather than a fact—Stevenson is signaling that action in *The Ebb-Tide* is also, at best, in the conditional mood (67). The defense of the crew, having virtually no result in the story, seems part of this mood. Herrick's surrender to Huish's fatal plan is described not as a choice but as a sudden "orgasm," "placid with the placidity of despair" (94). And Herrick's resistance to conversion is, at least as he expresses it, not a deliberate choice but an aspect of his continuing "cross," his "incredible submission," which, like his swimming, seems to override his will. Can will-less submission qualify as action?

The second counterargument, proposing that Stevenson uses *The Ebb-Tide* not to undo action altogether but to redefine it, is more in tune with the novel. Still, students will find that *The Ebb-Tide* exceeds a redefinition. Some historical context can help them in their deliberations. By 1894, literary realism understood action and events on a diminished scale, adjusting them to that of ordinary life. Stevenson practices such a diminution, but he goes further: he seems to want to undo action entirely. Herrick tells Attwater that he cannot accept religious salvation because he "must stagger on to the end with the pack of my responsibility; I cannot shift it" (92). Narrative staggers on because it is gripped by a similar compulsion to continue, but that compulsion results in the same indefiniteness for action and event, for narrative itself, that Herrick's attempted suicide expresses.

Does this indefiniteness predict the recent doubt that narratology has about the contrast between narrative and description? Bal has come to think that narrative might be "generated by the descriptive motor" rather than by the "action" one ("Over-writing" 572). In the light of that doubt students will see that narratives can be more than they seem; can undermine themselves, our theories about them, and even our appetite for stories. Students will wonder what motivated Stevenson to "stagger" his narrative. Was it his characteristic experimentation with the forms of fiction, his desire as a novelist to be new? Students also might consider the world-historical context in which *The Ebb-Tide*'s sympathy with inaction is rooted, a context that Attwater, in both his colonialist and religious imperialism, exemplifies. After a century of the action of world conquest by economic and spiritual powers, a full withdrawal from the tide of active affairs—not just a revision of them—might have seemed to Stevenson a better way to endure.

Gender and Genre

Fiona Wilson

Students are typically intrigued to match Robert Louis Stevenson, author of *Treasure Island* and *Kidnapped*, with the dandified figure that gazes at us from one well-known photograph. Thin as a pipe cleaner he stands, hand on hip, as if daring the viewer to find fault with his languid locks and especially the tatterdemalion sash slung about his slender waist. I like to begin class with this image because of the challenge it presents to vague, unexamined notions of Stevenson as the purveyor of a simplistic *Boy's Own* Victorian masculinity. "Robert Louis Stevenson?" as a colleague rather snidely put it. "You mean pistols and pirates?" The photograph reminds us of a more nuanced reality. This is the Stevenson whose dress as a teenager earned him the nickname "Velvet Coat," along with vociferous taunts on the streets of Edinburgh ("Hauf a laddie, hauf a lassie, hauf a yellow yite" [Masson 159]); who enjoyed exceptionally close, possibly homoerotic, bonds with other men; and who, in the face of convention, married an older American divorcée, Fanny Osbourne—a kind of New Woman *avant la lettre*, with a knack for rolling her own cigarettes and spinning yarns about the California gold rush. This is also the author who wrote with full consciousness of the hypocrisy underpinning bourgeois attitudes toward gender. Stevenson rejected those attitudes and, throughout his life, questioned notions of proper masculinity and femininity. In *Virginibus Puerisque* (1876), he wrote dryly:

> [I]t is the object of liberal education not only to obscure the knowledge of one sex by another, but to magnify the natural differences between the two. Man is a creature who lives not upon bread alone, but principally by catchwords; and the little rift between the sexes is astonishingly widened by simply teaching one set of catchwords to the girls and another to the boys. . . . What should be the result of such a course? (*Works* 25: 18)

What indeed? The query is offered lightly enough—like an earlier passage in which marriage is amusingly described as "a sort of friendship recognised by the police" (6)—but, as so often in Stevenson's prose, there's steel beneath the velvet: culture either conceals or exaggerates sexual difference; gender codes are a "set of catchwords" taught to girls and boys; adult women and men are ignorant of each other's needs and desires; society denies modes of feeling not recognized by the police. In fact, a heightened, sometimes anxious, awareness of the sheer strangeness of prescribed gender roles returns over and over in Stevenson's work and has been the subject of much recent critical commentary. Pistols and pirates, for sure—but also swindlers, soldiers, strolling players, bank clerks, cigar smokers, and lady con artists.

Talking about Stevenson and gender in the classroom, then, offers thought-provoking possibilities for critical analysis, possibilities richly displayed in his short story collection *New Arabian Nights* (1882). While some of the stories in this offbeat, self-consciously bohemian volume can be productively read on their own, the most effective pedagogical approach, in my view, is to discuss the tales in comparison with one another. Because *New Arabian Nights* is a less canonical text and therefore has been less picked over by critics, it arrives in the classroom with a pleasing freshness that allows students to make their own discoveries. Still, as always, some historical and literary background is vital.

The first chapter of Elaine Showalter's *Sexual Anarchy* remains excellent background reading, placing Stevenson in relation to fin de siècle culture and a historical moment notable for both challenges to and outraged defenses of traditional gender roles. The final years of the nineteenth century witnessed the first fruits of the long struggle for women's legal equality, but the same period also saw the criminalization of homosexuality. Meanwhile, the psychologist Havelock Ellis was exploring notions of human sexuality as mutable—a line of thought that threatened to undermine standard binary models of gender as well as the prohibition of allegedly perverse sexual practices. John Addington Symonds, a friend of Stevenson and collaborator of Ellis, was about to write some of the first defenses of homosexual love in a series of privately distributed essays and books composed between 1883 and 1901, and Lydia Becker, a suffragist, was arguing that there is no fundamental intellectual difference between the sexes. Gender issues always invite reflection on broader historical themes, and students are invariably fascinated by the distant yet oddly familiar contours of British fin de siècle culture: distant for the obvious historical and geographic reasons, familiar because in many ways our cultural moment seems to have been anticipated, or even invented, by Stevenson's era. As students often point out, late-Victorian questions about gender and sexuality can seem startlingly modern. What does it mean to talk of men and women? Is gender performed or innate, a matter of learned catchwords or of natural difference? How does sexuality intersect with gender? Is the binary difference between the sexes absolute or continuous? Stevenson at once reflects and participates in the cultural ferment that produced such questions, and it appears throughout his work.

Stevenson began writing the stories that would become *New Arabian Nights* shortly after meeting Fanny Osbourne in September 1876. The collection was published in two volumes in 1882: volume 1 consisted of two groups of interlinked stories, "The Suicide Club" and "The Rajah's Diamond"; volume 2 presented the separate tales "The Pavilion on the Links," "A Lodging for the Night," "The Sire de Maletroit's Door," and "Providence and the Guitar." In obvious ways, the collection's title riffs on *One Thousand and One Nights*, generally available to British Victorians in Edward William Lane's bowdlerized translation (1840) and, after 1882, in John Payne's complete and unexpurgated version. Stevenson imports the well-known nested narrative technique from the *Arabian Nights* and makes allusions to specific stories and themes in that work (e.g., recurrent tales about thieves). But he features no caliphs or genies, and the role of Scheherazade has been completely annexed by the narrator, unidentified though presumably male. The settings of these "new" tales have shifted from Baghdad to the streets of London and Paris and, in one tale, to the harsh east coast of Scotland. Two stories take place in the fifteenth century; the rest are apparently contemporary. The carnivalesque style of the *Arabian Nights* is translated into a hothouse hyperfictiveness, with some distinctly nineteenth-century elements thrown in: dandified drollery, historical fiction, and Victorian gothic horror. The echoes between Stevenson's work and Richard Francis Burton's translation of the *Arabian Nights*, published just a few years later, are especially interesting. With its notorious "Terminal Essay," touching on homosexual practices in the East, Burton's text capitalized on preexisting notions of the Orient as a zone of romance where Western attitudes to gender and sexuality did not pertain (10: 63–302). Stevenson connected his love of romance with freedom from the moralizing demands of realism; he writes approvingly in his essay "A Gossip on Romance" (1882), "[Y]ou shall look in vain for moral or for intellectual interest. . . . Adventure, on the most naked terms, furnishes forth the entertainment and is found enough"; "picture-making romance" permits "the realisation and the apotheosis of the daydreams of common men . . . the nameless longings of the reader" (*Works* 29: 126, 125, 123). Statements like these raise important and provocative questions about gender, sexuality, and orientalism—as well as questions about the meaning and effect of genre.

For the most part, Stevenson's first readers found *New Arabian Nights* rather a rum go. What one critic praised as "a noble disregard of probability" another viewed as "feverish, unwholesome reading" (Maixner 107, 118). Concern about how to classify the collection was common, echoing general complaints about Stevenson's writing as "foppish" and "affected" (76). The *Saturday Review* liked the book but worried over its sudden breaches of literary decorum, particularly the "curiously ill-judged burlesque ending" of "The Suicide Club"; *The Spectator* openly worried about the "place" of these "grotesque romances" (110, 117).

I quote these early responses less to recommend classroom study of the volume's reception than to suggest one possible route into discussing gender and genre, both of which have much to do with the demarcation and policing of boundaries. If Stevenson's first readers had difficulty in placing the tales of *New Arabian Nights*, so too do twenty-first-century students, who tend to find the stories a rather strange brew. Where does this dissonance come from, and how is it expressed in the stories themselves? In part, it arises from the recognition that gender roles in *New Arabian Nights*, especially those associated with masculinity, are so exaggerated as to verge on camp. In part, it results from the suspicion that, as in opera, plot is not terribly consequential, merely a shortcut to the production of scenarios: "picture-making romance," in Stevenson's terms. But what exactly is being pictured here?

In "The Suicide Club" cluster of tales, the two central characters are Prince Florizel of Bohemia, a kind of Mittel-European detective royal, and his aide, the improbably named Colonel Geraldine. In the opening narrative, "The Story of the Young Man with the Cream Tarts," the Prince and Geraldine are inducted into the mysterious, all-male Suicide Club, the members of which draw lots to be killed by one another. Discreetly situated near Charing Cross Station, the club provides an outlet for publicly inadmissible desires. A young club member tells the Prince that they are not

> alone, or even exceptional, in the highly reasonable desire that we profess. A large number of our fellowmen, who have grown heartily sick of the performance in which they are expected to join daily and all their lives long, are only kept from flight by one or two considerations. Some have families who would be shocked, or even blamed, if the matter became public. (*Works* 1: 10)

The Prince is horrified but also secretly excited to discover "a degree of pleasure in his sensations" (23).

A similar aleatory thrill informs "The Adventure of the Hansom Cab." An officer recently returned from British India responds on a whim to an invitation from a London cabman and is transported to a mysterious establishment where young men are being selected for a secret task by a host so charming, he radiates an almost "feminine coquetry" (65). The cabman, the officer learns, has been instructed "to kidnap single gentlemen in evening dress, as many as I pleased" (60). A further twitch of the curtain reveals the cabman to be Geraldine and the host, Prince Florizel—"character," it seems, is unreliable, a form of dressing up, and narrative a form of open-ended play. Playfulness emanates too from the four interlinked stories that make up "The Rajah's Diamond." A cursed Indian gem is the overdetermined motif that connects these nested tales. The gem passes from story to story, from hand to hand, so lightly that one begins to suspect Stevenson might as well have titled the piece "The Rajah's MacGuffin." Here as elsewhere, Stevenson heightens narrative technique to elicit the types and situations of "picture-making romance."

This is where students can certainly make their own discoveries. For what are the types and situations presented in these stories? Students have no difficulty recognizing that "The Suicide Club" and "The Rajah's Diamond" are stuffed with characters so exaggerated as to suggest a parody of middle-class Victorian masculinity. Both stories feature a string of young men who struggle to embody chivalric ideals. Hapless, helpless, Silas Q. Scuddamore struts into a Paris ballroom "with the swagger of a cavalier" (35) but is quickly outwitted by a con woman mugging as a damsel in distress. Later, Scuddamore is ludicrously stuck with the disposal of a dead man discovered in his oversized Saratoga trunk. Dove-eyed Mr. Harry Hartley, having received all the advantages of a gentlemanly education, is "a graceful although a timid cavalier," delighted to serve his female employer in the role of "male lady's-maid and man milliner" (78, 80). The bank clerk Francis Scrymgeour indulges in the fantasy of being a knight-errant and legitimate heir to a fortune only to be roundly mocked for his presumption. Like Harry, none of these young men seem likely candidates for the imperial ideal, men who "lead armaments of war, or direct councils of State" (78). Yet as Dennis Denisoff points out, men of that sort are satirized too, as either puffing buffoons or sinister patriarchs. Masculinity, as conventionally imagined, is in these stories just a poor fit. Thus, General Vandeleur, the legal owner of the diamond, is a red-faced imperialist boor, "loud-spoken, boisterous, and domineering," and his brother, John Vandeleur ("The Dictator"), is a pastiche of more of the same (78). Florizel himself, the putative hero of both tales, is described from the beginning as "travestied . . . by the addition of false whiskers and a pair of large adhesive eyebrows" (2). Travesty is the style too of the narrator's final comments on Florizel—the breech of decorum that so bothered the critics:

> As for the Prince, that sublime person, having now served his turn, may go, along with the *Arabian Author*, topsy-turvy into space. But if the reader insists on more specific information, I am happy to say that a recent revolution hurled him from the throne of Bohemia, in consequence of his continued absence and edifying neglect of public business; and that his Highness now keeps a cigar store in Rupert Street. . . . I go there from time to time to smoke and have a chat, and find him as great a creature as in the days of his prosperity; he has an Olympian air behind the counter . . . the handsomest tobacconist in London. (155)

This is, as Denisoff writes, "masculine drag" (sometimes, one wants to say, a cigar is *not* a cigar) (295).

Up for debate, however, is the effect. Is this parody evidence of Stevenson's discomfort with existing models of heterosexual Victorian masculinity? or a piece of lighthearted frippery reminiscent of Stevenson's student hijinks in Edinburgh (Bell 75)? Is Stevenson's travesty of imperial heroism a critique of empire itself? How is one to judge, for example, the parallels between the history of the Rajah's diamond and the history of *One Thousand and One Nights*, a work passed from one Western translator to another? Showalter links the depiction of homosocial bonds in *Jekyll and Hyde* to what she calls "Clubland," the world of exclusively male private clubs that underpinned imperial Britain, and ties both to the fear of hidden homosexuality (12–13). Does the Suicide Club, with its cigar-chewing president and its thrillingly secret criminal activities ("the back stairs to liberty"), present a coded version of a homosexual subculture with its own private language (*Works* 1: 9)? If so, what is Stevenson's attitude to such a subculture? In Wayne Koestenbaum's view, Stevenson engages in "double talk," at once confessing and sequestering same-sex love, through the use of what the critic describes as "a dishonest genre—romance"; for Koestenbaum, Stevenson relies on the permissions of romance to disguise and deny what is essentially a literature of the closet (*Double Talk* 149). Koestenbaum's largely negative judgment of Stevenson can be usefully complicated in class, however, by consideration of the stories in the second volume of *New Arabian Nights*.

At first glance, the somber mood of much of volume 2 seems a strange fit with the camp excesses of volume 1. Stevenson's turn to historical fiction and gothic melodrama is a decided change of tone. Attention to detail, however, shows that this shift is less absolute than it might seem, raising important questions about genre, as well as the treatment of gender. Both volumes, for example, return repeatedly to the chivalric ideals idolized by Victorian culture. Given the spectacular puncturing of those ideals in "The Suicide Club" and "The Rajah's Diamond," one might expect to see their reclamation in the two medieval stories, "The Sire de Maletroit's Door" and "A Lodging for the Night." But Stevenson is interested less in comparing modern degeneracy with a purer, idealized past than in tracing the genealogy of a culturally powerful concept. In the first tale, the Sire de Maletroit reprises the role of malevolent patriarch but with nary a cigar in sight. Described as having "a strongly masculine cast; not properly human, but such as we see in the bull, the goat, or the domestic boar; something equivocal and wheedling, something greedy, brutal, and dangerous," the Sire seeks to force his niece into an arranged marriage in order to restore family honor (248). Honor—and the masculine codes associated with that idea—is the object of skeptical scrutiny too in "Lodging." This piece manufactures a dialogue between an aristocrat who embodies the chivalric code and the poet-thief François Villon. When the Lord of Brisetour lays claim to honor by virtue of his class (and sex), Villon sharply reminds him that honor is a culturally specific practice: "I've an honour of my own, as good as yours" (239). The notion of an alternative honor reappears toward the end of the collection, in "Providence and the Guitar," in which a pair of married strolling players, extravagant bohemians like Stevenson and Fanny Osbourne, are evicted by the police from a French town for not having an official license to perform. As a visiting Englishman remarks about the alternative society of artists and musicians, "They are all mad . . . all mad—but wonderfully decent" (297).

Perhaps the most interesting story in volume 2 is "The Pavilion on the Links," a weirdly haunting piece that can be read productively against "The Suicide Club." Once again, the gender codes embodied in the chivalric ideal take center stage. As the narrator, Frank Cassilis, tells it, "The Pavilion on the Links" is about how he came to meet his future wife, Clara Huddlestone. Halfway through the story, Clara is introduced as the fiancée of his old friend Northmour; she is also the daughter of a disgraced banker on the run from the vengeance of the Italian Carbonari. Cassilis and Northmour compete for Clara's hand, and the story's pivotal scene takes place in the pavilion of the title as both men attempt to defend the Huddlestones from the Carbonari. When Bernard Huddlestone is killed, the Carbonari retreat, and Frank claims Clara's hand. Northmour vows never to return, and the final words of the story describe how, years later, the defeated suitor "was killed fighting under the colours of Garibaldi for the liberation of the Tyrol" (216).

Of all the tales in *New Arabian Nights*, "Pavilion" lends itself most readily to a stand-alone treatment. This short story can be considered in terms of genre—that is, as an instance of gothic romance—or as an example of the Victorian adventure story, with fewer pirates and pistols, this time, than carbines and Carbonari. Another approach might be to pursue the line of argument proposed by Koestenbaum, through Eve Kosofsky Sedgwick's analysis of homosocial bonds in *Between Men*. Certainly, the heterosexual love story is counterpointed by images and allusions (picture making) that suggest the existence of another, unspoken narrative—a strong candidate for a case of double talk. In the opening paragraphs, we learn that both men once spent "four tempestuous winter months" in the pavilion, a period ended by a fistfight. "[I]t was only with a great effort that I mastered him," Frank recalls, "for he was near as strong in body as myself, and seemed filled with the devil" (160). The near-erotic image of the struggling men exerts a vivid fascination, as does the setting of the story: the pavilion, with its multiple doors and windows; the shifting, unreliable land on which the pavilion is built; the pavilion besieged at night by the horde of faceless Carbonari. There is a visionary quality to all this, like the scenes Stevenson describes in his essay "A Chapter on Dreams" (*Works* 30: 41–53), and it provokes more questions than can be contained in the boundaries of the Frank-Clara plot. What is the nature of the bond between Frank and Northmour and of the triangle that links both men to Clara? What is conveyed by the contrast between north and south, Scotland and Italy, the domestic and foreign? In pursuing these issues, it is important to remember that much of the force of the story inheres in the way that it locates these binary contrasts in a strikingly liminal and lawless landscape, as if to place all absolute categories in doubt. One problem with Koestenbaum's view of Stevensonian romance is that it closes off argument by replacing one set of catchwords with another ("Here's the *real* truth about Stevenson"). Perhaps Stevenson is less about double talk than he is about multitalk. Reading "Pavilion" in the context of the whole of *New Arabian Nights* introduces all kinds of new angles, pushing to the foreground the very issues of genre and gender that Stevenson has sometimes been accused of suppressing.

The Gothic: Detection and Science Fiction

Linda Dryden

In the canon of English literature, Robert Louis Stevenson's position has oscillated between celebrated man of letters and popular writer of boys' adventure fiction. In his lifetime Stevenson was highly regarded as an essayist of considerable talent, a man who was seen as an equal to Henry James and whose literary reputation was guarded jealously by friends like W. E. Henley. During the twentieth century, however, this reputation became subordinated to his popularity as the writer of the best sellers *Treasure Island* (1883) and *Strange Case of Dr Jekyll and Mr Hyde* (1886). His contribution to genre fiction depends on both texts. This essay suggests ways to situate Stevenson in patterns of genre and influence that complicate his canonical designation and show his status in and contribution to a popular fiction that is also significant literature. In class, his works can be used to inform the history of numerous popular genres and yet to question their critical boundaries.

Much of Stevenson's fiction arises out of a Scottish Romantic tradition (see Fielding in this volume). *Treasure Island* further falls in the category of boys' adventure romance, a tradition established by James Fenimore Cooper, Captain Marryat, R. M. Ballantyne, W. H. G. Kingston, and G. A. Henty. In turn, Stevenson's stories helped generate the imperial romances of H. Rider Haggard, like *King Solomon's Mines* (1885) and *She* (1887)—Haggard was famously challenged by his brother to write anything "half so good" as *Treasure Island*; the result was *King Solomon's Mines*, an instant best seller that far outstripped the sales of Stevenson's novel (L. Haggard 122). But tales such as *Jekyll and Hyde*, *The Master of Ballantrae* (1889), "The Body Snatcher" (1884), "Olalla" (1887), and "Markheim" (1885) also emerge from the gothic tradition of duality and the macabre, bringing to mind E. T. A. Hoffmann, Mary Shelley's *Frankenstein* (1818), and the works of Edgar Allan Poe.

Stevenson's critical delimitation in imperial romance arises in part from his friends' desire to preserve a more sanitized reputation for the author; it ignores the darker side of his fiction. Since the 1990s, scholars have recognized the traditions from which this work emerged and now explore the reasons for his enduring popularity and influence. For example, *Jekyll and Hyde* has become part of our cultural heritage, and its presence is felt in adaptations for film and television and in references in newspapers and magazines (McCracken-Flesher, "Cultural Projections"; Veeder and Hirsch; Danahay in this volume). Its influence on detective fiction and on science fiction narratives of mad scientists, experiments gone wrong, and dreadful transformations of the human body is undeniable and can be usefully traced in genre courses (Dryden).

In a sense it was ever thus with Stevenson: his writing always moved effortlessly between genres and narrative modes, often involving more than one genre at a time. Peter Keating explains why:

> The attractiveness of Stevenson rested on his possession of two highly-developed qualities which are rarely found together. He was an Aesthete and a writer of exciting stories. In an age which was becoming obsessed with the need to separate Art from Entertainment, Stevenson spoke and acted on behalf of both. (347)

Indeed, Stevenson combined art and entertainment to dramatic effect—so much so that his influence over subsequent gothic and detective fictions remains undiminished, and his contribution to the tropes of science fiction endures to this day. The discussion that follows, therefore, locates his reputation in genre and influence and suggests ways to demonstrate for students his role in the past and present of genre fiction.

Beyond Adventure: Stevenson and the Gothic

James Hogg's *The Private Memoirs and Confessions of a Justified Sinner* (1824) is an early example of Scottish gothic, where the narrator, Robert Wringhim, is manipulated into murder by his evil doppelgänger, Gil-Martin. Stevenson's gothic fiction is obviously influenced by *Confessions*, but it also has antecedents in Poe's "William Wilson" (1839) and Herman Melville's "Bartleby the Scrivener" (1853). The gothic genre has always relied on horror and duality, and Stevenson continued the tradition with "Olalla," a tale of vampirism, and "Markheim," a tale, like Hogg's, of duality and demonic possession—reaching his gothic apotheosis with *Jekyll and Hyde*.

The comparison of Stevenson with his predecessors and of his numerous gothic texts with one another all proves fruitful in class. Gothic duality features strongly even in his imperial fiction. But the most obvious gothic text of his later career is *The Master of Ballantrae*, where the brothers Henry and James Durie seem to represent good and evil, respectively. Like *Jekyll and Hyde*, *Master* problematizes for students a simple dialectic conflict: in both stories the hypocrisy of the good, in Jekyll and Henry Durie, compromises them, and their stories become tales of self-absorption and ultimately self-destruction. Neither tale relies wholly on sensationalist horror: each is a deeply moral and deeply psychological exploration of human vanity, greed, and aggressive primal instincts.

Students can extrapolate from many comparable texts that the Victorian realist novel generally assumed a belief in Christian certainties and in the essential goodness of its heroes and heroines. Stevenson, in whose mode of storytelling J. B. Priestly found "nothing Victorian," can be seen to muddy those clear waters (117). He used the gothic to expose humanity's less savory impulses and more conflicted motivations, to expose the fact that we are all *homo duplex*. Adding this psychological dimension to the gothic, or at least providing a tale in which it came to the fore, he influenced the gothic genre for decades and perhaps for centuries to come. In Stevenson's gothic tales, like Hogg's and like Poe's, the integrity of self becomes compromised, and identity is split and fragmented.

Urban Gothic

Traditionally it is this process of disintegration that creates the horror in gothic fiction, because it is unlooked for and unwanted—it is literally forced on the unsuspecting victim. Jekyll, though, is no victim: he is the author of his fragmentation, seeking the "separation of these elements," these "polar twins," and the shaking of the "very fortress of identity" (*Works* 5: 58, 59). Ultimately he abhors the notion of good and evil coexisting in one frame, where the evil is suppressed as a necessary function of social morality: "It was the curse of mankind that these incongruous faggots were thus bound together" (58). In seeking the separation of the two sides of his nature, Jekyll reveals his innate hypocrisy: he wants the respectability afforded by his profession and social standing but yearns for the debauchery that Hyde can provide. He fails to see, or fails to admit to himself, that he is both Jekyll and Hyde. This idea gives gothic horror a new dimension, and students can track how Stevenson establishes a further trope of it when he locates this moral and psychological horror in the heart of the modern metropolis.

The conventional locale of the gothic in the eighteenth and early nineteenth centuries had been an ancient rural landscape with looming castles and crumbling graveyards. Increasingly, as the nineteenth century matured, gothic narratives began to shift, along with the population of the Industrial Revolution, from the countryside to the city. Students can play this forward, considering how Poe's Paris in "The Murders in the Rue Morgue" (1841), Hogg's Edinburgh in *Confessions*, and Melville's New York in "Bartleby" become locations of gothic horror. By the time Stevenson came to write *Jekyll and Hyde*, the modern city, and particularly London, was a teeming metropolis, a melting pot for "all sorts and conditions of men" (Besant, *All Sorts*). Here, any background in Charles Dickens is helpful, or Jerry White's *London in the Nineteenth Century* (2007). Through this lens, *Jekyll and Hyde* stands forth as the epitome of the urban gothic, where Hyde scuttles across the length and breadth of London to seek the nefarious, mostly unspecified, gratification of his perverse desires. The city has become a place of terror in which people are as vulnerable to acts of violence as they were in the remote lanes, inns, and decrepit, ancient structures of the countryside. More than any of his predecessors, Stevenson brought gothic horror to the metropolis, where it has remained ever since.

The shift in the gothic's geography can been seen most obviously in Bram Stoker's *Dracula* (1897), where a large part of the story takes place in fin de siècle London. Arthur Machen clearly followed Stevenson's lead for *The Great God Pan* (1890) and *The Three Impostors* (1895), both of which deal with the traditional duality of the gothic but are heavily influenced by Stevenson's imagination in the urban setting. In *Pan*, Helen Vaughan is a latter-day Jekyll and Hyde, a femme fatale who haunts the city's fashionable nightspots, preying on wealthy young men to sate her murderous sexuality. In *The Three Impostors* we encounter an even greater debt to Stevenson: the very narrative sequence and some of the events of the story are influenced by his *The Dynamiter* (1885), one of the books in the *New Arabian Nights* volumes. Machen admitted as much, writing:

> And it was in the early spring of 1894 that I set about the writing of the said "Three Impostors," a book which testifies to the vast respect I entertained for the fantastic, "New Arabian Nights" manner of R. L. Stevenson, to those curious researches in the byways of London which I have described already, and also, I hope, to a certain originality of experiment in the tale of terror. (*Things* 144)

The reader for Heinemann, overstating the matter, even commented that Machen's book was "Better than the best of Stevenson" (149). In *The Three Impostors* Machen returned to the terror tradition of the gothic, but he retained Stevenson's addition of the episodic format and the urban landscape, thus creating out of Stevenson's narrative inventions a new structure and a new narrative dynamic for the gothic tale of terror.

The Dynamiter can show students how Stevenson further parted from convention. Again in the urban context, he exploits the comic potential of the genre, adding wit, absurdity, and inconceivable coincidences. Using the device of a mysterious and beautiful young woman, Clara Luxmore, who is prone to flamboyant disguises and fabricating extravagant histories of her past, he constructs a series of gothic vignettes that traverse time and geography. Clara's flights of fancy lie at the center of the story and are as comic as they are gothic. This mixture enabled him to play with a genre that had largely been based on horror and sensationalism. In addition, he could take the gothic short story of the Poe tradition and stitch it into a larger, more coherent narrative through the motif of Clara's mischievous fabrications.

Stevenson had experimented with this episodic, gothic form in the earlier *New Arabian Nights* volume in 1882, creating a series of self-contained tales knitted together through the agency of his enigmatic central character, Prince Florizel (see Wilson in this volume). *The Dynamiter* has more internal narrative cohesion than the earlier *Arabian Nights* volume, but it too employs Florizel as a unifying character. However, it is the overarching story of Zero, the eponymous dynamiter, that ensures the story's narrative trajectory and its influence on writers of other genres.

Urban Terror and Detection

Stevenson's influence on urban terror can be tracked in Joseph Conrad's *The Secret Agent* (1907), also set in the city. Over twenty years before Conrad's novel, Stevenson had responded to dynamite campaigns in Ireland and London with *The Dynamiter*. The tone of the novel may be comic, but underlying its frivolity is the serious concern of actual urban terror, as Deaglán Ó'Donghaile has argued:

> Zero is killed within the circulation of modernity and its media, where the train platform, bustling crowds, and newspaper stand converge. The final explosion marks terrorism's absorption within the schema of urban modernity, so that instead of ending the city's cycle, the terrorist is appropriated by it. Exploding amid the crowd on the platform, Zero is atomized, fusing with the scattered remains of the daily papers, and achieves not the destruction of the system that he opposes but a literal synchronicity with it; instead of disrupting the metropolis, the terrorist—and his spectacularly violent campaign—is "processed" within it. (167)

If the fiction of terrorism is, as Ó'Donghaile argues, a fiction of modernity, it is also a new genre that, building on Poe's prototype Dupin (another useful comparison for classroom debate), inaugurates detective fiction. *The Dynamiter* is a gothic novel of terrorism and detection set in the modern urban landscape of London. This meeting of genres brings new possibilities for urban narratives, possibilities that were seized on by writers like Conrad and Arthur Conan Doyle.

As many have already observed, *Jekyll and Hyde* is also a detective story. Its very title suggests a police "case," and the various "statements" that form the novella's chapters read like witness accounts. Jekyll's "Full Statement of the

Case" is in itself like a convict's confession. "The Carew Murder Case" and the ensuing hunt for the culprit reprise the crime narratives of Poe, Wilkie Collins, Dickens, and Fyodr Dostoevsky. Utterson, the lawyer intent on protecting his friend's reputation, is transformed into an urban detective, stalking his prey, searching for clues, and formulating hypotheses. Finally, in possession of all the statements, he solves the crime.

Given its sensationalism, it is little wonder that *Jekyll and Hyde* influenced subsequent tales of crime and detection. Doyle even took Stevenson's lead by blending the gothic with the literature of detection when he wrote *The Hound of the Baskervilles* (1901–02). As Stevenson had demonstrated, gothic tropes mixed with murder and pursuit made for a potent mix: the most famous novels of Stevenson and Doyle rely on exactly that blend of horror, sensation, and mystery. As Owen Dudley Edwards says in *The Quest for Sherlock Holmes*, Stevenson had a close literary connection with Doyle: "Stevenson deeply admired his work, while having himself more influence on Doyle's literary formative years than any other contemporary writer" (14).

Stevenson brought duality to the fore in his tale of crime and terror, and it has remained at the heart of much detective fiction ever since. The troubled, flawed detective with his rational, reasoning brain and his poetic or artistic yearnings has become a staple of such fiction. This character endures through Inspector Morse and into Ian Rankin's Inspector Rebus. Keating rightly says that Dickens's *Bleak House* (1852–53) and Collins's *The Woman in White* (1859–60) were "rendered down into the tightly controlled solution-solving adventures of a Sherlock Holmes" and that such works are the precursors to twentieth- and twenty-first-century crime novels (342). However, between the mid-nineteenth-century stories of Dickens and Collins and the emergence of Sherlock Holmes in the fin de siècle, even before the demise of the three-decker novel, students can tease out Stevenson's use of the stripped-back novella format to create a protodetective story in *Jekyll and Hyde*.

From Gothic Horror to Science Fiction

Stevenson was writing on the cusp of burgeoning new directions for fiction. The emergence of the detective novel, the imperial romance of Haggard, the urban gothic, and tentative steps toward modernism coincided with another major development: the scientific romance, later to become what today we call science fiction. It is generally acknowledged that H. G. Wells's first novel, *The Time Machine* (1895), inaugurated science fiction, even though the genre had many precursors—in particular, Shelley's *Frankenstein* and Jules Verne's fantastical romances. New genres in literature do not emerge fully fledged; rather, they draw on and develop previous literary tropes and preoccupations, both established and marginal, and add a new, distinctive identity for emergent fiction.

For that reason, Stevenson can be included in the ranks of those who contributed to science fiction, and any course focused on science fiction would do well to include him.

Because Stevenson never wrote what we think of as science fiction, his texts prove useful to stimulate debate about genre boundaries and their privileged terms. His influence on science fiction is undeniable and wide. The mutation of a benign, respectable pillar of society into a grotesque creature resembling an evolutionary throwback has inspired comic book writers of superhero narratives since *Superman*. Hiding his identity from an enquiring public, Superman emulates Jekyll's dilemma and represents a reversal of Hyde's public threat by becoming a public hero. More derivative is the story of the Incredible Hulk, who actually does mutate into a threatening monster, like Hyde, through a scientist's experiment gone wrong, like Jekyll's. The notion of mutation, public threat, and existential angst lies at the heart of much of this type of science fiction and can be traced back to Stevenson's sensational narrative.

The Genre of RLS

Keating notes that Stevenson's ability to cross genre boundaries so effectively was unusual:

> One of the remarkable features of Stevenson's career is the way that he moved over so many different kinds of fiction, proving a commercial success in most of them, functioning as a powerful influence on their subsequent development, and ignoring the advice of friendly admirers that he should sit still and concentrate on being an Artist. (343)

Foremost among those "friendly admirers" was Henry James, who offered similar advice to Wells, hoping he would join the ranks of the emerging modernists. Wells declined. Like Stevenson, he was a gifted writer who worked successfully in different genres, and, like Stevenson, he was able to bring the reading public along with him and make a comfortable living from his literary pursuits.

Stevenson, traveling Europe, the United States, and the South Seas with an extended and dependent family, was aware of the wide potential audience for fiction, was heavily influenced by financial considerations, and knew that genre fiction would sell—often first in serial, then in book form. (His letters provide a rich mine of data for students to track his commercial and aesthetic considerations as he negotiates the best opportunities for his work.) *Treasure Island* began as a means of entertaining his stepson, Lloyd, but could become the byword for boys' adventure stories, as exemplified by Haggard's efforts to emulate its success. *Jekyll and Hyde*, though it was conceived in the tradition of Christmas ghost stories and was intended to appear in time to capitalize on the Christmas market for such fiction, has resonated far beyond that moment. Genre fiction thus provided Stevenson with a living to suit his very unusual personal circumstances, as it provided an outlet for his extraordinary talent.

Students reading the variety of Stevenson's work in the twenty-first century may learn to be grateful that Stevenson ignored the advice of literary friends like James and pursued his own inclinations to experiment and to entertain: genre fiction, literature in general, is the richer for his determination. Comparing the terms in which Wells and Stevenson were each encouraged to evade popularity and embrace aesthetics can reveal for students not just the critical mores of their moment but also the artistic and readerly importance of these authors' contrarian and commercial choices.

Travel Writing: Nonfiction into Fiction

Oliver S. Buckton

Travel was among the most significant sources for and enduring subjects of Stevenson's writing. Beginning with his early travels in Europe, which resulted in two published books—*An Inland Voyage* (1878) and *Travels with a Donkey in the Cevennes* (1879)—Stevenson widened his horizons and made ambitious and life-changing voyages to California and the South Seas. These were recorded in travel narratives such as *The Amateur Emigrant*, which narrates his journey by steamship and emigrant train to California (1892 and 1895), and *In the South Seas*, which is based on his cruises in the South Seas Islands (1896). Many of Stevenson's writings offer compelling accounts, in nonfictional and fictional texts, of his travels and of his encounters with new landscapes, peoples, and cultures. This essay outlines strategies for introducing students, in a course on the author or on travel literature, to Stevenson's travel writing and understanding its connection to his fiction.

In teaching Stevenson's travel writing, I find it useful to situate it against the prominence of travel for Herman Melville, Joseph Conrad, and Pierre Loti. We note that travel writing has marginal status in Stevenson's work, being cultural, economic, and biographical in nature. Recognizing that his reputation has been based on the popularity of a select group of fictional works—especially *Jekyll and Hyde* and *Treasure Island*—I begin by showing that Stevenson was himself involved in the exclusion of travel writing from his canon. I have students read "My First Book" (published in 1894, the year that he died), in which Stevenson writes, "I am not a novelist alone. But I am well aware that my paymaster, the great public, regards what else I have written with indifference, if not aversion. . . . [A]nd when I am asked to talk of my first book, no question in the world but what is meant is my first novel" (*Works* 2: xxiii). I draw students' attention to his reference to his "paymaster," foregrounding the economic factors that led him to devote his energy increasingly to the more lucrative market in fiction. From his biography, it emerges that after the publication of *Travels with a Donkey*, he made an epic journey by steamship and railway to California, in pursuit of Fanny Van der Grift Osbourne, an American whom he married in 1880. With a wife and two children to support (her offspring from her previous marriage), he was under pressure to increase his income (xxiv, xxvii) and thus turned to a "story for boys" to earn his first substantial paycheck (xxvi).

My approach is not to emphasize the differences between Stevenson's early travel writing and his first novel but to teach the two by tracing the similarities and continuities between them. While admitting the formal and commercial differences between genres, I interrogate the distinctions between nonfiction and fiction by focusing on Stevenson's use of travel and location as the foundation of plot and character development in all his texts. In an illuminating passage from "My First Book," Stevenson identifies a detailed knowledge of location as key to the writer's craft:

> [I]t is my contention—my superstition, if you like—that he who is faithful to his map, and consults it, and draws from it his inspiration, daily and hourly, gains positive support. . . . The tale has a root there; it grows in that soil. . . . Better if the country be real, and he has walked every foot of it and knows every milestone. But, even with imaginary places, he will do well in the beginning to provide a map. (xxxi)

The metaphor of the tale as a plant that grows in the soil of landscape is useful for making the related point that his fiction had its root in travel writing. The map he provides the reader in *Treasure Island*, though imaginary, is a figure for the central importance of the journey to the novel's plot: indeed, Stevenson states that the map is "all the plot" in this novel, as the journey is the basis of plot and character in *Travels with a Donkey* (xxxi).

With *Travels with a Donkey* I show students how in this nonfictional travel book Stevenson exhibits a novelistic sense of character and relationship and uses location to develop both practical and theoretical insights about the pleasures and burdens of travel. (In travel courses, Edward Said's *Orientalism*, James Buzard's *The Beaten Track*, Mary Louis Pratt's *Imperial Eyes*, and Nigel Leask's *Curiosity and the Aesthetics of Travel Writing, 1770–1840* can provide useful theoretical context.) We then proceed to *Treasure Island* to see how Stevenson transforms travel into a profitable commodity through the addition of two crucial elements: the treasure hunt as an objective of travel; the map as an object in the text that allures the reader. In both works, the narrator develops a relationship with an attractive yet troublesome character that functions as an ambivalent figure for the journey itself.

The advantage of beginning the course with *Travels with a Donkey* is that the narrative's focus on Modestine, the donkey, invites various psychological and figural readings that lead to productive discussion. For example, Stevenson's animation of the animal that carries his pack draws students' attention to the material practices of and obstructions to travel in the nineteenth century. *Travels* is unusual in this extended description of the means of travel, of its technical difficulties in the Victorian age. The author expresses his frustration with the labor of travel, as he "took in [his] right hand the unhallowed staff, and with a quaking spirit applied it to the donkey." He is "worthy [of] the name of an Englishman, and it goes against [his] conscience to lay [his] hand rudely on a female," which raises interesting issues of national identity and gender (*Works* 17: 150). He identifies as an "Englishman" partly to appeal to English readers, whom he, as a new Scottish writer, courted. But his pose as a chivalrous gentleman is undermined by his subsequent search for a more effective implement for inflicting pain on Modestine, culminating with a goad that made the donkey his "slave" (161).

The text is rich with biographical and historical implications. Stevenson finds parallels between the Camisards of the Cévennes and the Covenanters in his native Scotland: "Pont de Montvert, or Greenhill Bridge, as we might say at home, is a place memorable in the story of the Camisards. It was here that the war broke out; here that those southern Covenanters slew their Archbishop Sharpe" (219). He also finds topographic parallels: "It was like the worst of the Scottish Highlands, only worse; cold, naked, and . . . scant of life" (178). He sees in his journey through the valley of the Tarn "a pass like that of Killiecrankie; a deep turning gully in the hills, with the Tarn making a wonderful hoarse uproar far below" (224). Invoking one of the most famous Scottish battlefields, site of the defeat of Claverhouse at the hands of the Covenanters, this passage illustrates how Stevenson historicizes the landscape through which he travels.

To give the biographical context of *Travels*, I have students read Richard Holmes's fascinating chapter from *Footsteps* that interprets the Cévennes journey and Stevenson's relationship with Modestine as at once a preparation for his epic journey to America and a reflection of his ambivalence toward Fanny Osbourne. Holmes writes that "the whole Cevennes experience was a kind of initiation ceremony: a grappling with physical hardships, loneliness, religious doubts, the influence of his parents, and the overwhelming question of whether he should take the enormous risk of travelling to America and throwing his life in with Fanny's" (65). For Holmes, this journey exposed as a myth the notion of the solitary traveler that Stevenson cultivated: "My gradual discovery of Fanny Osbourne, and her hidden importance in Stevenson's journey, made me realize how Stevenson fitted into the enormously intricate emotional web of other people's lives" (68). This important insight supports the point that the subject of travel writing is the mental and emotional character of the traveler as much as if not more than the places that the traveler visits. Overall, *Travels with a Donkey* illustrates Stevenson's early, dilettante approach to travel, seen as a loosely structured, even random journey instead of a purposeful itinerary. Encapsulated in his remark that "[f]or my part, I travel not to go anywhere, but to go. I travel for travel's sake," this attitude suggests a leisurely approach to travel and invites comparisons with the philosophy of Victorian aestheticism, with its dictum of "art for art's sake" (*Works* 17: 178).

If we read *Travels* as a personal journey of emotional self-discovery, then Stevenson's response to the monastery of Our Lady of the Snows is illuminating: despite the monks' "solemn and cheerless isolation," Stevenson is attracted to some aspects of the monastic lifestyle: "I can see a certain policy, not only in the exclusion of women, but in this vow of silence." Apparently alluding to his seduction by or of Fanny Osbourne, he laments how "the dreams of boyhood, the schemes of youth, are . . . deserted at once for two sweet eyes and a caressing accent" (192). This passage helps students understand that his early travels were partly a flight from domestic life and from the feminine, hence his discomfort at being faced with the femininity of his donkey. The reference to the monks' "exclusion of women" also provides a transition to *Treasure Island*, of which he wrote in "My First Book," "there seemed elements of success about this enterprise. It was to be a story for boys; no need of psychology or fine writing; and I had a boy at hand to be a touchstone. Women were excluded" (*Works* 2: xxvi). Referring to his stepson, Lloyd Osbourne—the original boy audience of *Treasure Island* and Stevenson's later collaborator on *The Ebb-Tide*—Stevenson suggests the journey as an enterprise in which women have no place.

The *Hispaniola* in *Treasure Island* has no women on board, and it is precisely this absence that gives the grown men license to revert to childhood. Stevenson recalled, "I had counted on one boy; I found I had two in my audience. My father caught fire at once with all the romance and childishness of his original nature" (*Works* 2: xxvii). Yet this children's fantasy, as my class now realizes, is grounded in the experiences of travel Stevenson accumulated during his European journeys and his life-changing voyage to America. We explore the roots of the novel in his travel and knowledge of landscape. What has changed is that he jettisons the bohemian "travel for travel's sake" philosophy in favor of a commercially driven and end-oriented model of travel. The journey in *Treasure Island* has the specific goal of obtaining a hoard of money, a goal that mirrors Stevenson's move to achieve commercial success through fiction.

The map drives the plot, directing its possessor to wealth: Doctor Livesey's "fingers were itching to open it," while Jim's excitement at the voyage is bound up with its lucrative nature: "I was going to sea myself; to sea in a schooner, with a piping boatswain, and pig-tailed singing seamen; to sea, bound for an unknown island, and to seek for buried treasures!" (*Works* 2: 35, 47). Long John Silver's ambiguity as a villain derives partly from the fact that he shares the desire for wealth with Livesey, Trelawney, Jim, and Stevenson himself. I direct students' attention to the parallels between wealth as a motivation for travel in *Treasure Island* and the excitement of Stevenson at producing a text that would yield him profit. As he wrote his parents, "There has been offered for *Treasure Island*—how much do you suppose? . . . A hundred pounds, all alive, oh! A hundred jingling, tingling, golden, minted quid. Is not this wonderful?" (*Letters* 4: 119–20). Travel was henceforth intimately bound up with money.

The journey in *Treasure Island* is referred to as a "cruise," as when Captain Smollett states, "I don't like this cruise; I don't like the men; and I don't like my officer" (*Works* 2: 54). This term alerts students to a significant change in Stevenson's travel writing, from travel on land to travel at sea. His previous journeys had either been on foot or traveling inland waterways. Now his travel writing would be based on journeys by steamship to New York or by schooners in the South Seas (the *Casco* and the *Equator*), journeys that move away from Europe toward the distant places in which he would make his home. The term *cruise*, as I use it in teaching Stevenson's travel writings, applies to both fiction and nonfiction and denotes an approach to travel that might seem at odds with the quest for profit in *Treasure Island*. Yet the abrupt shifts in direction and narrative style characteristic of his first novel reveal cruising as narrative that is open-ended, sacrificing definite structure and closure for a more exploratory, experimental pleasure in the literary journey (see Buckton, ch. 1).

Of course, as we discover in shifting our focus to Stevenson's travel in and writing about the South Seas, cruising too was a source of profit. *In the South Seas*, Stevenson's major work about the South Pacific, began when Stevenson was invited by the American newspaper entrepreneur Samuel McClure to write a series of "fifty letters (2–3,000 words each) from the Pacific on subjects of his own choice, for which he would receive a fee of £20 per letter in England and a further $200 each in the USA" (McLynn 313). Stevenson was drawn to the South Seas Islands because they were conducive to leisure and possessed a climate that would benefit his fragile health. In the first of his South Seas letters, he portrays himself as an invalid in search of rejuvenation: "For nearly ten years my health had been declining; and for some while before I set forth upon my voyage, I believed I was come to the afterpiece of life, and had only the nurse and undertaker to expect. It was suggested that I should try the South Seas" (*Works* 20: 3).

Students therefore find interesting Stevenson's dissatisfaction with his literary output during his cruises (from 1889) and residence on Samoa (from 1890), far from both his native Scotland and what his friend Edmund Gosse, expressing "disappointment" at the South Seas letters, termed the "literary atmosphere" of London (McLynn 408). Gosse's criticism notwithstanding, a significant source of Stevenson's dismay about the letters was his inability to produce the magnum opus on the history, society, traditions, and culture of the South Seas that he had envisaged almost from the beginning of his cruise. He described his purpose in a letter to Marcel Schwob: "I am about waist-deep in my big book on the South Seas: *the* big book on the South Seas it ought to be, and shall" (*Letters* 6: 401). Stevenson conceived of this book as an ethnographic "prose-epic" that would undo generations of misrepresentation of Polynesia and portray "the unjust (yet I can see the inevitable) extinction of the Polynesian Islanders by our shabby civilization" (Johnstone 103). The lack of a settled home at first hampered the execution of his ambitious South Seas project, even while the cruises were providing the material for his writing. The spontaneous and random excursions by ship, his preferred mode of travel, proved far from ideal for the production of a major volume of historical, cultural, and anthropological analysis. Cruising was conducive to the writing of more informal texts, such as journals, letters, and yarns, which would be published in installments. Daunted by the scale and complexity of such a big book, Stevenson finally abandoned this project and found other outlets for his South Seas material: letters and yarns were marketable commodities that would both mine his experience and yield profit.

The metaphor of quarrying provides students with a key to Stevenson's conception of his literary labor in the South Seas, evident in his emphatic response to Sidney Colvin's Gosse-like criticism. Stevenson declares, "*These letters were never meant, and are not now meant, to be other than a quarry of materials from which the book may be drawn*" (*Letters* 7: 115). In teaching these travels,

I draw the class's attention to specific examples of his quarrying his journals (the basis for his letters, serialized in Britain and the United States) for material to be incorporated into his fiction. Stevenson and Fanny made a visit to the island that he described in "A Pearl Island: Penrhyn." Illustrating the fragmentary nature of his South Seas writing, this piece appeared in the letters' serialization in the *New York Sun* but not in *Black and White*, and it was not published in the 1896 edition of *The South Seas* (Swearingen, *Prose Writings* 134–43). The local sailors on Penrhyn possessed a figurehead, Lloyd Osbourne's photographs of which are included in Fanny's book *Cruise of the* Janet Nichol. Stevenson noted:

> [O]n the verandah, the figure head of the lost ship stood sentinel: a very white and haughty lady, roman nosed and dressed in the costume of the directory. . . . [W]ith head thrown back, she gazed on the house and the crowding natives . . . I thought it strange to stand by the figure head, in the tropic sun, beset by a throng of Penrhyn Islanders, and be talking of the Glasgow road.
>
> ("Pearl Island" 20–21; Natl. Lib. of Scotland MS 9892 [Balfour Papers])

Fanny wrote a description of this figurehead that echoes Stevenson's. She describes "a very haughty lady in a magnificent costume. She held her head proudly in the air and had a fine, hooked nose" (F. Stevenson 55). She goes on to relate the troubling influence of the figurehead on the natives of Penrhyn: "When the figurehead came ashore people were terribly alarmed by the appearance of the 'white lady.' The children are still frightened into submission by threats of being handed over to her" (56). Given its regal bearing and "magnificent costume," the figurehead may represent Queen Victoria, the distant monarch who authorized much of the travel and exploration during the Victorian period.

This figurehead makes a good transition to the class's discussion of *The Ebb-Tide*—originally titled "The Pearl Fisher"—which, according to Roger Swearingen, was begun "after the cruise of the *Casco* in 1888–89" (*Prose Writings* 184). By August 1890, Stevenson was writing, "I have two huge novels on hand—*The Wrecker* and *The Pearl Fisher*. . . [the latter] I think highly of, for black, ugly, trampling, violent story, full of strange scenes and striking characters" (*Letters* 6: 401). The narrator of *Ebb-Tide* notes a large discarded object that, despite its femininity, serves as an emblem of the white man's colonization of the islands: "[O]n the top of the beach and hard by the flagstaff, a woman of exorbitant stature and as white as snow was to be seen beckoning with uplifted arm. The second glance identified her as a piece of naval sculpture, the figurehead of a ship" (*Works* 14: 74). Stevenson takes a thing he saw on his travels and transforms it into one of the most powerful symbols of his South Seas fiction.

Some of the novel's "striking characters" also came from Stevenson's travel writing. In concluding the course or unit, we focus on Tembinoka, the king of

Apemama in the Gilbert Islands. The figure of Tembinoka was one of the main reasons why, according to Colvin, "no less a person than Mr. Joseph Conrad . . . prefers *In the South Seas* to *Treasure Island*" (Colvin [1911] 3: 308). My claim here is bound to strike some students as controversial: that Tembinoka is the model for the British colonialist Attwater in *Ebb-Tide*. Ann Colley has argued that Attwater is based on missionaries in the South Seas, asking, "What is Stevenson implying about missionary culture in his depiction of this towering Attwater?" (*Robert Louis Stevenson* 39). By contrast, Tembinoka would have been viewed by most Victorians as a savage, in stark opposition to the eloquent and outwardly refined Cambridge-educated Attwater.

By pointing to parallels between these two characters in Stevenson's writing, I conclude the course with two essential ideas about his travel writing. First, Stevenson quarried people as well as locations, landscapes, and objects for the enrichment of his fiction. Second, by transforming into fiction an original object or figure from his travels, he had an ideological agenda. Presenting Modestine, his donkey, as a symbol of the burden carried by all travelers suggests practices of travel ignored by many travel writers. Making legible a connection between a Polynesian king and a British colonial tyrant suggests that the sharp distinction between savage and civilized is a myth.

Children's Literature

Barbara Chatton

Robert Louis Stevenson's works aimed at children enjoy a rare distinction as we enter the twenty-first century: today's children still read them. Works for young people achieve the status of classic in two ways: because they have historical importance for the field of children's literature or because they continue to be read (and in many cases watched or heard) by children. Stevenson's books are classics in both senses. They changed the literature created for young people, and they stand the test of time with young readers. They thus offer an important opportunity to those of us who teach students who will in turn cultivate young readers, starting in the elementary classroom. *A Child's Garden of Verses*, *Treasure Island*, and *Kidnapped* invite us to consider just how a text becomes a classic in children's perception and what important classroom work can be achieved through the appeal children recognize in such books.

In this essay I provide historical information to help situate Stevenson's writing for children and review his influence to show what features of his writing have proved most compelling for young people over time. As a teacher of students working toward careers in elementary classrooms, I focus too on the immediate appeal of his writing and throughout imply the virtue of students' consulting their own responses as a way to chart and engage the reactions of the children those students will be teaching. A further route to such engagement lies in texts derived from Stevenson's work and in the powerful illustrations Stevenson has inspired. These texts and illustrations both are good materials for a classroom analysis of cultural history, literary and artistic resonance, and the interaction between child and text.

Classroom discussion in courses on children's literature might begin with *A Child's Garden of Verses*, which has been continuously in print since Stevenson first published the collection in 1885. Its verses continue to be shared with young children, and many of our students know them from their own childhood. Indeed, children often encounter Stevenson first through his poetry. Because of this familiarity, it is instructive for students to learn the historical context of these verses and to consider the degree of their innovation. After reading the poems in Kate Greenaway's *Birthday Book* (written by Sale Barker, illustrated by Greenaway, and published in 1880), Stevenson began writing verse about his own experiences as a child. He wrote these poems while confined to bed in a darkened room as he recovered from a serious illness. Dedicated to his childhood nurse, Alison Cunningham, they capture the joyful moments and imaginative play of his youth.

The poems in Greenaway's collection are moralistic and sentimental, while those in *A Child's Garden* reveal the imaginative life of real children. Most of Stevenson's poems remain fresh and relevant today. Classroom discussion can demonstrate that freshness simply by having students quote from childhood memory. Often they can recite verses from "The Land of Counterpane,"

"My Shadow," and "The Swing." A mother I know recites the two short lines of "Happy Thought" to her children whenever they encounter something new.

Reading through Stevenson biographies (and there are many), students are struck by how much he accomplished despite his being sickly most of his life. They might consider how rarely his illnesses appear in these poems. "The Land of Counterpane" alludes briefly to being ill but focuses on the elaborate imaginative games played with a collection of lead soldiers. Classroom debate can track the invitations of voice, or the lure of imaginative play. Modern children hearing the verse can easily imagine the play they might experience when confined to bed with a cold. Verses such as "Pirate Story," "Armies in the Fire," and "The Dumb Soldier" show Stevenson's lifelong love of adventure, and "Travel" and "Foreign Lands" his love of travel.

But students should recognize that despite the collection's childlike and contemporary feel, a few verses don't entirely escape the nineteenth-century urge to preach to children—for example, "Whole Duty of Children" and "System." Others reflect the Eurocentric values of Stevenson's time. Several verses describe playing "wild Indians," perhaps arising from Stevenson's childhood enjoyment of the books of James Fenimore Cooper. "A Thought" speaks of children saying grace "[i]n every Christian kind of place" (*Collected Poems* 25); "Foreign Children" describes the habits of children of other places around the world and ends with "O! don't you wish that you were me?" (38). Such moments provide an opportunity to review cultural differences over time and to discuss the necessity for thoughtful selection of poems in elementary classrooms.

Stevenson's books also raise questions about the relation between text and audience through illustration and about the role of illustration in elementary teaching. In 1895, ten years after the publication of *A Child's Garden,* Charles Robinson created the first illustrated edition. Modern editions of the volume tend to feature tidy, well-dressed children painted in the pastel style of Greenaway, perhaps a bow to the classic status of the poetry. Tasha Tudor's illustrated edition (1947), created in her signature nineteenth-century romantic style, remains in print. Diane Goode's delicate watercolors in a 1998 edition also portray sweet, innocent children. Picture book versions of individual poems, on the other hand, feature modern settings, contemporary children, and vibrant color. Glenna Lang and Ted Rand have each illustrated "My Shadow," and Ashley Wolff and Daniel Kirk have each created a version of "Block City." Kim Fernandes's illustrations in *The Little Land* are almost three-dimensional and dreamlike. Tracy Campbell Pearson's illustrations for *The Moon* tell a completely modern story of a father and son's boat trip by moonlight. Max Grover's *Where Go the Boats?* includes four verses illustrated in bright acrylics and set in a modern city. Each of these picture books introduces the poems to a new generation of children through a modern context.

Stevenson's first successful book for children, *Treasure Island*, appeared in serial form in *Young Folks* magazine in 1881 and 1882 and was published in book form in 1883. Here, students can discuss the influence of working with and for children on Stevenson's writing. As Stevenson recounts in "My First

Book," the story began when he created a map of an island while he was drawing with his stepson, Lloyd. Stevenson shaped the island to be similar to one he had visited off the coast of Scotland as a young man but included pirate features, like "Captain Kidd's Anchorage" and an X to mark the spot where the treasure was buried. With that map as a starting point, he began writing chapters of his novel, sharing them each evening with his family. Lloyd responded enthusiastically to these readings and suggested that the book would be better with no women characters. Except for a mention of Long John Silver's native wife and early chapters that include descriptions of Jim Hawkins's helplessly weak mother, Stevenson complied with this request. Stevenson's father, a lighthouse engineer who knew much of the sea, responded with "all the romance and childishness of his original nature" and added comments and suggestions on the setting (*Works* 2: xxvii).

It is often illuminating for students of Stevenson and children's literature to read along with a child. My friend Mark and his ten-year-old son Ky followed in the footsteps of the Stevenson family, reading *Treasure Island* together this past summer. Mark observed that Ky was interested in pirates from seeing *Pirates of the Caribbean* movies and from reading Dugald Steer's *Pirateology*, an elaborately illustrated fictional sea journal that contains a great deal of actual history. When I asked Ky what he knew about pirates before he read *Treasure Island*, these influences clearly had affected his understandings of pirate life: he replied, "I know that pirates steal and fight and get drunk a lot. They wear baggy clothes and they sail on ships. They lived in the past. . . . They have to talk in a certain way. They say things like 'shiver me timbers' and 'arghhh.'"

Such responses invite students to think again about the author's own reading and about cycles of influence. Like Ky, Stevenson enjoyed reading adventure tales and stories about pirates when he was young, as he mentions in the introductory poem for *Treasure Island*:

> If sailor tales to sailor tunes,
>   Storm and adventure, heat and cold,
> . . . .
> And all the old romance, retold
> . . . .
> Can please, as me they pleased of old,
>   The wiser youngsters of to-day:
>
> —So be it, and fall on! If not,
>   If studious youth no longer crave,
> His ancient appetites forgot,
>   Kingston, or Ballantyne the brave,
> Or Cooper of the wood and wave:
>   So be it, also! . . .
>
> (*Works* 2: frontispiece)

Stevenson's novel is consequently full of action, and yet it has fully realized characters and settings, with neither the didactic tone nor the sensationalism typical of nineteenth-century adventure stories. Like Mark Twain, whose *Tom Sawyer* and *Huckleberry Finn* were published in the same time period, Stevenson wrote about young people who were not at the mercy of a hostile world but instead free to act with the authority of adults. *Treasure Island* is not a story of good versus evil, as many stories for the young at that time were, but one of nonstop adventure with little time for reflection. Although Jim Hawkins writes of his adventures after the fact, it is not to show the lessons learned but to relive an excellent if frightening adventure. Jim uses his courage, wits, and strength to save his crew members several times and proudly boasts of these feats when confronted by the pirates. This aspect of *Treasure Island* appealed to Ky, who wrote about his favorite part of the story: "I really liked it when Jim stole the ship. I liked that it was one kid against a man and the kid wins."

But Stevenson's texts can raise issues of empathy, even of moral relativism, that are challenging for students preparing to teach in the elementary classroom. Although Jim narrates and plays an active role in the story, the wily and charming Long John Silver, who changes sides and makes arguments to suit his purposes, continues to be the most memorable character. Stevenson's original title, "The Sea Cook," indicates his focus on and preference for Long John Silver (Swearingen, *Prose Writings* 64). Jim clearly finds the man both repugnant and fascinating. The pirate is, after all, a killer, a thief, and a liar. Jim is glad that Silver escapes in the end, saying it is because Jim no longer has to deal with him. But there is a grudging admiration for Silver's ability to survive and thrive in the world of pirates. Ky assumed that Silver had a change of heart at the end of the novel (a response not typical of adults). Ky wrote, "Long John Silver was my favorite character, because at first he was a bad guy and then he turned good. He respected the Captain, Doctor, and Jim. . . . I like that Long John Silver has a happy ending. It would be bad to hang Long John Silver."

Perhaps this feeling of Ky and children like him speaks to Stevenson's success at creating a fully realized world—another good topic for discussion among students of elementary education. In his dedication for *Kidnapped*, Stevenson confesses, "[H]ow little I am touched by the desire of accuracy. This is no furniture for the scholar's library, but a book for the winter evening school-room when the tasks are over and the hour for bed draws near" (*Works* 6: xi). Certainly the cold fogs, live oaks, and sea lions that Jim finds on the beaches of *Treasure Island* are more appropriate to the Pacific Coast at Monterey, where Stevenson waited to marry Fanny, than to the Atlantic. The captain of the ship that Stevenson and his family took to Samoa years later pointed out to Stevenson the factual errors he had made about ships and sailing. Yet if his works are not technically accurate, he vividly conveys a sense of the excitement of sailing the ocean and exploring new places. His clear delight in ocean travel, his lack of seasickness, and his vigorous activity while aboard ships come across in Jim's adventures at sea. Education students might select and parse some of their favorite passages of travel in an effort to understand how Stevenson persuades young readers to enjoy the adventures along with him.

Of course, ocean adventure books continue to be popular with young people. It is worth comparing these with their source in Stevenson, both to see what Stevensonian allure persists and what each new moment demands of and implies about its readers. Students might consider Brian Jacques's fantasy series *The Castaways of the Flying Dutchman*, one volume of which involves adventures with pirates; the series allows readers to pursue ocean adventures across space and time. Avi's *The True Confessions of Charlotte Doyle*, a Newbery Medal honor book, provides a comparison closer to Stevenson. It is set on a transatlantic voyage in 1832. The hardships of shipboard life, the nefarious doings of the ship's company, and the vital role of a young person echo *Treasure Island* but are modernized through a young girl narrator. That Avi wrote the introduction to the Aladdin edition of *Treasure Island* suggests Stevenson's influence on his work.

Since Stevenson's contemporaries too were influenced by stories of pirates, their work provides another, comparative line of influence. Here students can consider the role of intertextuality. Captain Kidd and Henry Morgan contribute to J. M. Barrie's tales of Peter Pan (the play in 1904 [Peter Pan], the novel in 1911 [*Peter Pan*]), which introduce Captain Hook and his crew, another classic group of pirates for young people. Stevenson's pirates are cruel and murderous men—worthy adversaries for young Jim Hawkins and his friends. In important contrast, Barrie's are comical and easily outwitted by children. Their influence appears in picture books for younger children, such as Mem Fox's *Tough Boris*, in which the pirate Boris cries when his parrot dies, and in Ridley Pearson and Dave Barry's *Peter and the Starcatchers*, a continuation of Barrie's story. The dark Stevenson tradition is developed in Philip Caveney's *Sebastian Darke: Prince of Pirates* and Sid Fleischman's *Giant Rat of Sumatra; or, Pirates Galore*. Together, Stevenson and Barrie's inventions for pirate appearance and behavior have shaped our notions of what pirates are like. Hook donates a coat and a hook; Long John Silver contributes a wooden leg and the parrot sitting on his shoulder and squawking, "Pieces of eight." But the influence is predominantly Stevenson's—the treasure map marked with an X, the black spot, and the sea chantey "Fifteen Men on a Dead Man's Chest," which has been included in pirate tales ever since.

There is an abundance of comparative material for those wishing to use adaptations: *Treasure Island* has achieved such classic status that it now exists in a large number of editions and formats. From N. C. Wyeth to Robert Ingpen, illustrators have visually reproduced Stevenson's images of pirates. There are two graphic novels, by Tim Hamilton and by Roy Thomas and Mario Gully. Stuart Paterson has adapted the novel as a play, and there are TV versions (e.g., Athanassiou's *The Legends of Treasure Island*), Brian Henson's Muppets version, and Ron Clements's recent Disney cartoon set in space (Clements and Musker). Editions of the novel with teaching guides (such as the Enriched Classic Series edition of *Treasure Island*) as well as Web sites like www.webenglishteacher.com/stevenson.html and www.robert-louis-stevenson.org indicate the continuing use of *Treasure Island* in classrooms.

Aids to classroom teaching of Stevenson include biographies of him for young people. Education students can study how lives are scripted for their schoolchildren and consider what makes a particular background choice helpful and appropriate. Carol Greene's *Robert Louis Stevenson: Author of* A Child's Garden of Verses appeals to younger readers; Angelica Carpenter's *Robert Louis Stevenson: Finding Treasure Island* and Beverly Gherman's *Robert Louis Stevenson, Teller of Tales* are written for older readers. When Stevenson traveled by steamer and train to California to be with his future wife, Fanny, he described the trip in *Across the Plains*. Jim Murphy uses entries from this work in his history of nineteenth-century emigration, *Across America on the Emigrant Train*. Stevenson was more prosperous on his second voyage to the United States, when he and his family sailed on a steamer with a cargo of exotic animals. This strange journey has been retold for children in the poet Nancy Willard's *The Voyage of the Ludgate Hill: Travels with Robert Louis Stevenson*.

Stevenson wrote books for the young that he would have liked to read as a child. It is for this reason that his works have achieved classic status. By putting his young characters at the center of his stories and giving them the life and personalities of real children, he helped change the course of children's literature. Both in his poetry and his adventure novels, children are allowed to explore and imagine, to have adventures and to play, instead of being lectured at and preached to. Robert Louis Stevenson wrote a number of works for young people, including *Kidnapped* and *David Balfour* (published as *Catriona* in the United States). But it is *A Child's Garden of Verses* and *Treasure Island* that have stood the test of time with young American readers. Both provide elementary education students with the unique privilege of standing at the center of a historic exchange between writer and reader.

The Essay and the Periodicals

Thomas Richardson

Although Robert Louis Stevenson's modern reputation rests largely with a small number of works of fiction and the poetry collection *A Child's Garden of Verses*, Stevenson was an essayist from the beginning of his writing career until the end and ranks among the most widely read and widely published essayists in his time. He thought the essay, or "short study," as important an art form as fiction and poetry: "Short studies are, or should be, things woven like a carpet, from which it is impossible to detach a strand" (*Works* 27: xiv [*Familiar Studies*]). His essays represent a significant literary output and cover a wide range of subjects, including personal reminiscences and autobiography, biography, social philosophy, love relationships, nature, and travel. He also produced many reviews and critical works that address literary form and function, the character of the imagination, and the achievement of individual authors. He published more than one hundred essays, nearly all of which first appeared in the burgeoning periodical press, and they featured in over thirty different periodicals, including all of the most highly regarded magazines of the 1870s and 1880s, such as the *Cornhill Magazine*, *Macmillan's*, *Longman's*, the *Athenaeum*, and *Scribner's*.

In terms of his achievement as a literary artist, his significance for literary history, and the diversity of his subjects, Stevenson the essayist offers opportunities for teaching in a variety of courses: Victorian prose, creative nonfiction, surveys of Scottish or British literature, fiction writing, literary criticism, life writing, and even first-year composition. He collected many of his essays for publication in book form soon after their periodical publication, and these volumes are available to students in the various editions of his collected works. For modern students the essay collections provide the easiest access to the most important of his essays, especially those in *Virginibus Puerisque* (1881), *Familiar Studies of Men and Books* (1882), and *Memories and Portraits* (1887). The essays were sometimes revised for book publication, but Stevenson always added an introductory essay to each volume that suggested new ways of thinking about his work; therefore these collections also offer approaches to teaching his essays beyond their original periodical contexts.

Stevenson was born in Edinburgh in 1850 and grew up in this city that was rich in literary tradition. Harriet Beecher Stowe, on visiting Edinburgh in 1853, wrote, "Edinburgh has had an effect on the literary history of the world for the last fifty years, that cannot be forgotten by any one approaching her. The air seemed to be full of spirits of those who, no longer living, have woven a part of the thread of our existence" (1: 80). Periodical literature was central to the literary culture of Stevenson's Edinburgh and an important element of that influential "thread" of the city's literary history—although it must be noted that the magazine "spirits" were sometimes malignant. The *Edinburgh Review*, a quarterly journal founded in 1802, initiated what became a very competitive and highly politicized periodical market. Edited by the author and advocate

Francis Jeffrey, the *Edinburgh* was published by Archibald Constable, who also published the long-standing monthly literary miscellany the *Scots Magazine*, which in 1817 was renamed *Edinburgh Magazine and Literary Miscellany*. The *Edinburgh Review* quickly became a popular publication and well respected for the quality of its articles, but the review was aligned with Whig politics and in the midst of the tension of the Napoleonic era eventually alienated some of its neutral or Tory supporters, including Walter Scott. In 1809, with Scott's support, the London publisher John Murray (also a Scot) established the *Quarterly Review* as a Tory counterpart to the *Edinburgh*. Then in 1817, encouraged by the review and magazine successes of both Constable, his Edinburgh rival, and Murray, his London ally, William Blackwood established *Blackwood's Edinburgh Magazine* as a Tory voice in Edinburgh. Other important early-nineteenth-century periodicals are the *London Magazine*, with John Scott as editor, which began publication in 1820 in direct competition with *Blackwood's* and in opposition to its political and philosophical ideologies; *The Westminster Review* (1823), which supported radical politics and utilitarian philosophy; and *Fraser's Magazine* (1830), which was also a Tory mouthpiece.

The periodical press for most of the first half of the nineteenth century had a reputation for its heated political rivalries and its pointed—sometimes vicious—attacks, not only on literary texts but also on the personal character of their authors. Examples are numerous, such as the famous opening sentence of Jeffrey's review of William Wordsworth's *The Excursion* in the *Edinburgh Review*—"This will never do!" (1 [Nov. 1814]); John Lockhart's and John Wilson's series of articles in *Blackwood's* "On the Cockney School of Poetry" that condemned Leigh Hunt's poetry and character as well as those associated with Hunt, most notably John Keats (beginning October 1817); and John Scott's indignation at the insults from *Blackwood's*, which he took so far as to challenge Lockhart to a duel over magazine matters. The duel resulted in Scott's being killed by Lockhart's friend, Jonathan Christie.

Critical discussion of the periodicals of the early nineteenth century often focuses on the scandalous, the personal, and the political. These were significant aspects of the magazine world, certainly, but it must also be remembered that while the negative writing received the lion's share of attention, in large measure the content of the magazines was broadly literary, nonpartisan, and uncontroversial. *Blackwood's* combined review essays with diverse literary offerings—poetry, tales, serialized novels, and general essays—that explored a variety of topics, from scientific discoveries to classical literature to travel and exploration. The *London Magazine* published some of the most enduring essays of the early nineteenth century, Charles Lamb's Elia essays and William Hazlitt's *Table Talk*. A lasting, positive benefit of the periodical controversies is that they, providing popular topics of conversation, served to create interest in the magazines.

By the time Stevenson was writing, however, the political and social conditions of Britain were more secure, and the magazines had become more focused on literary content without the limitations of the political and philosophical biases of earlier times. There had also emerged a large middle-class reading population that included women and young readers, thus creating a market for a wide range of magazines. The second half of the nineteenth century saw hundreds of new periodicals. Many were short-lived, but many others became thriving, quality publications, among them the *Cornhill Magazine*, *Macmillan's*, *Longman's*, *Scribner's*, *Saturday Review*, and the *Fortnightly Review*. There were lesser or more-specialized publications, such as *Temple Bar*, the *Magazine of Art*, the *English Illustrated Magazine*, *Young Folks*, and the *Contemporary Review*. All were publishing outlets for Stevenson.

Stevenson as essayist merits study in the context of the history and development of nineteenth-century periodicals as a whole. Indeed, the range of his periodical contributions makes him a model "magazinist" for the study of late-nineteenth-century periodicals. He began his career as an essayist in earnest in 1871 while still a student at the University of Edinburgh, publishing six essays in the short-lived *Edinburgh University Magazine*. Only two years later his essay "Roads" appeared in a national periodical, the *Portfolio* (Dec. 1873). In 1874 he firmly established himself as an essayist of importance, publishing again in the *Portfolio* (twice); the *Academy* (four times); the *Fortnightly Review*; *Macmillan's Magazine*; and, of special importance for his magazine career, the *Cornhill Magazine*. "Victor Hugo's Romances" was published in the *Cornhill* in August, the first of twenty-three works to appear in the *Cornhill* over the next eight years. The *Cornhill* is the magazine to which Stevenson contributed the largest number of essays, and it was also probably the most important magazine of that time. It was published by the well-established London publisher George Smith, who engaged William Makepeace Thackeray as its first editor. The contributors' list reads like a who's who of Victorian writers: Thackeray, Anthony Trollope, Elizabeth Gaskell, George Eliot, Margaret Oliphant, Thomas Hardy, and Henry James. Leslie Stephen became the editor in 1871, and Stevenson developed a close friendly as well as professional relationship with Stephen; Stevenson ceased his contributions to the *Cornhill* about the time that Stephen left the editorship in 1882.

A study of Stevenson's publications in the *Cornhill* alone would provide an effective representation of his achievement as a periodical essayist. The magazine contains several of his most important essays on writers—Robert Burns, Samuel Pepys, Henry David Thoreau, and Victor Hugo—but also many of his most successful general, human-interest essays. As one contemporary reviewer suggested, writing of *Virginibus Puerisque and Other Papers* (1881), the volume in which Stevenson collected ten of his *Cornhill* essays, "[Although to say] since the days of Charles Lamb there has appeared nothing in the way of personal essays so spirited and so engaging as these" might be problematic, Stevenson was "nothing if not original" (Maixner 78). The variety of Stevenson's essays in the *Cornhill* clearly showcases his art, but—useful for teaching—it also models the character of the periodical culture of the late nineteenth century. There is another dimension to his periodical contributions that must be considered in any study of Stevenson in the context of magazine literature. The magazine market was important to him as a poet and fiction writer. Many of his short stories were published in the magazines before being collected in book form—"Thrawn Janet" (Oct. 1881) and "The Merry Men" (June and July 1882) appeared in the *Cornhill*, and both *Treasure Island* (Oct. 1881–Jan. 1882) and *Kidnapped* (May through July 1886) were first serialized in *Young Folks*. He also contributed numerous poems to periodicals in the 1880s and 1890s. A complete view of the magazine industry and Stevenson's place in it should include the fiction and poetry. But I am focusing on the essays and their role in class.

"A Humble Remonstrance" is probably the best known of Stevenson's essays. It was first published in *Longman's Magazine* (Dec. 1884) and written in response to Henry James's essay "The Art of Fiction," which had appeared in *Longman's* in September 1884 and which itself was a response to Walter Besant's lecture "The Art of Fiction," which had been published as a pamphlet earlier that year. "A Humble Remonstrance" is Stevenson's most fully developed statement on fiction writing. Identifying an essential element of the debate with Besant and James, Stevenson addresses the characteristics of the form of the novel, although he distinguishes three different "classes of novels":

> first, the novel of adventure, which appeals to certain almost sensual and quite illogical tendencies in man; second, the novel of character, which appeals to our intellectual appreciation of man's foibles and mingled and inconstant motives; and third, the dramatic novel, which deals with the same stuff as the serious theatre, and appeals to our emotional nature and moral judgment. (*Works* 29: 137)

He proceeds to discuss the three forms in greater detail. Yet, despite the expansion of the genre offered by the consideration of these three classes, he objects to the restrictions imposed by Besant, especially, and James on the terms of the debate and the narrow limits implied by "the art of fiction." Instead of considering only "prose" fiction, Stevenson broadens the discussion to the "art of narrative": "The art of narrative, in fact, is the same, whether it is applied to the selection and illustration of a real series of events or of an imaginary series" (134). Stevenson names particularly *The Odyssey*, *The Lady of the Lake*, *The Faery Queen* (his spelling), *Paradise Lost*, *Don Juan*, and James Boswell's *Life of Johnson* as works in which "the novelist will find many of his own methods most conspicuously and adroitly handled," works that are successful for the same technical reasons that *Tom Jones* and *The Scarlet Letter* are: "the clear conception of certain characters of man, the choice and presentation of certain incidents out of a great number that offered, and the invention (yes, invention) and preservation of a certain key in dialogue" (134). "A Humble Remonstrance" provides interesting theoretical perspectives from which to approach Stevenson's fiction, but clearly these terms apply equally well to the art of his essays.

When Stevenson republished "A Humble Remonstrance" in the collection of essays *Memories and Portraits*, he added a sharply critical paragraph on William Dean Howells, who, following the periodical publication of "A Humble Remonstrance," "entered repeatedly the lists of theory" (142–43). He also added a note to the beginning of the essay to indicate that it was "the proper continuation" of the essay that immediately preceded it, "A Gossip on Romance," which originally appeared in *Longman's* in November 1882 (132). He essentially considered these two essays as the culmination of the development of his ideas about fiction, romance, and narrative. More important for *Memories and Portraits* as a whole, in the brief introductory note to the volume Stevenson advises that the volume should be read as a book rather than as a collection of essays: "This volume of papers, unconnected as they are, it will be better to read through from the beginning, rather than dip into at random" (frontispiece). Although the essays were "unconnected" in their original publication, the note suggests that there is a unifying thread running through them, that the ordering of the essays has a definite literary purpose, and that the reader should see much more in the whole book than in its individual parts. The essays taken together seem to establish a narrative of the growth of an essayist's mind, beginning with Stevenson's sense of the identity of the Scottish imagination and character in the opening essay, "The Foreigner at Home," and developing to an important concluding theory of imaginative literature in general in "A Humble Remonstrance." In terms of teaching Stevenson, *Memories and Portraits* provides an opportunity to explore approaches to the same texts in different contexts and to discuss what happens to periodical texts when they are arranged into a single text under the author's direction.

Stevenson's transformation of a collection of essays into a book is also evident in an earlier volume, *Familiar Studies of Men and Books*, a collection of his essays on individual authors that had appeared in various magazines, primarily in the *Cornhill*. Stevenson wrote an introduction to the collection, titled "Preface, by Way of Criticism," in which he in part responds to critics of the original magazine versions of the essays and in part rethinks the ideas of the earlier publications. This preface is an important statement on the art and purpose of essay writing, especially as it attempts in "brief representations" to elucidate such noteworthy—and sometimes controversial—topics as the "various sides of human life and manners" represented by the "nine worthies" that are discussed in the volume's essays: Hugo, Burns, Walt Whitman, Thoreau, Yoshida-Torajiro, François Villon, Charles of Orleans, Pepys, and John Knox (*Works* 27: xiii, xi). Implicit also in the preface is the acknowledgment of differences between magazine publication and book publication as well as differences between the audiences of each and the differing expectations of those audiences.

Stevenson notes that he did not substantially revise the essays for book publication, but his preface inserts revisions to individual works while also giving a sense of unity to the entire volume. Because each essay addresses a different person, it can be read for its insights into the life or works of the essay's subject, and Stevenson offers fresh, sometimes controversial perspectives. He also raises questions that are larger than the significance of the individual authors discussed: what literary criticism should be, what biography should be, the relation between the author and the author's works, and the relation between form and content in literature. These questions show Stevenson's value in criticism and theory classes.

"Walt Whitman" originally appeared in the *New Quarterly Magazine* (Oct. 1878) under the title "The Gospel according to Walt Whitman." In the preface to *Familiar Studies*, Stevenson addresses the challenge of an author's balancing his critical opinion with the expectations of his audience: "This is a case of a second difficulty which lies continually before the writer of critical studies: that he has to mediate between the author whom he loves and the public who are certainly indifferent and frequently averse" (*Works* 27: xvi). His response to Whitman had been mixed. On the one hand, Stevenson played down the technical success of the poetry: "But when all is said, Walt Whitman is neither a Milton nor a Shakespeare; to appreciate his works is not a condition necessary to salvation; and I would not disinherit a son upon the question, nor even think much the worse of a critic, for I should always have an idea what he meant." On the other hand, he regarded the message of Whitman's poetry as a high achievement: "Not as a poet, but as what we must call (for lack of a more exact expression) a prophet, he occupies a curious and prominent position" (56). A question that arises in *Familiar Studies*, though, is to what extent a reader-critic may make such conflicting judgments. Stevenson's two-part essay "John Knox and His Relations to Women" was included in the volume "in the interest of the next biographer of Knox." Stevenson argued that Knox had been "buried" by his most recent biographer, Thomas McCrie, and Stevenson's intention was to introduce ideas—essentially, biographical theory—that would encourage a new writer "to break the tomb and bring him forth, alive again and breathing, in a human book" (xxii). In "Some Aspects of Robert Burns," the debate about the relation between judgments of a writer's character and the writer's work is forcefully presented.

My own teaching of Stevenson's essays occurs primarily in an upper-level undergraduate Victorian literature course and a lower-level survey of Scottish literature. For the Scottish literature course, "The Foreigner at Home," "Some Aspects of Robert Burns," and "John Knox and His Relations to Women" are particularly useful background to a common issue in Scottish literature: the characteristics of and influences on the Scottish national identity. For the Victorian literature course, I take two approaches. First, I look at the significance of the essay genre for Victorian writers and Stevenson's role in the history and art of periodical literature. Students read Stevenson along with two large figures in Victorian prose that he regarded as masters of essay style, Thomas Babington Macaulay and Thomas Carlyle. Second, I include discussion of Stevenson's essays on writing along with discussion of his fiction and of how his ideas can be applied to other writers. Victorian literature has a substantial body of literature marketed to younger audiences. Assigning Stevenson's essays on writing and the childhood imagination provokes interesting discussions of such writers as Lewis Carroll and George MacDonald. In addition to "A Humble Remonstrance" and "A Gossip on Romance," "The Lantern-Bearers" is an excellent essay to teach in conjunction with Victorian fiction. Appearing first in *Scribner's* (Feb. 1888) and collected for the volume *Across the Plains* (1892), it is a delightful and powerful essay about memories of childhood and the childhood imagination that lead to adult ideas about the function of the imagination in writers and readers. Overall, Stevenson's essays teach well. His style is engaging, his content is approachable and interesting to students, and his ideas generate meaningful discussion.

Two twentieth-century collections of essays are good resources for study and provide little overlap of contents: *The Lantern Bearers*, edited by Jeremy Treglown, provides a broad representative selection of Stevenson's essays as well as an excellent introduction to his achievement as an essayist; Glenda Norquay's *R. L. Stevenson on Fiction* provides a thorough introduction to Stevenson as a literary essayist as well as a brief introduction to each essay in the volume. Roger G. Swearingen's *Prose Writings* is the major resource on Stevenson's stages of publication, and Paul Maixner's *Robert Louis Stevenson: The Critical Heritage* provides a valuable selection of reviews of Stevenson's works that helps set the author's periodical writings in the context of his time. Both my own teaching of Stevenson and the present essay are indebted to the work of these Stevenson scholars.

Stevenson's Scotland: History and Topography in the Classroom

Ian Duncan

Stevenson wrote four novels set in Scotland, all of which are historical novels set in the second half of the long eighteenth century (1680–1830): *Kidnapped* (1886) and its sequel, *David Balfour* (1893; published as *Catriona* in the United Kingdom); *The Master of Ballantrae* (1889); and *Weir of Hermiston* (1896; unfinished, published posthumously). Born and bred in Edinburgh, Stevenson spent the greater part of his writing life elsewhere, leaving forever in 1887 (see Calder in this volume). He made Scotland a setting for his fiction the farther he moved away from it: *Kidnapped* was written in Bournemouth, *The Master of Ballantrae* in the Adirondacks, and *David Balfour* and *Weir of Hermiston* in Samoa. In his last years he became a Pacific writer, taking literary possession of his new home in a series of essays and works of fiction (see Tulloch in this volume; V. Smith). At the same time, his imagination returned with redoubled intensity to Scotland.

History

Exile is a pervasive theme in Stevenson's Scottish tales, which can play a strong role in courses on historical fiction as well as on Scottish literature. Exile determines the historical topic, Jacobitism, of *Kidnapped*, *David Balfour*, and *The Master of Ballantrae*, all of which take place in the wake of the 1745 Jacobite rising, the last attempt by a banished dynasty to reclaim the British throne. Students often need a summary of this history. The term *Jacobite* comes from *Jacobus*—James II of England and Ireland, James VII of Scotland, the last

Stuart king to occupy the British throne in the late seventeenth century. James's grandfather, James VI of Scotland, had become James I of England and Ireland in 1603 after the death without issue of the English queen Elizabeth I. This Union of Crowns inaugurated Scotland's century-long decline from independent state to province of a modern multinational empire. The Stuart monarchs' claims on absolute sovereignty, overriding the authority of Parliament, as well as their hostility to Presbyterianism, the form of Protestantism established in Scotland at the Reformation, fueled a series of civil wars until a constitutional coup, the so-called Glorious Revolution (1688–89), drove James II and VII into exile and replaced him with his daughter Mary and son-in-law William III (William II in Scotland). The new dispensation, Whig in politics and Protestant in religion, was secured with a Treaty of Union of Scotland and England (1707), which dissolved the Scottish parliament for a joint assembly in Westminster, and with the Hanover succession (1714), which settled the descendants of George I, elector of Hanover, on the British throne.

Throughout the first half of the eighteenth century the old regime maintained a court in exile in France and a base of domestic support in the north of Scotland, reinforced by residual clan and feudal loyalties. Jacobite enthusiasts plotted to reinstate the Stuarts and repeal the Anglo-Scottish Union. The equation between the fall of the dynasty and the end of an independent Scotland would remain central to the ideological appeal of Jacobitism long after it ceased to be a viable political movement, charging it with an aura of romantic loss. A major uprising failed to install James II's son, James Francis Stuart, on the British throne in 1715. Thirty years later, James Francis's son Charles Edward Stuart—Bonnie Prince Charlie, the Young Pretender, the Chevalier—landed with a handful of followers in the West Highlands and rallied the disaffected clans. The rebels took Edinburgh, routed a government army, and marched halfway down to London before turning back, pursued by another army, led by George II's son, the duke of Cumberland. Cumberland crushed the Jacobite regiments at Culloden in April 1746; Charles Edward fled back into exile, while his followers were put down in a ferocious campaign of pacification. The longer-term consequences of the rising included the legislative dismantling of the political and cultural structures of Highland clan society, followed by the region's economic and demographic collapse. Although Stevenson's tales can stand alone, further knowledge of this history enriches the reading experience. Many resources can help (though students should exercise caution on the Web, which tends to romanticize this past). Fitzroy Maclean and Bruce Lenman both provide reliable overviews, supported by illustrations and maps.

Historical Fiction

Kidnapped is set a few years after the last of the Jacobite risings, in the spring of 1751. Wandering in the Highlands, David Balfour witnesses the assassination of the Red Fox, Colin Roy Campbell, a government administrator of confiscated

Jacobite estates. The outlaw Alan Breck Stewart, who has befriended David, is accused of the crime, and the two men flee across country. The so-called Appin murder was a historical event, the main marker of unrest in the Highlands after Culloden. Its sequel, the trial and condemnation of Alan Breck's kinsman James Stewart of the Glens, provides the historical frame for *David Balfour*. In that novel, David tries to save James Stewart, whom he knows to be innocent; he is thwarted by Lord Advocate Prestongrange, who sanctions James's conviction—in what amounts to a judicial revenge killing—for reasons of national security. The identity of the Appin murderer remains controversial to this day. Despite moving the date of the murder forward by one year (from May 1752), Stevenson paid serious attention to the historical substance of both novels, as Barry Menikoff has shown in *Narrating Scotland*. A contemporary pamphlet, *The Trial of James Stewart for the Murder of Colin Campbell* (1753), gave Stevenson the idea for what he at first intended to be a factual history, and he researched the subject with some care. Menikoff provides a detailed account of Stevenson's use of his sources to depict social and economic conditions in the Highlands as well as historical events.

Instructors might want to balance Menikoff's argument for the historical verisimilitude of *Kidnapped* with Matthew Wickman's more speculative, theoretically sophisticated treatment of the "aftershocks of the Appin murder" in *The Ruins of Experience* (43). A comparison of these quite different critical approaches can raise fruitful questions about the status of *Kidnapped* and *David Balfour* as historical novels. Crucially, the history that Stevenson took up was far from being empty ground in Scottish literature. It was the Scottish history that had already been turned into fiction by Walter Scott in a series of major novels set around the Jacobite risings: *Waverley* (1814), *Rob Roy* (1818), and *Redgauntlet* (1824). Scott's enormous prestige throughout the nineteenth century ensured that Jacobitism and its cultural fallout were inescapably associated with his achievement, especially for Scottish writers. It was Scott who was credited (not altogether accurately) with giving Jacobitism its mythic charge as the romance of a lost heroic Scotland. In *Kidnapped*, Stevenson is working, with a high degree of self-consciousness, in territory that he and his contemporaries acknowledged to be charted and occupied by Scott. The story takes place shortly after the close of *Waverley*, while its central situation distills, to a pure essence of adventure, the bond between Highland outlaw and first-person protagonist developed in *Rob Roy*. The very term *kidnapped*, signaling a central theme in Scott's novels, prepares us to understand David's friendship with Alan as a kidnapping of a more profound kind than the brutal abduction that takes place in the opening chapters: a kidnapping of the imagination and affections. (On this aspect of Scott, see Wilt.)

Students can see, even from a few Scott excerpts, how the "flight in the heather" that occupies chapters 20 through 26 of *Kidnapped* takes its cue from the great sequences of cross-country wandering and escape in *Waverley* (chs. 37–39) and *Rob Roy* (chs. 27–31). Of course *Kidnapped* is more than an imitation of Scott. While David's adventures may give us a series of crisp, exact glimpses of the breakup of the clan system after Culloden, *Kidnapped* is not a historical novel as Scott practiced it. Despite his care for accurate detail, Stevenson's novel is not as concerned as Scott's novels are with the philosophical and anthropological dynamics of modernization, the grand theme of Scottish Enlightenment inquiry. David's and Alan's adventures "are remote from history," as F. R. Hart observes; instead, "[t]opography is the pervasive reality. . . . [I]t is the physical impression of place and movement that matters" (158). Stevenson renders with an unprecedented intensity the trials of the body exposed to rugged terrain and climate. The rush and friction of their flight sustains the purity of masculine friendship between David and Alan, so that it replaces, for the duration of the adventure, all other social and emotional bonds and needs. *Kidnapped* converts the Scott novel into a boys' book with such bravura that afterward Scott's own novels were routinely mistaken for boys' books, which they are not.

Place and Movement

A frontispiece to *Kidnapped* provides an abstract of the story in the form of a map of David's journey across the Highlands. *Treasure Island* also includes a map, in imitation of the maps of imaginary lands in Jonathan Swift's *Gulliver's Travels*. *Kidnapped* goes further, making its map represent the progress of the story, not just its locations. Some sense of Stevenson's concern for topographic precision may be gained from looking at contemporary sources that recreate David's itinerary, such as the Web sites www.robert-louis-stevenson.org/highlands-and-islands and www.booksfromscotland.com/Settings/Kidnapped-Map. It is worth reminding students of the rich tradition of adventure fiction focused on deadly games of cross-country hide-and-seek that flowed out of *Kidnapped*, from John Buchan and Geoffrey Household to Alfred Hitchcock, Ian Fleming, and their current followers. Such comparisons, positioning Stevenson between the historical novel and adventure fiction, illuminate the relations between history and topography, place and progress, state power and physical terrain, which structure these stories.

Students can track Stevenson's shifting use of history through the figure of Alan Breck Stewart, who appears in all three of the novels set in the aftermath of the 1745 rising. The character's recurrence tracks a successive deflation of the Romantic Jacobite myth of a lost authentic Scotland. In *Kidnapped*, Alan befriends David and helps him reclaim his stolen inheritance—a marvelous alliance of Jacobite adventurer with dour Whig, which repairs the antagonisms of history, very much according to a formula associated with Scott. If *Kidnapped* sublimates the romance of Jacobitism in a glow of youthful adventure, *The Master of Ballantrae* and *David Balfour* return it to the cooling pressure of history. In *Master*, the eponymous Master, James Durie, makes Alan look ridiculous by outrunning him in the retreat from Culloden—writing Alan out of the story, in effect, and replacing him with a diabolical mutation of the Jacobite outlaw. The novel yields something like the opposite of *Kidnapped*'s condensation of history into topography. As Penny Fielding argues in her contribution to this volume, the scattering of action and narration rehearses a dislocation of Scotland itself in the globalizing force field of the British Empire in the era of the Seven Years' War (1756–63) (see also Duncan, "Stevenson" 23). That national dislocation frames, in turn, the ideological fraud of Jacobitism and the moral corruption of the house of Durrisdeer. The novel closes with the extinction of the family in the American wilderness—a final, irremediable loss of Scotland. Also closing abroad, on the seashore at Dunkirk, *David Balfour* reflects back on *Kidnapped* to reveal that novel's lost terrain as youthful innocence itself, which the hero seeks to reclaim as a private and erotic property through his courtship of Catriona, pure daughter of the despicable James More Drummond. Alan returns, his dashing old self, but now his main function in the story is to be safely removed from it. Instead, David's future father-in-law plays a terminally sordid version of the role of Jacobite trickster.

David Balfour is so radically different a novel from *Kidnapped* that students may have trouble understanding it (as I did when I first read it), and this difficulty can be productive in the classroom. This most subtle of Stevenson's Scottish novels yields his most profound essay in disillusionment. As with *Kidnapped*, topography can provide a useful teaching tool. *Kidnapped* breaks off with David's arrival in front of the British Linen Company's bank in Edinburgh. Written after a gap of six years (a long time in Stevenson's short career), *David Balfour* takes up the story mere minutes later: "Here I was in this old, black city, which was for all the world like a rabbit-warren, not only by the number of its indwellers, but the complication of its passages and holes" (*Works* 7: 4). This labyrinthine Edinburgh remains oddly underparticularized, however, in the story that follows. Its key locations are left studiously vague; we never even find out the address of the most important place in the novel, the town house of the lord advocate, William Grant of Prestongrange. An exact topography comes into focus only when David leaves the city—when he accompanies the Miss Grants to Hope Park, for instance, and walks a few hundred yards more to fight a duel in the "rough rocky desert of the King's Park" (69). Once we are back inside its bounds, the Edinburgh Old Town of *David Balfour* becomes a blur.

In contrast, Stevenson gives David's excursions north of the city a crystalline clarity of topographic and historical detail. Here eighteenth- and nineteenth-century maps of Edinburgh, accessible in the National Library of Scotland's online map collection (www.nls.uk/maps/towns/index.html), make attractive teaching aids. David heads out of the city by Leith Wynd past the villages of Picardy and Broughton to visit his kinsman Balfour of Pilrig, or else along the Lang Dykes, a "rural road" to the north of the city which is now (a footnote tells us) Princes Street, to visit Catriona Drummond beyond "the village of Dean" (54, 55). From there he follows Leith Water through Stockbridge to the wood at Silvermills, where Alan Breck is hiding. These itineraries flank the suburb of Canonmills, where Stevenson was born and spent the first seven years of his life. The story keeps veering out of the city to fix on the districts of its author's childhood, imagined one hundred years before his birth, when they were outlying villages. It is here that David runs to meet his sweetheart and the comrade of his romantic adventure. In these idyllic episodes, *David Balfour* fleetingly recaptures the spirit of *Kidnapped*.

Edinburgh accommodates the altogether murkier relations with fathers, two of whom overcast the tale: the weak rogue James Drummond and the formidable Prestongrange. In their shadow, David and the reader discover what was left out of *Kidnapped*: the bloody, dirty domain of national and tribal politics, of disappointment, betrayal, and compromise that is the domain of the fathers. David's failed attempt to save James Stewart recasts the ethos of adventure as a boyish idealism that is now all too easily overcome, not by the machinations of flagrant villains like Fraser of Lovat but by the potent, sophisticated, at once admirable and sinister figure of the lord advocate. One of Stevenson's triumphs of characterization, Prestongrange personifies the grown-up world—and stands at one of the limits of Stevenson's imagined Scotland. Classroom discussion of him can be productively contentious.

Stevenson as Transatlantic Romanticism

Susan Oliver

I teach Stevenson's *The Master of Ballantrae* as the final text on my Transatlantic Romanticisms senior undergraduate module. Among the reasons that I place the novel at the end of our studies is the obvious matter of chronology. Another reason is that the text gives a British and American Romantic studies course a fully nineteenth-century perspective. Transatlantic studies is about more than intercontinental influence in works written in Europe and North America; it is concerned with reciprocal literary and intercultural relations. In that framework, oceanic travel and the Atlantic as a geographic fact must be regarded as phenomena that both connect and separate. Many of my students, having studied British and American Romantic writing from their second year on, are ready to consider advanced concepts of transcontinental literary relations. In this essay, I put forward ideas that can be used with classes from the sophomore level up, after Romantic studies has been covered in a survey form.

The date of *Master*, 1889, makes it a good choice for Victorian literature modules, where it exemplifies the relation between late-Victorian fiction and Romantic precursors. Its Scottishness makes it eminently suitable for Scottish literature courses, because it provides one of the finest examples of Gothic adventure fiction and a late-century comparison with Walter Scott's works (such as *The Bride of Lammermoor* [1819]) and with James Hogg's *Private Memoirs and Confessions of a Justified Sinner* (1824). A transatlantic studies approach can be used as a full theoretical framework or as a complement to such programs.

The Master of Ballantrae is an ideal text for getting students to explore the ambiguities and anxieties surrounding such issues as cultural migration. James Durie's and Henry Durie's travels from Britain to the northeastern United States exemplify the spread of popular stereotypes, myth, and adventure literature. My teaching looks at Stevenson's treatment of the ways in which conscience and desire travel and become reconfigured, through being symbolically buried, unearthed, and reburied. Throughout *Master*, encounters with Irish Jacobite chevaliers, pirates, Native Americans, and Indian mystics make accessible to students the manner in which myths and legends are reshaped to acquire currency. I ask my seminar to what extent Chevalier Burke's narration can be considered reliable and how far it might be touched with blarney. The students' response is likely to be inflected by popular perceptions about that character's fictionalized Irishness, so I follow with the same question about the trusted servant and main narrator, Ephraim Mackellar, and about the Chinese-box style editorial agency through which the story is told. (Students who have read Scott's *Tales of My Landlord* novels will recognize the origins and implications of that frame-narrative technique.) Then there is Stevenson's trademark plotline of the quest for buried treasure, which almost all students know from *Treasure Island* or else from the recent film series *Pirates of the Caribbean*—a way in for those who do not know Long John Silver. The treasure represents all that is valued and hoarded but that cannot ultimately be certified genuine or safeguarded from theft. It has been taken from other romanticized characters—pirates who themselves are nomadic thieves. The exotic appeal of treasure raises questions about authenticity and cultural memory: how can we determine what genuinely belongs to a people, what is stolen, and what has acquired a false luster? Discussion can lead to consideration of how societies and their histories travel through "contact zones" of contested representation (Pratt 6). Just as Scottish emigration affected the demography of nineteenth-century North America, so the literature of that nation and its Romantic relation with a series of tragic human circumstances (centuries of confrontation, then Culloden, followed by the Highland clearances) traveled across an ocean to become implanted in the cultural landscape of a new country. The proximity to the border with Canada of the concluding "melodrama in the wilderness" of *Master,* which takes place in the hills above Albany, encourages students to explore differences and connections in Canadian and American transatlantic relations with Scotland, Ireland, and Europe more generally (*Works* 10: 239). The memorial that an unnamed man, "skilled in stone-cutting," finally chisels into a boulder in a sublime landscape to commemorate the "heir to a Scottish Title . . . admired in Europe, Asia, America . . . in the tents of savage hunters and the citadels of Kings. . . . [and] his brother" should generate some lively discussion about irony, punning, memorialization, and the matter of legend (233). Attention to the very word *title* opens a way into critical understanding: valuable discussion in my group arises from considering ambiguities in the title of the novel and the title of "Master" linking the two brothers. The subtitle, *A Winter's Tale,* has ambiguities that simultaneously suggest Shakespeare's tragicomedy and the howling, frigid landscape in which the Duries die.

The richly transatlantic context of *Master* is another reason for putting it at the end of a course that presents students with challenging theoretical material. By the time they have consulted secondary sources in transatlantic studies, alongside readings from a selection of fiction, poetry, essays, and travelogue, they should be prepared to interrogate ideas about genre, particular historiographies, and intercontinental relations. Stevenson's introduction of the Master's Indian manservant, Secundra Dass, in the second half of the novel adds a British imperial dimension that stretches the mythic, cultural, and literary trajectories eastward to India. Students can be encouraged to consider how Secundra Dass's physical condition marks the character as old and primitive, suggesting extreme cultural lateness. A placard above the hovel in which he lives with the Master in "a poor quarter of town" in New York describes him as a "Decayed Gentleman of India" (182). Perceptions of presettlement America as a degenerating land undeveloped by its inhabitants were used in the eighteenth and nineteenth centuries to justify the removal from the land of Native Americans, "Indians." I use paintings from the Hudson River school, such as Thomas Cole's 1825 *Lake with Dead Trees (Catskill)*, to demonstrate that idea of decay. Students respond well to visual artworks, and Cole, Frederic Edwin Church, and Albert Bierstadt are all effective in demonstrating perceptions of landscape (www.the-athenaeum.org/). Ecocritical readings can be introduced as an approach to Stevenson's study of human beings and the environment. There are many good, recent works of ecocriticism. I recommend Lawrence Buell's conceptualization of socioecological issues in *The Future of Environmental Criticism* as likely to challenge adventurous students. I encourage my class to think about why Secundra's brand of wisdom does not travel well, ultimately failing in the New World. By aligning the Master with a figure already in a condition of deterioration, Stevenson adopts Scott's method of marking an irrevocable turning point in history. Students can easily identify the point where a culture makes a choice that fatally connects it to the past and ensures that it can move into the future only in the form of myth history. At this point, some information can be introduced about the Scottish Enlightenment and theories of human development. Those theories can be compared with Darwinian evolution and treated as complexly as time will allow.

Anxieties about arcane practices in non-Christian religions and about secrets conveyed in languages that are not commonly understood make possible Secundra Dass's role in *The Master of Ballantrae*. The gothic and orientalist implications of him as an Asian character who brings about the gripping denouement to a tale of endless tit-for-tat rivalry between two faces of Scottish identity ask the reader to reconsider the relation between British and American literature. Students who have read Byron's Eastern tale *Lara* (1814) will notice an intertextual acknowledgment in figures of the exiled European and his Eastern servant who converse in an unfamiliar tongue. They will identify the fearfulness generated by conversations conducted in other languages and the parallel that Stevenson draws with Native American speech and European Americans' suspicion of treachery. Students can be shown that it is an easy step from that suspicion to attempts to suppress Gaelic in Scotland after the 1745 Jacobite rebellion. The manner in which the Romantic status of the Highlands inexorably grew as a result of fictional representation can be considered alongside politically driven programs of cultural erasure. *Master* explores the difficulties associated with assimilation into a nation (the United States of America) of immigrant communities and the failure of immigrant peoples to understand codes of survival that the natives know. Secundra Dass's final words, "Too cold . . . good way in India, no good here" as he lies down to sleep by the fire, always generate discussion of the obvious play on Indian as other (233). The Native Americans have at that point retreated into the woods, where they remain an unseen presence. I particularly like the notion of a binocular transatlantic that *The Master of Ballantrae* raises through its Eastern and American Indian contexts, for the lands of both had been colonized by the British. My students find this line of inquiry enlightening. In the Transatlantic Romanticisms course they have already read Henry David Thoreau's *Walden*, where there is an engagement with Eastern philosophies, and Nathaniel Hawthorne's short story "Rappaccini's Daughter," with its reference to the westward travel of a deadly but fascinating myth. In each case, a transatlantic relation is uncovered in which a deep, non-European literary past is manifest.

My students begin the course with a week of critical study, followed by novels that establish forms of gothic and historical fiction: Charles Brockden Brown's *Wieland* (1798; some will have read *Arthur Mervyn* [1799] and *Edgar Huntly* [1799] in other of my modules), Scott's *Waverley* (1814), and James Fenimore Cooper's *The Pioneers* (1823). Hogg's *Private Memoirs* is a set text in a sophomore course, so they will have read that novel, with its themes of haunted brotherhood, guilt, and double burial. Each work engages with anxieties about cultural confrontation and change. *Wieland* and *Edgar Huntly* specifically identify a problematic relation between Europe and North America that haunts the landscape. *Waverley* treats Scotland's guilt over its divided past. The 1745 Jacobite uprising is variously referred to as "that memorable year" (ch. 2) and "the troubles" (all other chapters) in *Master*, and in both novels history renders inevitable the loss of cultural authenticity and recall. Students can easily follow the trajectory from Scott's 1814 novel: the '45 and Culloden are the point of departure for Stevenson's 1889 adventure tale. Similarly, students are able to trace the development of ideas that cross and complicate cultural as well as national boundaries. Stevenson's letters to Charles Scribner, Sidney Colvin, and Henry James in December 1887 and January 1888 provide valuable context (*Letters*, vol. 7). Stevenson wrote to James in late January that the Master, supposedly killed at Culloden, is like an "INCUBUS" that keeps returning, not quite dying, living and traveling along with the tragedy in which he is the protagonist (105). I encourage students to consider the tragedy as national as well as personal, and to think about how tragedy helps myth travel.

Recent developments in transatlantic studies shape my theoretical and critical approach to Stevenson. The course focuses on twenty-first-century texts, although some are from the last quarter of the twentieth century. For budgetary reasons, it is appropriate to work with an anthology supplemented by library holdings and journals. We use Susan Manning and Andrew Taylor's *Transatlantic Literary Studies: A Reader*, because that volume contains extracts from a wide variety of recent works by writers from either side of the Atlantic. Manning and Taylor's introduction is accessible and illuminating, providing students with a point of departure for thinking about a range of texts. Of further value to our work on Stevenson is Wai Chee Dimock's *Through Other Continents*. Dimock argues that North American literature is informed by a cultural history and prehistory that stretch far into the past and across intercontinental trajectories. Although *The Master of Ballantrae* is not American literature, the two strands of Scottish myth that Stevenson plants in American soil through the burial of the Durie brothers in the woods of upstate New York make Dimock's ideas relevant to the novel. This approach has generated original and lively discussion in presentations, essays, and examinations. Other texts that help students understand transatlantic studies critical approaches are William Keach's seminal

"A Transatlantic Romantic Century," Manning's *Fragments of Union*, Joel Pace's "Towards a Taxonomy of Transatlantic Romanticism(s)," and the electronic collection *Sullen Fires across the Atlantic: Essays in Transatlantic Romanticism* (Newman). I recommend two journals: *Symbiosis*, which is student-friendly and accessible, and the *Journal of Transatlantic Studies,* which is not specifically a literature journal but contains thought-provoking articles that challenge the most able students.

Class activities and assignments have their own pedagogical value. My students are graded according to three types of work that require them to consider texts comparatively: group oral presentation, essay, and unseen written examination. I teach *Master* in weeks dedicated to "Transatlanticizing Myths and Migration," so questions relating to that topic are most commonly chosen. However, students should be able to look across the full course and use texts in a range of ways. Group presentations are a particularly valuable form of assessment, because they encourage discussion beyond the confines of the seminar and require students to carry out their own research. Stevenson is a popular choice for presentations, featuring in sessions with titles such as "Transatlantic Conscience, the Gothic and the Exotic," "Ways of Seeing the Nation," and "Arcadias and Exotic Locations: Reading Cultural Otherness." One of my most popular topics is "The Backwoodsman and the Dying Indian as Figures in Transatlantic Romanticism": it has students thoughtfully discuss *Master* as a text concerned with Scottish and migrant myths in the process of becoming part of national consciousness, alongside more regular, American fiction. Film and television versions help students studying literature with film or media. The advantages of framing the module with Brown, Scott, Hogg, and Cooper at the beginning and Stevenson at the end become evident in such assignments. Students who want to investigate further Stevenson's writing in a transatlantic context and choose our undergraduate dissertation option are encouraged to extend their reading to *Treasure Island* (1883) and *Kidnapped* (1886) as adventure novels and *Across the Plains* (1883) and *The Amateur Emigrant* (1895) as prose nonfiction about travel and other matters. Those works are open to readings that employ transatlantic methodologies.

To conclude, the strategies outlined here are designed to help students from a wide variety of backgrounds and ability levels read Stevenson with critical acuity and enjoyment. Transatlantic studies is a theoretical and critical apparatus for achieving that end. Challenging the strongest students to stretch their inquiries into new and original areas is not incompatible with helping those who need to progress from a more fundamental level. Although *The Master of Ballantrae* is among the most complex works that I teach, my students derive both pleasure and benefit from studying it. I am humbled by the appreciation they often show at the end of their studies.

Boys' Adventure and the Allure of Violence in the Postcolonialism Class: *Treasure Island*

H. Aram Veeser

Students at an urban public university such as mine, the City College of New York, find racial and ethnic otherness fascinating, and that is a good point of entry for the postcolonial analysis of Stevenson's imperial romances, thrillers, and shilling shockers. These books, stuffed with monstrous others, so readily lend themselves to postcolonial analysis that elaborate, mannered, and specialized vocabularies may be omitted.

The ultimate purpose of my course is to explore the ways in which canonical literature and popular classics express England's position as a world power that governed colonies stretching across the globe. Power and violence assume considerable importance as themes in England's late-imperial literary works. The evidence may be laid out alongside compelling passages from Frantz Fanon on the divided colonial city, from William Butler Yeats on the evils of partition (Said, *Yeats*), from Antonio Gramsci on the propagandistic role of brainy humanists, and from Sigmund Freud on the curious time warp caused by trauma (Laplanche and Pontalis). Critical readings can address the late-Victorian moment in class struggle (Honaker; Moretti) or draw attention to *Treasure Island* as a debate over monetary policy (N. Wood) and as an exploration of competing styles of sadomasochism (Kucich). Students bring their own interests: their familiarity with beast fables such as Rudyard Kipling's "Rikki-Tikki-Tavi" inclines them to consider *Treasure Island* as a political parable, while their interest in psychology encourages them to dig beneath the dazzling surface action and seek *Treasure Island*'s rich value to Hollywood and pop culture and to high-culture figures such as Paul Muldoon (his poem "Yarrow").

Treasure Island invariably raises a set of enticing and valuable problems. Each classroom experience generates another problem set, and each set grows organically from those in earlier classes. In this essay I describe how, in a typical semester, the class and I move through a series of stages. The sequence that a class follows derives from my general practice, which is to find puzzles that I myself cannot readily solve and to engage the students in the effort to find answers. This practice involves risk and allows for spontaneity: students feel that the teacher hasn't worked it all out ahead of time and is struggling and seeking their aid. In the fall semesters of 2008 and 2009, using a range of Stevenson's texts, we took up the themes of brute force, sexy primitive criminality, geographic partition, patriotic nationalism, foreign plunder, live burial, enlightened benevolence, and clueless condescension. We asked why characters are divided with apartheidesque finality into one group of average, normal Brits and another group of radically exotic others. We exposed layered narrative structures that model a dissection not unlike the pattern of exploration or penetration to the heart of a conquered, unknown territory. Following clues or maps (in the style of Sherlock Holmes or John Buchan) or peeling the onionskin layers of a framed narrative (like Stevenson's *Jekyll and Hyde*) may be compared at this point with the late-Victorian, early-high-modernist narrative method, which is to bring out the story as "a glow brings out a haze" (Conrad 6). But throughout the semester I am using as my reference point, violence and power were the touchstone to which we always returned.

My first question to students generally requires them to investigate the sources of literary value. Few books have commanded as much popular attention as *Treasure Island*, yet the average melodrama rarely outlasts its first season. What makes *Treasure Island* so enduring? As a first pass at the question, I ask my class to look at the structure of trauma and the response to it embedded in the sudden, violent deaths and displacements that launch the book. Shockingly violent events happen quickly but are only later absorbed by Jim Hawkins in their full significance. These are the two parts of trauma: event and delayed response (see Caruth). In-class writing and group reports involve exercises that bring out this two-part temporality. Students have reported on the custom of marooning, the lag time built into the black spot, and Jim's initial blackout after killing Israel Hands.

Brute force and the threat of death make *Treasure Island* suspenseful. Among possible deaths, violent death is preferred by the author. Of the three deaths in part 1, the tranquil passing of Jim's father merits not even a paragraph. Billy Bones's apoplexy is more vivid, but the final death is the most horrific: a blind man crashing through unknown woods only to be run down and trampled by galloping steeds. Helplessness and victimization also press to their most extreme expression. Jim is small; the men are all large. He is gripped, restrained, and physically threatened by Billy Bones, Black Dog, Blind Pew, even the stolid gamekeeper.

Since violence shades into bondage, I introduce the theme of masochism. Jim experiences pain. Blind Pew wrenches his arm to the breaking point. The gamekeeper awakens him "by a punch in the ribs" (*Works* 2: 47). Silver holds him fast or binds and drags him with a rope. Hands puts a knife through his shoulder and pins him to the mast. Drawing attention to the kinky aspects of tying up and forcibly restricting movement, not to mention penetrating, I summarize some of the psychological theories of masochism. I also remind students that queer readings of *Jekyll and Hyde*, as well as of Stevenson's own sexual preferences, are abundant (Koestenbaum, *Double Talk*; Linehan, "'Closer'"). We follow the biographical subtext of masochism: Stevenson wrote that he first came to love literature in a rush of sadomasochistic delight. He gushes in "Popular Authors" that, on hearing *Macbeth*, "it was something new and shocking to be thus ravished by a giant, and I shrank under the brutal grasp" (*Works* 28: 26). Literary power ravishes (a sexual word) in the form of a (male) giant grasping a young boy. Add to these suggestive biographical details the scenes in which Silver repeatedly cajoles and, it might be said, seduces Jim and renders him available to

Silver's purposes or consider the way Stevenson composed the book in a series of nightly readings to a thirteen-year-old boy, and you have a pederastic scenario. In highlighting this scenario, I plant the seed for our final topic, the relation of violence to seduction, particularly to seduction by means of persuasion.

Masochism has a politics of gender, race, or power. The genres that converge in *Treasure Island*—conversion narrative, domestic romance, and adventure fiction—are all caught up in masochistic fantasies of omnipotence (Kucich). Omnipotence in psychoanalysis is the delusion that one's wishes will come true. Such magical thinking is linked to antipatriarchal rebellion, though a rebellion that is passive and indeed hypocritical. The masochist relishes her own brutalization as a sure sign that she possesses an annoying moral superiority. "I am more civil, more subtle, more refined than you": competition for social status turns on such claims.

In recent classes, when it came time to introduce the political valences of masochism, I outlined theories of cultural capital (see Guillory). Students were eager to discuss what gave the gentlemen in truth, as opposed to the gentlemen of fortune, their distinction and social standing. Masochism's importance to claims of moral-cultural superiority has been linked by John Kucich to the revival of evangelical Christian missionary work. The prominent examples of masochistic pleasure in *Treasure Island* might be considered personal erotic delight or private pathology, but they might also be understood as a bid for political superiority and moral authority in a world of brutish badness. In the latter case, masochism shows its kinship to that other political weapon, brute force.

In moving the class toward rhetoric and persuasion as political weapons, I have to concede first that brutish badness on its own makes a strong case for rightness and efficacy. Is *Treasure Island* not a political laboratory in which the state's monopoly on violence has been canceled and competing groups struggle for dominance? I ask students to consider the book as a contest of hypocrisy against its opposite, acknowledged badness. I ask them to find examples of hypocrisy—the squire's, the doctor's, the captain's. They should now consider how the book presents the British establishment. The monied men, capitalists, are needed to bankroll the whole adventure: they hire the ship and the crew, provision the journey, and rule the floating commonwealth. But have they any more right than the pirates to the treasure? The gentlemen in earnest are gentlemen in interest: they are the bank. The silly squire is an inheritor of land, what analysts of capitalism call a rentier, one who builds wealth by renting out his land. The pirates or gentlemen of fortune, by contrast, have produced the wealth, pillaging towns and boarding other ships: the loot is the result of their labor. Thus the capitalists are differentiated from the gentlemen of fortune. Unlike the profligate gentlemen of fortune, the squire, doctor, and captain use money as capitalists should: they invest it and make it reproduce. The journey to the treasure island is a capital investment for profit, after all—whether the profit is rightly theirs lurks in the book as an unconfronted question: Just how good are the gentlemen in truth?

Notably, Flint's gunner, Israel Hands, makes a case for badness. In an odd lull, when Jim has proclaimed himself captain and Hands is prostrate before him, the boy gets on a high horse and criticizes the gunner for having "lived in sin and lies and blood." Hands gives a surprisingly reflective answer: "For thirty years . . . I've sailed the seas, and seen good and bad, better and worse, fair weather and foul, provisions running out, knives going, and what not. Well, now I tell you, I never seen good come o' goodness yet. Him as strikes first is my fancy" (162). This statement is eloquent, and the book might be said finally to endorse Hands's view. Silver is a murderer, an opportunist, and pirate, but in the end he is rewarded with money, freedom, and domestic tranquillity. I put the question to the students: What is the ethical stance of this book in its contest between physical and rhetorical violence? And if the book has no ethical stance, why has it not joined *Ulysses* on the list of banned books?

Now it is time in class to consider that perhaps badness and brute force have a politics in excess of their unquestionable aesthetic appeal. Violence has a persuasive weight comparable to that of its competitor, masochism. Violence and brutality represent, in this political reading, an advantage to the nation. *Treasure Island's* unquestioned victories of brute power gain a share of explicit praise amounting to a reasoned defense. Even the lesser thug Billy Bones is admired by many of the local men as being just "the sort of man that made England terrible at sea" (6). A social pillar like the squire has nothing but praise for lawless violence as a benefit to the nation: "Blackbeard was a child to Flint," the squire declares, all admiration for the criminal buccaneers. "The Spaniards were so prodigiously afraid of him, that, I tell you, sir, I was sometimes proud he was an Englishman" (36). The link between savagery and patriotism, between the nation and the pirate, is solid. And of course there are the guns, germs, and steel that are the furniture of imperial conquest: from the cutlasses and pistols of part 1, through the gallows, daggers, muskets, and ship's cannon of the later parts, *Treasure Island* gives a more than respectful nod to the bluntest forms of brute force. At this point in my class, a group compared Somali pirates and Flint's crew. Students began to consider piracy as a form of ongoing resistance to European domination.

The question now forces itself: Is *Treasure Island* a pro-English, imperialist book? Hands's disillusioned bluntness can be taken in two opposite ways. It can be a resounding affirmation of violence in defense of empire, and in this sense the monied gentlemen would have to endorse Hands's ruthlessness. Or it may be considered an endorsement of liberatory, anticolonial violence. Fanon's poetry about a Manichaean colonial world where natives, to become free, must bathe in settlers' blood (88), suggests to students new puzzles in *Treasure Island*.

It is now time to disentangle the confusing mélange of the three instruments of power: masochism, violence, and eloquence. To get to a more nuanced post-colonial reading of *Treasure Island*, I ask students whether power comes in forms other than a knife or cannon. I ask them to consider whether Gramsci's "organic intellectual" (14–23) is akin to Long John Silver, Jim, and others who speak or think well. To Gramsci, official intellectuals simply mouth ruling class ideas, whereas new intellectuals go beyond oratory to active and sometimes forceful resistance. I ask how these big-brained yet unofficial orators manage to outwit, in argument, the more traditional pontificators such as Dr. Livesey, who uses verbal eloquence and the state's monopoly of violence to threaten Billy Bones and shore up the existing relations of production and society.

Having discussed braininess, we move to the question of mental agility and its relation to power. I read Yeats's short lyric "Leda and the Swan." I pose the problem of how to apply the final line to colonialism: "Did she put on his knowledge with his power / Before the indifferent beak could let her drop?" Yeats, a high modernist if ever there was one, is like Stevenson concerned with brutality and withheld information as the bases of state formation (Helen, Leda's child, is accountable for the burning of Troy). Map-centered (as is Haggard's *King Solomon's Mines*) or based on a cryptogram (as is Buchan's *Greenmantle*), *Treasure Island* also weighs mental alacrity against brute force. I circulate among students a *New York Times* story about the United States joint chiefs of staff and their imperatives to supplement force with persuasion in Iraq (Rohde). Physical force and rhetorical power, like Hyde and Jekyll, have the same address and write the same script.

Adventure novels such as Kipling's *Kim* anticipate "Leda and the Swan" in that both equate knowledge with political power. *Treasure Island* turns on privileged and withheld knowledge. Billy Bones owes his centrality in the plot to his possession of special directions to find the treasure. Livesey, Smollett, and the squire survive the voyage out only because they have exclusive knowledge of the treasure's location. Silver changes sides every time he gets a new piece of information. If the brainy characters win directive power over others, what role does their language—beyond their intelligence—play in their success? For example, I have asked students to discuss the following: How does Silver convince Jim to whitewash the Black Dog sighting? How does Silver convince the reticent hand to join the conspiracy or persuade the mutineers not to depose him? What is it in Jim's stockade speech that persuades Silver to save his life? My students compared such acts of persuasion with acts of negotiation—for example, Captain Smollett's negotiation with Silver—or they compared the doctor's speeches with Silver's. A debate ensued as to whether Silver represents a new force in society, perhaps a class in society that is just now coming into being—the working class, the hybrid natives of the colonies, Jewish cosmopolitans, or some other disenfranchised or marginalized social force. Some students suggested that he instead represents a noble relic, a Byronic holdover, the remnant of a feudal age when a precapitalist aristocracy tyrannized over decent burghers and threw money out of windows.

Classroom opportunities abound. We can read Stevenson's boys' adventure, with its disturbing yet alluring mix of violence and power, from the standpoint of a postcolonial moment or from the operational perspective of today's joint chiefs of staff. We can read it as a simple allegory about capitalist monetary policy (silver vs. gold) or a jungle story about investment capital (the squire's, the doctor's, the captain's) triumphing over the decayed remnants of a spendthrift aristocracy (Silver, gentlemen of fortune). We can read its memorable scenes of bondage and cruelty as Stevenson's tapping into erotic desire or as a canny dissection of imperial fantasies of omnipotence and self-effacement. In all these readings, students will be spurred to reconsider the ties between thrilling narrative and colonial empire.

Exposure and Image: A Visual Approach

Ann C. Colley

Stevenson as Photographer

When Robert Louis Stevenson and his family were residing and cruising in the South Seas between 1888 and 1894, they hauled with them cameras; large numbers of cumbersome, ill-fitting photographic plates; and flash powder (they were experimenting with flash photography). Intent on recording images of their unique experiences for themselves as well as for their European friends, they carried this burdensome cargo wherever they sailed. During a brief period, Stevenson, anxious about his finances, was also interested in using some of these pictures to help him construct a portable diorama that would tour Europe as a money-making project (Colley, *Robert Louis Stevenson* 115–16).

These photographs can stand at the crux of nuanced student discussions about experience, art, and commerce in Stevenson and modernism. These images have no connection with either the commercial demand for pictures of exotic Samoan belles or the anthropometric photographs depicting naked native subjects in front of a measuring grid. Nor do they fully participate in what Susan Sontag, in *On Photography*, identifies as the camera's imperialistic scope. Photography for the Stevensons was not necessarily an articulation of colonial power and authority, even though there were moments when they delighted in dressing and arranging their native subjects, as well as occasions when they experimented with a detective camera worn secretly underneath the shirt so as to take pictures without people's knowledge. For the most part, the Stevensons' photos are simply amateur snapshots of the landscape, special celebrations, the people they met, the family, and their dwellings. Naturally, some of these images have perished. Once a camera fell overboard, and later fireworks accidentally destroyed about ninety exposed plates. Some of the photographs that have survived can be viewed online at www.robert-louis-stevenson.org/gallery; most are to be found in four South Seas albums at the Writers' Museum in Edinburgh.

What can students make of these pictures? At first they seem to be no more than items of curiosity, especially since a few were probably taken by Stevenson, a figure not usually associated with photography. (Most were shot by his stepson, Lloyd Osbourne; some by his son-in-law, Joe Strong.) However, when students learn that Stevenson intended to publish many of these photographs with his semianthropological study *In the South Seas* (1896) and that he sent photographs to such journals as *Scribner's* and the *Illustrated London News* so that there would be a more accurate representation of what he was writing about, they begin to realize that these images were not incidental but, rather, integral to his writing: they complemented his wish to correct the generic verbal and visual portraits of life in the South Seas. Displeased with the stereotypical images that perpetuated racial types, he planned to use his own, more realistic photographs to support his corrective observations. (A list of these photographs and where Stevenson would have placed them in the text of *In the South Seas* is in the Beinecke Rare Book and Manuscript Library at Yale University.) Unfortunately, this project never reached fruition.

To understand Stevenson's impulse to catch a more realistic image of the Pacific cultures and its peoples, it is helpful to compare the Stevenson snapshots, available online, with the stereotypical ones featured in Casey Blanton's *Picturing Paradise: Colonial Photography of Samoa, 1875 to 1925* (1995). The differences between them illustrate Stevenson's commitment to offering a portrait of the Pacific area that is neither distorted nor indebted to exotic fantasies. Extending the exercise, students should also read *In the South Seas* (*Works* 20) and note how Stevenson attempts to offer a more complicated, and therefore more realistic, notion of the people and life on these islands. Students would better understand Stevenson's desire to include the images and also begin to appreciate that this study of Pacific cultures is essentially a series of snapshots. *In the South Seas* presents a collage of illuminated episodes surrounded by areas of obscurity and dogged by shifting shadows of meaning—an acknowledgment by Stevenson that much about the South Seas eluded him. A panoramic, inclusive portrait of this complex society was impossible for him; he could only take one picture at a time.

Stevenson and the Landscape of Light and Darkness

Stevenson's commitment to these photographic records understandably tends to be overlooked in favor of his Pacific writing and his interest in capturing in words the complex flavor of island life. However, there is a vital connection between image and word that can be helpful not only when teaching his South Seas fiction, poetry, and semianthropological prose but also when considering his work written before he entered the Pacific regions. Working backward from the texts and pictures belonging to his last years in the South Seas, students will recognize similar impulses at play in his earlier poetry and prose. They will realize that, contrary to received opinion, which sharply distinguishes Stevenson's Pacific writings from his earlier oeuvre, there are ways of bringing meaning to light that link the earlier to the later work. Not all gets left behind when Stevenson explores new methods of writing while in the South Seas. (Roslyn Jolly's *Robert Louis Stevenson in the Pacific* helpfully teases out relations between Stevenson's pre-Pacific and Pacific writing.) In particular, Stevenson's habit of letting meaning emerge from darkness, as if it were a negative exposed to light, runs throughout his work.

Lighting Up the Darkness

The relation between the photographic image and Stevenson's writing, his Pacific as well as earlier work, goes beyond the obvious opportunity of actually looking at the people or landscape written about. There is also the similarity between the act of bringing a snapshot into view and the ways in which Stevenson's plots emerge. His writing develops as a photographic negative or plate: gradually the darkness of a page is exposed to illuminated moments, and, by degrees, the full meaning of the text appears. The photograph can serve as a metaphor to help students appreciate that much of Stevenson's prose and poetry originates in the contrast of light and darkness. The metaphor is imperfect, of course, because the process of developing a film is a physical thing, whereas the creating of a fiction is an act of will. Still the metaphor can enhance an awareness of the play of light on the black of night in Stevenson's work.

In his Pacific writing Stevenson positions both himself and his reader in a landscape oriented by lights shining in the darkness. Students might read this positioning against his earlier poems. As if he were still the child following his shadow ("My Shadow" [*Collected Poems* 32–34]), admiring the lamps that mapped the city of Edinburgh ("The Lamplighter" [39] and "A Plea for Gas Lamps" [*Works* 25: 129–32]), or the young boy carrying a bull's-eye lantern so he could illuminate the black night of a Scottish fishing village ("The Lantern-Bearers" [*Works* 30: 29–40]), Stevenson continues to follow the glow of lanterns or the sight of a young moon on his nocturnal journeys through the Pacific islands. His letters written in the South Seas show that he was using spots of light to map his way through darkness as he had done years before in Edinburgh. As if using a draftsman's grid, he finds his way back from Apia to Vailima, his home in Samoa, by tracing the patterns of the phosphorescent deadwood strewn over the ground "like a grating over a pale hell" (*Letters* 7: 56). These luminous points of reference shine not only on the dense thickets and rough roads of the islands' trackless interiors but also on the ill-charted seas that lie about their shores. In this world oriented by lights shining in the darkness, Stevenson's daily habit of writing early and late by lamplight seems apt. In Samoa, he would arise as early as four and work until "the lamp has once more to be lighted" (136). The lamp's rays overspread his manuscript pages, to reappear in his South Seas fiction as scattered beams glowing in a green thicket (*The Wrecker* [*Works* 12: 13]), as the street lamps' trembling reflections on the waters of the port (*The Ebb-Tide* [14: 1]), and as distant light from fires and "torches of many fishers moving on the reef" (*The Beach of Falesá* [13: 64]).

Stevenson's interest in photography and his continuing references to a light penetrating the dark shape his prose. In the opening passages of *In the South Seas*, when Stevenson describes his first view of the Marquesas, it is as if his words, like a photographic image, emanate from the disappearing night. The contrast between light and dark brings into view the black line of the horizon on which stands a "morning bank" as "black as ink" and exposes a prospect in which the dark peaks or needles of Va-pu show themselves in outline against the first rays of the sun (*Works* 20: 4). These passages create the lines, the ink, and the letters that mark his arrival as the dawn slowly reveals the landscape "in the attenuating darkness" (4). But although these patches of light help him articulate what he sees, their patchiness reflects his sense that his knowledge of the island cultures and peoples is by no means complete.

On his journey through the islands, Stevenson is never content to rest in the full, whitewashed blaze of day but returns, as if to refurbish his vocabulary, to an obscure landscape, where he remarks on "the hour of dusk, when the fire blazes, and . . . the lamp glints . . . between the pillars of the house" and where the fronds of the palm trees "stand out dark upon the distance, glisten against the sun, and flash like silver fountains in the assault of the wind" (15, 90). He orients himself to a new island by concentrating on how the light punctuates and contrasts with the darkness of what he cannot see or know. He looks up at "clouds of an inky blackness" shattered at times by lightning and walks "perhaps till twelve or one in the morning" on "the bright sand and in the tossing shadow" of the Gilbert Island palms (127, 301). These episodes recall the genesis of *The Wrecker* and *The Master of Ballantrae*, novels that came to him on dark nights sporadically illuminated by the rays of the moon or by a few lights scattered in the darkness. As he explained, these were "fine conditions" for the making of a story (*Works* 10: xxiii ["The Genesis of *The Master of Ballantrae*"]).

In looking at Stevenson's fiction, it is helpful to consider how his imagination thrives on an alternating, uneven dispersal of light and darkness. As I have pointed out in *Robert Louis Stevenson and the Colonial Imagination*, his characters and their stories "seem to step out of the shadows onto the brightness of the page." "Like the native women in *The Wrecker* who 'came by twos and threes out of the darkness' . . . and into the glow of the scattered lights, his characters emerge" from the negative plate, as if from oblivion, onto the text. "Their succession of illuminated faces stirs [Stevenson's] fancy and stimulates him to explore the mystery of what surrounds them" (109).

In his Pacific texts, Stevenson transplants an earlier perspective in which intermittent light is prominent. Just as when he placed his characters in the half-lit streets and drawing rooms of London (*Jekyll and Hyde*) and positioned Mr. Utterson waiting for a glimpse of Mr. Hyde under the gas lamps that draw "a regular pattern of light and shadow" (*Works* 5: 11), he must now, in the South Seas, enter areas where the unseen and the unarticulated are merely partially visible and where a flickering light illuminates a dark place but not in its entirety. The full picture of *Jekyll and Hyde* develops gradually through a maze of city lights, the flame of a drawing room fire, and the small beam of a candle. Only when the truth is fully known about Dr. Jekyll's doubleness is there the full light of Dr. Lanyon's consulting room—an illumination that both overexposes and destroys. Otherwise, the characters are kept in the half-developed knowledge of an undeveloped plate. The plot emerges like the scroll of pictures that run, one at a time, through Mr. Utterson's mind when "he recalls, at night in bed, what Mr. Enfield has told him about a Mr. Hyde" (Colley, *Robert Louis Stevenson* 110). Like the magic lantern slides with which Stevenson was familiar, these images disappear back into the darkness.

Stevenson occasionally opens his narrative in the full light but soon retreats into episodes of interrupted darkness and discontinuous light in which metonymic figures and fragments replace the full, inclusive prospect. The opening chapter of *Jekyll and Hyde* offers an easy example in class: Mr. Utterson and his "distant kinsman" Enfield walk in the bright light of a Sunday stroll, but soon, as the subject of Mr. Hyde emerges, that Sunday glow is replaced by a half-concealing, half-revealing light that only partially illuminates the black night (2). In *The Beach of Falesá*, we move from the full brightness of the morning to a sporadically illuminated setting where the lantern, the candles, the torches, and matches punctuate the nocturnal landscape and reveal silhouettes of incomplete meaning. If there is class time, it is worth tracking how this story shifts from the sun-baked beach to the dark interior of the bush and gradually, as the narrative develops, exposes and explains the mystery of the taboo and the devil work. The backdrop of contrasting light and darkness continues what was essential to Stevenson's composing of *Jekyll and Hyde,* where most of the action plays on a shadowy set of images—until the truth is revealed and the mystery solved and the full image developed.

In Stevenson, as in the photographic negative, it is the dark, obscure moment that brings to view an event, a sighting. This metaphor allows readers to understand that darkness is the foundation of seeing and knowing. Without the dark, light has no significance. Therefore I encourage a reading of *In the South Seas* and *The Beach of Falesá* coupled with his earlier "My Shadow" and "The Lamplighter" from *A Child's Garden of Verses*, his essays "A Plea for Gas Lamps" and "The Lantern-Bearers," as well as *Strange Case of Dr Jekyll and Mr Hyde*. Students will better understand that Stevenson's plots emerge, that meaning is incomplete and gradual in its development into consciousness. They may also begin to grasp how the obscurities of a poorly lit Victorian age give way to the abstractions of modernism.

The *Jekyll and Hyde* Class: Overcoming Strangeness

Wendy R. Katz

A Teachable Text

Strange Case of Dr Jekyll and Mr Hyde is an eminently teachable text that instructors can approach in various ways for different levels of students. I have taught it in a first-year introduction to literature course and in upper-level courses in late-Victorian fiction. Instructors who like to introduce authorial context will find useful material in Stevenson's explanation of the genesis of his text in the 1888 essay "A Chapter on Dreams" (*Works* 30: 41–53) as well as in his remarks on the text in his correspondence, the most notable being the comment on Jekyll as a hypocrite (*Letters* 6: 56–57). For instructors who want to establish intertextual links as essential interpretive tools, *Jekyll and Hyde* can be set beside Stevenson's own "Markheim" (1886), Edgar Allan Poe's "William Wilson" (1839), Oscar Wilde's *The Picture of Dorian Gray* (1891), or even Mary Shelley's *Frankenstein* (1818), that other gothic tale of a creature born of scientific experiment. For instructors who prefer to bring not much more than the text to class, *Jekyll and Hyde* lends itself admirably to the tracking of key images and motifs or discussions of the nature of allegory, the gothic tale, the detective story, and narrative itself. Its brevity contributes further to its pedagogical adaptability.

More advanced readers of this text can examine the plentiful supplementary material on *Jekyll and Hyde*. Instructors who favor a cultural studies approach with a psychoanalytic leaning can indicate the novella's anticipation of Freudian theory. Those who favor a framework of intellectual and social history will find opportunities to discuss the developing field of psychology, Victorian morality, Victorian sexuality, and the Victorian city. Instructors could choose to examine the text in the context of late-Victorian discourse on criminality and urban poverty. Students unfamiliar with late-Victorian anxieties about class, masculinity, sexuality, urbanization, or scientific advances and their ensuing assaults on established values and religion will find abundant material. An excellent choice for a cultural studies approach is Martin Danahay's Broadview edition, with its selected passages on Victorian theories of crime and degeneracy from Cesare Lombroso and from Max Nordau. Students will find a gold mine of background, critical essays, and textual history in the critical editions of Katherine Linehan and of Richard Dury. Not to be overlooked is the Stevenson Web site, which includes notes and packages for *Jekyll and Hyde* complete with assignments, questions, and links (and now folds in Dury's previous site): www.robert-louis-stevenson.org.

The Motif of the Double

Teachers will probably want to deal with the motif of the double, for which *Jekyll and Hyde* is famous. An instructor can quickly sketch concepts of identity and otherness along with the specific Victorian duality that seems to have sunk deep roots into a period known for its ostensible repression of the passions. Students will be interested to learn that the language of pre-Freudian psychology was largely literary. Allegories of moral monsters made Dr. Jekyll and Dorian Gray bywords for the double self. Students who focus on Dr. Jekyll's final confession of his misdeeds and explanation of his experiments with the borders of personality may welcome an extended discussion of the double that reaches into the area of late-nineteenth-century science and evolutionary psychology. The experiments of Dr. Jekyll not only free him to indulge his concealed desires but also release the ties to scientific rationality that bind his professional community.

One way to examine the double is to assign "A Chapter on Dreams," in which Stevenson writes about the "case" of a dreamer who begins "to lead a double life" of waking and sleeping (*Works* 30: 43). Stevenson ultimately confesses to being the dreamer, trying to explain his unconscious self and its effect on the creative imagination that shaped *Jekyll and Hyde*. Students should be asked to consider the nonfictional double in "Dreams" as a counterpart to the fictional motif in *Jekyll*. Alternatively, they may start identifying the doubles that appear in the text: the strange pairing of the disparate characters Utterson and Enfield at the outset of the tale; the contrasting medical doctors Jekyll and Lanyon, whose divergent views deepen the tale's conflict; and the cluster of minor references to the biblical Cain and Abel and the legendary Damon and Pythias. Instructors can ask students to identify other binaries, such as the images of windows and doors. Such work will allow students to prepare for the paramount double of Stevenson's title. The double can be discussed in terms of moral responsibility, suggested by biblical references to sibling rivalry in the figures of Cain and Abel. Peripheral binaries are threads of the central binary of Jekyll's "profound duplicity of life," his struggling "polar twins" (*Works* 5: 57, 58). Students might be asked if the double identity is a binary that Stevenson eventually challenges when Jekyll considers the possibility of a multiplicity of selves in his final statement, speculating that "man will be ultimately known for a mere polity of multifarious, incongruous and independent denizens" (58). Does this final pointing beyond the binary view of life make the late-Victorian writer an early modernist?

Getting beyond the Double: Overcoming Narrative Strangeness

While a discussion of the double is necessary, it depends largely on instructors' bringing their knowledge of Victorian culture, science, or psychology to the students or requiring students to do their own research. Getting beyond the double, however, is essential for the pedagogy of the classroom. My way of taking this step is to explore the notion of strangeness proposed by the title of *Strange Case*. Although Jonathan Culler's notion of "naturalizing" a text, a process of reducing the artifice of literary conventions to the familiar by "simultaneously cherishing and overcoming . . . strangeness" refers to reading literature in general (67), it is rarely more useful than in Stevenson's strange tale. Strangeness is the insistent keynote of the text. Indeed, students can profitably track all occurrences of the word *strange* in a searchable e-text (such as the *Project Gutenberg* version of *Dr. Jekyll*). Although strangeness clamors for attention as part of the text's title, many students ignore it. But the strangeness of the text must be embraced and, to use Culler's word, overcome for a satisfying interpretive workout.

Instructors might point out that strangeness is immediate in the opacity of the familiar—for example, the habitual Sunday walks of two distant relatives, Utterson and Enfield, who otherwise have nothing in common. The upright lawyer, determinedly averse to any levity and "embarrassed in discourse," seems an incongruous companion for Enfield, "the man about town," whose narrative of horror introduces the Hyde story almost as an entertainment (1, 2). Students should consider the effect of introducing Hyde through Enfield's narrative. As they proceed through the text, they might ponder the whole as a narrative of narratives, a layering of meaning. The language of the Stevenson text is another place to focus for the interrogation of strangeness. Ostensibly simple and straightforward, it restrains, defers, or perplexes meaning. Information is carefully withheld or given in a way that is tantalizingly opaque.

As strange as the incongruous pair who walk the streets of London on Sunday afternoons is the street scene itself. Stevenson teases the reader with descriptions that appear almost mathematically precise, but the reader digs at the text only to come up against strangeness. The house "two doors from one corner on the left hand going east," which turns out to be Jekyll's, promises a clarity that vanishes immediately in its upper-story "blind forehead of discoloured wall" (2–3). Direct and unproblematic on the surface, the language draws the reader into a puzzle. The atmospheric setting of night and fog also creates opacity. Although Utterson rides to Hyde's lodgings in Soho in the morning, the light seems "like the back-end of evening; and there would be a glow of a rich, lurid brown, like the light of some strange conflagration" (22). Students may discover that their gradual immersion in strangeness allows them to accept the ambiguities of Jekyll's final confession.

Moving from the general stylistic opacity of the text to the examination of material objects that function as symbols, instructors can draw attention to doors in Enfield's narrative. Here is another opportunity for students to examine a searchable text, finding both "doors" and "windows" with the goal of working up to that final forcing of the door to Jekyll's laboratory. Discussion of doors and windows should guide students to thematic concerns of freedom and imprisonment. Finally, students should confront the strangeness of Hyde's seemingly motiveless attack on the girl and his similarly inexplicable act of murdering Danvers Carew.

Narrative Indeterminacy

Strangeness continues in the story's several narratives. Although a traditional third person tells the lion's share of the story, supplementary narratives, letters, and notes complicate and destabilize meaning. The first narrative is Enfield's tale of Hyde, in which the teller reveals more than he intends to Utterson about the lawyer's friend, Dr. Jekyll. Later, students learn of the murder of Danvers Carew through the indirect narrative of a maidservant whose account is filtered through the third-person narrator. In addition, there is a putative letter from Hyde to Jekyll, a letter from Jekyll to Utterson, an envelope from Lanyon to Utterson containing a sealed envelope, a series of notes from Jekyll to Poole, Dr. Lanyon's narrative, and Dr. Jekyll's full statement. It is essential to underline Stevenson's deliberate complicating of the narrative structure. Like the streets of London that draw the reader into a world of labyrinthine confusion, the narrators and the concluding narrative of Jekyll's confession in particular, found in an envelope along with other written enclosures, establish an ambiguity that reinforces the strangeness of the text. Dr. Jekyll's narrative offers the biggest challenge, but it is one that students willingly work at for clues to the puzzle. Instructors should remind students of the general caveats inherent in first-person narration. Jekyll is hardly reliable. Students should be asked to consider the ambiguity of pronouns ("I," "he," and "it") and nouns ("Jekyll," "Hyde") in the final statement. The confusion provokes questions about Jekyll's identity and the way Jekyll perceives it. Once students embrace the novella's narrative strangeness, they will become less willing to satisfy themselves with easy answers about the text and more willing to discuss narrative strategy. The indeterminacy of the narrative, instructors should stress, is highlighted by Stevenson's leaving the reader with the final first-person narratives (Dr. Lanyon's and Henry Jekyll's) to work out without further commentary. A final suggestion for instructors in late-Victorian literature courses: having covered the narrative enclosures in *Jekyll and Hyde*, they may wish to adduce these as anticipating the narrative enclosures that Joseph Conrad later uses in *Lord Jim*.

Reading Literary Conventions: A Final Note on Strangeness

Instructors can also examine the value of using literary genres to generate meaning, specifically allegory, the gothic tale, and detective fiction. Students might eventually debate the merits of each. I discuss here only the first two (for an excellent treatment of *Jekyll and Hyde* as detective fiction, see Hirsch, who also looks at the gothic). Some instructors may begin by discussing *Jekyll and*

Hyde as an allegory of human conflict, the definition of which may vary from a spiritual battle between good and evil to a psychological battle between the primitive passions and the strictures of civil society. Others may want to view the text as an allegorical conflict between science and metaphysics, concentrating on the quarrel between Lanyon and Jekyll. The character of Hyde, however, the quintessentially demonic monster, garners the most attention from readers, gently nudging discussion from allegory to the gothic, a form students find appealing. This inherently strange literary genre, with its horror and terror, bizarre settings, irrational or supernatural occurrences, and monstrous characters, offers not only an apt but also a lively literary context for Stevenson's story. Because of their relevance to the present discussion of strangeness, Judith Halberstam's remarks on the gothic are particularly suggestive here; speaking of a "riot" of meaning in the gothic tale, she singles out the monster as "a symbol for this interpretive mayhem" (128). I suggest focusing on the symbolic monster Hyde for discussion of the gothic, then refining the discussion with an emphasis on masculinity.

It is not unusual to view the gothic through the lens of gender studies. Critics have long done that with Charlotte Perkins Gilman's "The Yellow Wall-Paper," maintaining that it is difficult to follow the path of the narrator as she loses her senses without acknowledging her plight as an oppressed woman. One could argue, similarly, that it is difficult to understand Hyde without trying to fathom the nature of his aggressive and sinister maleness and his peculiar threat to the almost exclusively male environment of this tale. Students who suspend judgment throughout the text may be prepared to see Hyde as providing a chemical avenue for otherwise forbidden sexual freedom to the respected but repressed Dr. Jekyll. (But they should be reminded that Stevenson said that Hyde was not "a mere voluptuary" [*Letters* 6: 56]). Many critics see a homosexual subtext, citing the covert nature of Hyde's activities and the sexually symbolic resonance of the back door to Jekyll's house, Hyde's chief access to the residence. (Students need to know that the Labouchere Amendment criminalizing so-called acts of gross indecency was passed in 1895 and that homosexual acts were not decriminalized in England and Wales until 1967.) Elaine Showalter's commentary on *Jekyll and Hyde* in *Sexual Anarchy* is arguably the best-known analysis identifying a homosexual subtext. Other commentaries on the novella have looked closely at its intense maleness as corroborating evidence for this interpretation. It is true that Utterson dreams of Hyde's "stealing like a thief to Harry's bedside" (16), but Bertha Mason, another atavistic creature of gothic sensuality, steals to the bedside of Jane Eyre (241–42). The image seems more a recurring gothic trope than decisive evidence of sexual intent. Besides the single male state of the text's characters and their solitary existences, students should examine their near obsessive concern with respectability and social standing. These characters insist on a code of silence, preventing any scandal from threatening the reputation of the respectable Dr. Jekyll. Students might be directed to the conversation about silence between Utterson and Enfield that ends the "Story of the Door" and asked what silence signifies when upheld by that principled representative of the legal system, Utterson, who apparently is more concerned with Dr. Jekyll's respectability than with finding the murderer of Danvers Carew. How does Hyde threaten these men? He remains an enigmatic menace, the puzzle expressed by his very name. Hyde cannot be described by anyone who sees him, except in vague terms as a deformed and savage creature, but he seems nonetheless to infect everyone with loathing. Regarding the question of what danger Hyde poses to this group of reputable men, readers don't know exactly what Jekyll wants to do when he seeks a second identity or what Hyde does when he goes in search of pleasure. It's all a mystery. A tentative solution may emerge from asking students why the borders between Jekyll and Hyde become increasingly soft, if not porous, and why the room finally entered by Utterson and Poole discloses a dead Hyde as well as a picture of truly strange civility:

> There lay the cabinet before their eyes in the quiet lamplight, a good fire glowing and chattering on the hearth, the kettle singing its thin strain, a drawer or two open, papers neatly set forth on the business-table, and, nearer the fire, the things laid out for tea: the quietest room, you would have said, and . . . the most commonplace that night in London. (44)

"Commonplace," ironically, may be the strangest word in this passage. Stephen Arata convincingly argues that "Hyde acts out the aggressions of timid bourgeois gentlemen," and he suggests further that Hyde is "a figure whose rage is the rage of a threatened patriarchy" (*Fictions* 39). Hyde, in other words, winds up being very close indeed to Jekyll. This treatment of the gothic through the lens of gender should provide a great deal for students to discuss.

Having taught *Dr. Jekyll and Mr. Hyde* over the course of several years, I can only reiterate the importance of insisting on the text's strangeness and reminding instructors that students, usually uncomfortable with uncertainty and ambiguity, often reach for easy answers, especially given our society's inclination for over-the-counter psychologizing and easygoing familiarity with terms such as *the unconscious* and *repressed*. Students will arrive gratefully at Dr. Jekyll's "Full Statement," ready to accept it as a true confession and to disregard its problems. They need to be encouraged to read the text with a clear eye to its internal contradictions, encouraged to see that the text's strangeness is its most enduring and endearing feature.

Jekyll and Hyde as Science Fiction

Anne Stiles

Stevenson's works often have been overlooked by guardians of the literary canon, whose preferences for realism and literary experimentation in a modernist vein seemingly left little room for the author's delightful romances (Ambrosini and Dury, Introduction). Even *Jekyll and Hyde* was not included in the *Norton Anthology of English Literature* until the eighth edition (2006). But Stevenson's renowned shilling shocker has long been welcome in courses devoted to science fiction, another literary tradition that inhabits the margins of academic respectability. Critics and historians of science fiction generally acknowledge the novella's status as a seminal work of science fiction or scientific romance in the tradition of Mary Shelley's *Frankenstein* (1818) or H. G. Wells's *War of the Worlds* (1898).

This essay explores how one might teach *Jekyll and Hyde* as science fiction, using approaches different from those normally employed in a Victorian literature class or literary survey, and how instructors can help students situate the novella with reference to nineteenth-century scientific disciplines, especially medicine, psychology, and evolutionary theory. Stevenson's greatest achievement as an author of science fiction, I suggest, is his appropriation and critique of these discourses in his most famous work.

First of all, how might we contextualize *Jekyll and Hyde* in a science fiction syllabus? How does the novella fit in a genre that has evolved into a predominantly American, multimedia art form with mass popular appeal? Purists may argue that *Jekyll and Hyde* does not belong in the canon of science fiction because of its early publication date, Scottish author, and the absence of robots, spaceships, and other familiar science fiction paraphernalia. While most science fiction scholars accept Brian Aldiss's assertion that the genre began with Shelley's *Frankenstein*, a significant minority feel that science fiction originated in American pulp magazines of the 1920s and enjoyed its golden age from 1937 to 1950 (see Aldiss and Wingrove 18–19; Le Guin and Attebery 7). For an explanation of the unique role of Scotland in this debate, see Caroline McCracken-Flesher's introduction to *Scotland as Science Fiction*.

Instructors wishing to step around this debate and the anachronistic label "science fiction," which took on its modern meaning around 1929, can follow Brooks Landon to place *Jekyll and Hyde* as a scientific romance (51). This earlier literary tradition flourished in Britain from the 1880s until around 1940, culminating in works such as Wells's *The Island of Dr. Moreau* (1896), Grant Allen's *The British Barbarians* (1895), and Aldous Huxley's *Brave New World* (1932). In *Scientific Romance in Britain*, Brian Stableford explains how scientific romances developed apart from the American tradition and placed greater emphasis on evolutionary narratives (3, 6). The late-Victorian scientific romance emerged alongside a parallel tradition of science writing in a quasi-Romantic vein. One thinks, for instance, of Charles Darwin's *Descent of Man* (1871), with its dramatic narrative of human origins, or Thomas Henry Huxley's eminently readable popular science essays in *Evolution and Ethics* (1893). *Jekyll and Hyde*, in its sustained focus on Hyde's atavism and in its indebtedness to discourses surrounding evolution, dual personality, and other topics, fits the mold of scientific romance.

What might it mean to teach this novella as science fiction or scientific romance rather than as fantasy or late-Victorian gothic? To be sure, these categories frequently overlap, and their histories intertwine. Aldiss argues, for instance, that science fiction descended from the gothic and that both genres helped nineteenth-century Britons grapple with the overwhelming consequences of the Industrial Revolution. He points out that *Frankenstein*, arguably the first work of science fiction, was known in its time as a highly successful gothic novel (Aldiss and Wingrove 16). Similarly, Patrick Brantlinger contends that gothic romance and science fiction are "both forms of apocalyptic nightmare fantasy" that are antithetical to realism (Brantlinger 31).

Critics likewise acknowledge the difficulty distinguishing science fiction and fantasy, genres that feed off of each other's popularity. In the late nineteenth century, supernatural fiction and heroic fantasy flourished in tandem with scientific romance, as shown by the simultaneous popularity of Marie Corelli's occult fantasies and of gothic horror extravaganzas like *Dracula* (1897). When attempting to separate science fiction from fantasy, scholars sometimes point out more similarities than differences. Brian Attebery describes fantasy as "science fiction's other: magical instead of scientific, backward-looking instead of prophetic, but full of the same kinds of adventure, mystery, and metamorphosis" (10). The boundaries between magic and science blur when scientific experiments boast improbable or miraculous results, such as a character's division into good and evil avatars. Thus, as Donald Lawler observes, *Jekyll and Hyde* might reasonably be considered a science fantasy, especially since Jekyll's chemical process operates "more like alchemy than pharmacology or chemistry" (250).

Whether one considers *Jekyll and Hyde* a fantastic, gothic, or scientific romance, the novella clearly diverges from mainstream realist narratives. Stevenson famously championed romance over realism in "A Humble Remonstrance" (1884), where he argued that the reader of fiction should "be submerged by the tale as by a billow" (*Works* 29: 137). Yet the content of *Jekyll and Hyde* is not entirely fantastical. Students might consider where the novella most closely approaches realism: in its skillful appropriation of mid-Victorian scientific discourses surrounding evolution, sexology, and dual personality. In fact, it so convincingly utilizes medical concepts that some Victorian physicians cited it in psychiatric case studies (Mighall 194; J. Reid, *Robert Louis Stevenson* 96). The novella's scientific verisimilitude earns it a place on a science fiction course syllabus.

Instructors wishing to foreground scientific aspects of *Jekyll and Hyde* may consult an impressive range of scholarship on this subject. Several critics explore

Stevenson's attitude toward evolution and related discourses such as degeneration theory. Robert Mighall analyzes Hyde's appearance and behavior in terms of Victorian anthropology, criminology, and psychiatry, disciplines that could be described as "'gothic' versions of evolutionism" (131). According to these discourses, Hyde is an anachronism, a throwback to humankind's savage past living in the body of a Victorian bourgeois gentleman. Stephen Arata likewise focuses on Hyde's atavism but identifies a different form of degeneracy lurking in the text. Noting Hyde's tastefully furnished Soho apartment, Arata suggests "how easily Stevenson's Hyde could be taken not for a brute but for a dandy" (*Fictions* 37). He reminds us that Victorian writings on evolutionary regression, such as Max Nordau's *Degeneration* (1892, trans. 1895), emphasized the dangers of an effete aristocracy riddled with sexual vice.

Many Victorians feared the prospect of evolutionary regression, whether it surfaced in the person of the criminal or in the degenerate vices of an entire class. By contrast, Stevenson encouraged readers to access primitive instincts by means of fiction, especially romances featuring adventure and danger. Such tales invigorated readers by hearkening back to "the first men who told their stories round the savage camp-fire" (*Works* 29: 136 ["Humble Remonstrance"]). While *Jekyll and Hyde* is hardly escapist fare, the novella features a protagonist whose failure to embrace his instincts brings about his downfall. Julia Reid reminds us that Stevenson disapproved of "civilized" repression and hypocrisy far more than the "lower elements" derived from man's evolutionary prehistory (*Robert Louis Stevenson* 104). (On evolution and degeneracy in Stevenson's writings, see Punter; Pick; Greenslade; and Brantlinger.)

Still, most of the criticism on Stevenson and science focuses on psychology. Many scholars take a Freudian approach to *Jekyll and Hyde* (Beattie; Veeder and Hirsch), but I would avoid this route in class, since Sigmund Freud's first psychoanalytic publications appeared after Stevenson's death. Students can better understand the author and his period by focusing on evolutionary psychology, dual brain theory, and dual consciousness. Stevenson's interest in evolutionary psychology stemmed from his friendship with James Sully, who is now best known for his work on child development (Block). Sully's writing addressed the relation between genius and insanity, alongside "duality, primitive consciousness, illusions, and madness," issues that surface repeatedly in *Jekyll and Hyde* (Block 447; see also Davis 214–17).

Victorian ideas of dual and multiple personality can provoke lively class discussion. Fanny Osborne Stevenson traced her spouse's interest in dual personality to a "paper he read in a French scientific journal on sub-consciousness" (*Works* 5: xvi). Elaine Showalter suggests that he might have read an essay about Louis Vivet, the first case of multiple personality, published in the *Archives de neurologie* in 1885 (105). Vivet's case was described in "Multiplex Personality" (1886), a celebrated article by Frederic W. H. Myers, which Stevenson read after the publication of *Jekyll and Hyde* (Dury, "Crossing" 237). Richard Dury provides evidence for an earlier source: one of Étienne Eugène Azam's essays about his famous patient, Félida X (243). Félida was a florid hysteric who alternated between a gloomy "first state" and a cheerful "second state," during which she was promiscuous. Félida may have served as a model for Jekyll, since her case was relatively well known in Britain (243). Her illness was even discussed in the *Cornhill* during the years when Stevenson contributed to the periodical (J. Reid, *Robert Louis Stevenson* 96; Stiles 891–94). In articles like "Have We Two Brains?" (1875) and "Dual Consciousness" (1877), Richard Proctor, a journalist, described Félida X alongside another French dual personality, Sergeant F.

According to Victorian psychologists, dual personality was caused by brain hemisphere asymmetry. Nineteenth-century physicians proposed that the left brain housed higher, civilized faculties such as reason and linguistic ability, while the atavistic right brain controlled emotions and instincts. If the emotional right brain routinely overruled the civilized left brain, it was thought, dual personality or criminal tendencies could emerge. (For the history of this idea and its application to *Jekyll and Hyde*, see Harrington; Finger; Showalter 114–15; Stiles 884–88; also appendices in the Luckhurst [2008] and Danahay [2005] editions of the novella.)

When introducing these ideas in class, instructors must remind students that dual personality differs significantly from multiple personality disorder. Whereas dual personality was attributed to physical causes, including brain hemisphere asymmetry, multiple personality has long been understood as a reaction to severe childhood trauma. The multiple personality diagnosis first surfaced in France in July 1885, about six months before the publication of Stevenson's novella (Hacking 171–72). It is unclear whether Stevenson had heard of Vivet and multiple personality disorder before writing *Jekyll and Hyde*. However, the novella amply demonstrates his familiarity with discourses surrounding dual consciousness (Stiles 884–88).

A few critics have looked beyond psychological discourses to explain Jekyll's pathology, and their comments can enrich class discussion. Stephen Heath turns to Richard von Krafft-Ebing's sexology and the concept of the "Lust-Murder," in which "killing replaces the sexual act" (103). Hyde's brutal murder of Sir Danvers Carew, or his trampling of a little girl, may well stand in for "something unsuitable for fiction," as Gerard Manley Hopkins noted (Linehan, *Strange Case* 101). By writing a story bereft of female characters, Heath suggests, Stevenson was able to highlight the normally unspeakable subject of male sexual deviance. Daniel Wright, meanwhile, convincingly argues that *Jekyll and Hyde* is a narrative of chemical addiction, and Thomas L. Reed considers it an allegory for alcoholism.

Instructors might also ask students to consider the novel as a medical case study. Oscar Wilde observed in "The Decay of Lying" that the tale "reads dangerously like an experiment out of *The Lancet*" (167). As a case study, however, *Jekyll and Hyde* is inconclusive, since the patient under investigation commits suicide. Moreover, the physician is also the patient, in a conflation of roles that destabilizes Victorian medical hierarchies. *Jekyll and Hyde* can thus be read as a parody of the case study, in which the objective physician becomes abject patient (see Mighall 191; Heath 102; Stiles 888–91).

Various resources and activities can help introduce scientific aspects of *Jekyll and Hyde* in undergraduate courses. The Martin Danahay, Katherine Linehan, and Roger Luckhurst editions of *Jekyll and Hyde* provide useful excerpts and reviews of specific sciences for preparatory reading. I often supplement these readings with a lecture or slide show covering scientific interpretations of *Jekyll and Hyde* not addressed by the assigned texts. After this lecture, I make a table on the blackboard with several headings: "Sexology," "Dual Brain Theory," "Evolutionary Regression," "Addiction," and so on. I ask students, "If you could vote for only one of these scientific explanations of Jekyll's behavior, which would it be?" Then I ask why they voted the way they did and enter their responses under the appropriate heading. Generally my students favor the addiction narrative, though the dual brain theory and related psychological explanations are also popular. This exercise introduces undergraduates to a broad range of Victorian scientific theories and allows them to consider why some scientific explanations are more convincing than others. The resulting discussion might highlight the rhetorical power of scientific discourse or the near mythic power of a scientific theory to alter how we think about human behavior and the physical world.

In an advanced undergraduate seminar or graduate course, students might focus on one or two scientific explanations of Jekyll's behavior and research them more thoroughly. I have asked graduate students to read *Jekyll and Hyde* alongside articles about dual personality, including Proctor's *Cornhill* essays and various secondary sources (e.g., Dury, "Crossing"; Stiles; Hacking). I may also assign Victorian accounts of dual brain theory available in Jenny Bourne Taylor and Sally Shuttleworth's anthology *Embodied Selves*. Students thereby develop an excellent understanding of dual consciousness in *Jekyll and Hyde* and even begin to apply this theory beyond Stevenson's work. They also start to grasp the historical contingency of medical and scientific ideas. One can apply this same in-depth approach to other scientific theories that surface in *Jekyll and Hyde*, such as evolutionary debates (drawing on J. Reid, *Robert Louis Stevenson*; Arata, *Fictions*; Mighall).

My goal here is to encourage instructors to present the science behind *Jekyll and Hyde*, not to dictate how they present it. Teaching *Jekyll and Hyde* as science fiction allows one to highlight aspects of Stevenson's artistry that are not usually emphasized in literature courses, including the author's impressive grasp of Victorian scientific ideas and his independence of mind. Instead of accepting scientific theories at face value, Stevenson often turned ideas against the institutions that created them, as in his decision to upend medical hierarchies by housing doctor and patient in one body. Students can find in *Jekyll and Hyde* a critique of scientific hubris every bit as powerful as *Frankenstein* or *Brave New World*.

Stevenson and Adaptation: Resources and Methods

Martin Danahay

Stevenson's stories have been widely adapted. There are plays and musicals, TV shows and movies, many available internationally on DVD or online. Classroom uses for these materials include tracking the story's prevalence — for the stage alone, reviews reach from Australia to France and from South Korea to California — or noting differences and the shifting cultural anxieties that they express. In this essay I indicate the span of materials and their possible uses but focus on films, since these are so readily available.

The most widely adapted Stevenson works are *Treasure Island* and *Jekyll and Hyde*. Because both have an interesting life through adaptation and thereby an influence on popular culture, they are rewarding subjects for analysis. Students already know of *Treasure Island*, if only through Long John Silver, and *Jekyll and Hyde* they recognize as a synonym for split personality. From this awareness, they can build an understanding of the mutual entanglements of text and audience through popular culture. Related to this topic is the question of how far from the original an adaptation can move without becoming a completely new text in its own right.

Jekyll and Hyde

Jekyll and Hyde was immediately adapted for the stage. In 1887, two versions competed in America; they then raced across the Atlantic to claim boasting rights as the first to be performed in London. Daniel Bandmann's version has been largely forgotten (Danahay and Chisholm 133–66), but the second, with a script by T. R. Sullivan and performed by Richard Mansfield (41–80), was a commercial success that became the template for many film adaptations. The Mansfield version adds a romance to the Stevenson original, as do most subsequent retellings. Jekyll is given a fiancée, the daughter of Sir Danvers Carew. The play also rehabilitates Jekyll, making him more appealing than Stevenson intended. When interviewed about the Sullivan play, the author insisted that the story was not about sexuality but hypocrisy and that Jekyll was, above all, a hypocrite (*Letters* 6: 56). Yet Stevenson endorsed the play after Sullivan read it to him.

There have been many dramatic adaptations since. In 2008, Jeffrey Hatcher proffered a script to the Arizona Theatre Company in which Jekyll and Hyde are each played by a different actor. The story was turned into a musical that had a long run on Broadway. Scripted by Leslie Bricusse, the musical continues to be performed by touring companies around the world. It would have appealed to Mansfield, who became famous for his onstage transformation from Jekyll into Hyde, which involves a duet with himself by the actor playing Jekyll/Hyde as he switches from one side of his face to another. The musical follows Mansfield's leads in having a romantic interest for Dr. Jekyll and making him into a more appealing character; indeed the musical had a sizable online fan base of women who viewed the story as a romance. Class consideration of these materials can revolve around issues of stage convention and commerce. Resources include *Jekyll and Hyde Dramatized* (Danahay and Chisholm).

The many films of *Jekyll and Hyde* pose questions about the lure of particular texts for adaptation. The earliest commercially available film is the 1912 Thanhouser–Kino International version (Henderson; see Bowers). Silent and only twelve minutes long, it is an extremely low-budget piece that sets the action in a village. The film is notable for the first use of special effects in the transformation scene—it exploits the possibilities of film through stop-motion techniques. In a 1920 version, more successful, John Barrymore uses his body and expression to suggest the transformation from Jekyll into Hyde. Students laugh at the low-budget Thanhouser version, at the trampling of the little girl. Their response might start a discussion of the difference between horror in Stevenson's time and in the 1912 version as opposed to the high body count and gore of horror today. David J. Skal's *Hollywood Gothic*, which tracks *Dracula* in the movies, provides a useful comparison.

The Barrymore version introduces an exotic dancer, and in 1931 Rouben Mamoulian introduces a prostitute. Mamoulian's version is a remarkable erotic achievement, considering that it was produced at a time when censorship made it difficult to address sexuality onscreen. The film turns Jekyll's internal divisions into a conflict in which male desire is split between a good woman, the fiancée, and a bad woman, who is openly sexual. Whereas the Stevenson story took place in an almost completely male environment and can be read in the context of antihomosexual legislation in the late nineteenth century, Mamoulian turns the story into a parable of divided male heterosexual desire. Paramount marketed the film as ideal for a first date, recasting the story into a romance despite the violence against women that it depicted. Students might consider this film and the Spencer Tracy 1941 version in connection with Laura Mulvey's "Visual Pleasure and Narrative Cinema" to debate the role of scopophilia and the narrative drives of Hollywood. The Mamoulian version adopts the perspective of Jekyll/Hyde when the prostitute Ivy is on the screen, implicating the audience as voyeurs in his desire for her and in her later murder. Scopophilia raises unsettling questions about the relation among film, sexuality, violence, and the gender of the viewer.

These films also show how the story, so spare in its telling and so allegorical in its method, can be adapted to express different cultural anxieties. Where Stevenson's original registered Victorian concerns about degeneration, Mamoulian reflects racial tensions in the United States. In Bricusse's musical, Jekyll becomes a drug addict, injecting himself with a bright red liquid. In two different BBC television versions, one turns Hyde into a pedophile (A. Reid), and one makes the story a meditation on surveillance (Mackinnon and Lipsey). Caroline McCracken-Flesher ("Cultural Projections") and Brian Rose provide resources here, reviewing cases and positing theories of adaptation according to anxiety.

Jekyll and Hyde has also inspired retellings that do not owe so much to the original. Chuck Palahniuk, author of *Fight Club*, draws on Stevenson's story, as does Stan Lee for the Hulk, and these tales have been made into films. The overlarge and hugely muscled Hulk is in turn a progenitor of a later Mr. Hyde, who, in films like the adaptation by Stephen Norrington of Alan Moore's *The League of Extraordinary Gentlemen*, has clearly been taking steroids and working out in the gym. Stevenson's Hyde was smaller and lighter than Jekyll, but now Hyde is a symbol of masculine rage and power. Companion reading for this approach can be found in Virginia Wright Wexman and in Janice Doane and Devon Hodges, all of whom give nuanced readings of the original Jekyll/Hyde relationship. Susan Jeffords's *Hard Bodies: Hollywood Masculinity in the Reagan Era* and David Greven's *Manhood in Hollywood from Bush to Bush* discuss the hypermasculinity of more recent filmic Jekylls and Hydes.

Treasure Island

Like *Jekyll and Hyde*, *Treasure Island* has entered popular consciousness—unwitting students sing "Fifteen men on the dead man's chest / Yo ho ho, and a bottle of rum!" (*Works* 2: 3). The book's most enduring legacy is not the bildungsroman of Jim Hawkins but the character of Long John Silver. This morally ambiguous figure, with his wooden leg and the parrot on his shoulder, has become the stereotypical image of the pirate (see Chatton in this volume). The influence of the story was enhanced by N. C. Wyeth's illustrations from the 1911 Scribner edition, which established the outfit that is still found in Halloween pirate costumes. Comparison of Stevenson's descriptions and Wyeth's illustrations, available at www.ncwyeth.org, yields good classroom discussion on the relation between literature and its art.

Because the Wyeth illustrations shaped perceptions not only of the story but of pirates generally, they foreground the problem that we cannot read the narrative in the same way that the Victorians first did. Our readings will always be a retelling, because our imagination of the characters is indelibly marked by later interpretations. Students might consider whether, even using contemporary reviews and letters, we can ever reconstruct how a story was interpreted at the time of publication.

The many film versions of the story include a 1972 rendition, directed by John Hough, in which Orson Welles plays Long John Silver. The 1950 version, directed by Byron Haskin and with Robert Newton as Long John Silver, is considered one of the best in terms of cinematography. The 1990 TV retelling, starring Charlton Heston and directed by Fraser Clarke Heston, offers an accurate representation of the relationship between Jim Hawkins and Long John Silver. No copies seem to exist of the 1908 silent *The Story of Treasure Island*, directed by J. Stuart Blackton, or the 1920 film that has costumes inspired by the Wyeth illustrations and directed by Maurice Tourneur. Students might discuss how texts influenced by Stevenson's tale in turn inflect remakes of it. There is the great advantage of tapping students' recent reading and viewing. *Treasure*

Planet, a science fiction animated adventure for children (Clements and Musker), parallels ideas (e.g., sailing ships in space) from the Edge Chronicles (Riddell and Stewart), which itself owes a debt to *Treasure Island*. There is a wide range of materials on which to draw. The *Pirates of the Caribbean* film series (Verbinski) is influenced by *Treasure Island* through the Wyeth illustrations, as was Sid Meier's video game, *Pirates!*, which self-consciously tried to re-create the costumes from the 1911 edition.

Even fast food can be considered an adaptation, for Long John Silver's, the fish restaurant, clearly refers to the Stevenson story. Bizarrely enough, *Jekyll and Hyde* has inspired many restaurants in Britain and the United States. The best known is the Jekyll and Hyde Club in New York. Such restaurants can encourage discussion of how far from the original the reference to a text can stray—Jekyll and Hyde became part of the "dining as entertainment" movement started by the Rainforest Café and Chuck E. Cheese chains. The Jekyll and Hyde Club uses actors to portray Henry Jekyll and Edward Hyde, and animatronic figures for stock horror characters like Frankenstein and his monster. "Jekyll and Hyde" in this context seems more a synonym for *horror* and a locus for commerce than an interpretation of Stevenson's text.

Kidnapped

Kidnapped remakes allow a different type of analysis. The novel was first adapted for the screen in 1917 (Crosland). Prints for this film are no longer available. A Disney production (1960), directed by Robert Stevenson, remains faithful to the original and is memorable for the first onscreen appearance of Peter O'Toole. A 1971 version combines *Kidnapped* with *Catriona* (also called *David Balfour*), which follows the further adventures of the eponymous hero and allows the romance so beloved of Hollywood (Mann). This version, featuring Donald Pleasance and Michael Caine, is considered a success both technically and as an adaptation. There have been several feature-length, made-for-TV versions by the BBC. A miniseries lists Francis Ford Coppola as an executive producer; it was directed by Ivan Passer and starred Armand Assante. At 180 minutes, this television series may be too lengthy for classroom use. But one can fast-forward to the scenery. In classes interested in cultural appropriation through Hollywood visualization, this fast-forwarding can provide rich data for analysis of place, the past, and nostalgia. Books such as David McCrone's *Scotland—the Brand* (McCrone, Morris, and Kiely) and Cairns Craig's *Out of History* can lay the groundwork for a discussion of Scotland as a space colonized by the cinematic gaze.

Audio Stevenson

Some of Stevenson's work has a further life in song: poems from *A Child's Garden of Verses* have been set to music. Seymour Barab published sheet music composed for voice and piano with settings for most of the poems. Howard

Blake, an English composer chiefly known for film scores, composed *The Land of Counterpane* for the tricentenary of the Mary Erskine School in Edinburgh in May 1993 (the recording can be purchased from the composer's Web site). For smaller children, Steve Klaper's 2005 *I Have a Little Shadow* uses folk guitar to interpret Stevenson's poems in various soothing adaptations (Klaper and Klaper). There is no rock version of *A Child's Garden of Verses*—but there is for *Jekyll and Hyde*, directed by Andre Champagne.

Stevenson in Circulation

Bringing together *Jekyll and Hyde* and *A Child's Garden of Verses* in one paragraph on music shows not only the extraordinary scope of adaptations to Stevenson's work but also the extraordinary diversity of the work itself. Students raised on *A Child's Garden* can be shocked to know he also wrote *Jekyll and Hyde*; students fascinated by *Fight Club* might have the opposite surprise. This conflict in part comes from the fact that even when Stevenson wrote boys' stories, his young protagonists navigated an adult world. His texts may have a light touch yet grapple with the darkest aspects of human behavior. Adaptations of his work can thus run the gamut from X-rated versions suitable only for adults (as in both the rock musical and pornographic versions of *Jekyll and Hyde*) to lullabies for children.

Stevenson was a vagabond. Just as his life encompassed diverse landscapes, from the Scottish Highlands to tropical isles, a journey through his writings can open up diverse vistas. His texts have wandered, and been recognized far and wide, in modern media. In their many versions, they can be used to address questions of gender, violence, sexuality, culture, adaptation, and influence.

It is impossible to pigeonhole Stevenson as a writer of adventure yarns, of a famous horror story, or of verses for children. How one writer could produce great works in so many genres is a central question for any class that tries to address the full range of his accomplishments and his enduring influence on popular culture. Classroom possibilities are limited only by the questions at hand. There is an adaptation to inform almost every text, whether *Jekyll and Hyde* in the survey, *Treasure Island* in gender studies, or *Kidnapped* in Scottish literature and culture. Best of all, with this selection to choose from, students can chart the course themselves.

NOTE

For an indication of the many adaptations of Stevenson, see Richard Dury's list at www.robert-louis-stevenson.org and *The Internet Movie Database* Web site. Of particular note for other Stevenson texts are versions of *The Master*, directed by Fiona Cumming, by Pharic Maclaren, by William Keighley, and by Douglas Hickox; of *The Black Arrow*, by John Hough and by Gordon Douglas; of *The Wrong Box*, by Bryan Forbes; of "The Bottle Imp," by Marshall Neilan; of *The Ebb-Tide*, by Nicholas Renton; *Muppet Treasure Island*, by Brian Henson; and "The Suicide Club," by Rachel Samuels.

The Stevenson-Osbourne Collaboration

Gordon Hirsch

For students accustomed to discussing great books produced by a single author, Stevenson presents an interesting complication, as he seems always to have been willing to collaborate. He attempted a number of dramatic collaborations (*Deacon Brodie*, *Beau Austin*, *Admiral Guinea*, and *Macaire*) with his friend William Ernest Henley (*Works* 24). Stevenson's wife, Fanny, contributed ideas for some early work as well as portions of the text for *The Dynamiter*. Stevenson's most important collaborator, however, was his stepson, Lloyd Osbourne. When Osbourne was twelve years old, they together created a map to represent the principal setting for *Treasure Island*, though their more significant literary collaborations occurred in three novels published late in Stevenson's career: *The Wrong Box* (1889), *The Wrecker* (1892), and *The Ebb-Tide* (1894).

When students learn of this collaboration, they often ask whether the authors' respective contributions can be discerned from the manuscripts. Lacking access to the manuscripts, they are best referred to discussions of them and of proof sheets in Roger Swearingen's *Prose Writings* as well as to the introductions and notes in Ernest Mehew's edition of *The Wrong Box* and in the Peter Hinchcliffe and Catherine Kerrigan edition of *The Ebb-Tide*. There are also substantial (but not always consistent or uncontested) reports of what each author of the collaborative novels contributed in Stevenson's letters, Lloyd Osbourne's *Intimate Portrait*, and Graham Balfour's *Life*—especially in Osbourne's account there of their collaborative methods (Balfour 2: 40–42).

Another frequent question is: Why did Stevenson collaborate? He supported a large, blended family by his writing, and throughout his life he was shrewd about tracking sales and finding outlets that would prove lucrative. He recognized that novels were not just aesthetic objects but also commodities and that fiction writing was, among other things, a commercial proposition. For example, as Hinchcliffe and Kerrigan note, having the American Osbourne as coauthor strengthened Stevenson's claim to copyright protection in the United States (157–58). In recent years scholars have called attention to the substantial number of nineteenth-century collaborative works, noting that collaboration was particularly likely for plot-driven fiction, such as novels of adventure or detection—the sorts of popular genres in which Stevenson tended to work (see Ashton 8). It is worth noting, too, that nineteenth-century literary theory had developed its own arguments in favor of collaboration; Brander Matthews and Walter Besant ("On Literary Collaboration") both pointed to the stimulation of collaborative effort.

Still, Stevenson's collaborations with Osbourne have drawn fire from their time to our own, perhaps because although Stevenson was widely liked and admired, Osbourne was and remains decidedly less so. Stevenson's biographers point out that Osbourne neither earned a university degree nor developed an independent profession. After his stepfather's death, he supported himself largely by revenues from Stevenson's literary estate and from his own writings—allegedly published only by virtue of his connection with Stevenson. Indeed, Osbourne seems to have enjoyed his social status, membership in elite clubs, and driving fast motorcars. Frank McLynn, in his 1993 biography of Stevenson, likens Osbourne to "Mr Toad, with a mindless devotion to fast roadsters," and considers his collaboration with Stevenson "disastrous" (511, 345; see also Harman, *Myself* 384, 352).

Nonetheless, Stevenson encouraged his stepson, asking him to generate ideas, plots, and some incidents and characters for their collaborative works, each of which evolved somewhat differently. *The Wrong Box*, a comic novel with a bizarre plot having to do with a train wreck and a roving corpse that must remain hidden in order to secure a tontine fortune, was essentially Osbourne's story, begun at age nineteen, which Stevenson rewrote. That Stevenson was engaged by this collaboration and used Osbourne's material is evident from a letter he wrote while the book was in process: "Lloyd's story was so damned funny and absurd that I lost my heart to it, and am now about half through my version. Lots of the lad's stuff stands; he has a genuine talent of a kind, and a fine idea of fun" (*Letters* 6: 125). Osbourne himself felt that "*The Wrong Box* was more mine as a whole than either" of the other collaborations, though Mehew's edition assigns more credit to Stevenson, noting that 106 of the manuscript pages are in Stevenson's hand and that Osbourne's 23 are heavily amended by his stepfather (Balfour 2: 42; Mehew, Introduction xiv, xx).

The next completed collaboration, *The Wrecker*, is a peripatetic novel—set variously in the American state of "Muskegon," Britain, France, San Francisco, Hawai'i, and the South Seas. It conjoins depictions of shady business and trade, murder, mystery, adventure, and bits of autobiographical reminiscence by Stevenson. He characterized the book as "a long tough yarn with some pictures of the manners of today in the greater world—not the shoddy sham world of cities, clubs and college—but the world where men still live a man's life" (*Letters* 7: 181). The collaborators agree that Osbourne had no part in writing the Paris and Barbizon scenes, which drew on Stevenson's experience, but that Osbourne had a fair amount to do with the representation of certain characters (Nares, Pinkerton, Loudon Dodd, and Captain Brown), where he was familiar with the real-life models (8: 364; Balfour 2: 41–42; Harman, however, minimizes Osbourne's contribution [*Myself* 388–89]). Apparently Stevenson and Osbourne planned *The Wrecker* together in considerable detail. Osbourne later recalled that he would draft a chapter, Stevenson would revise it, and they would discuss their product as well as future sections (107–08). Collaboration proved especially problematic when Stevenson stayed in Samoa while Osbourne traveled to England. Stevenson clearly remained the final authority and would send the chapters off for the initial periodical publication.

Of the three collaborative novels, *The Wrecker* seems to have been the one on which Stevenson and Osborne collaborated most fully. In his *Intimate Portrait*, Osbourne asserts, "Every page of it was a joy—to us," and wonders, "Am

I wrong in thinking that some of that zest is to be found in *The Wrecker*?" (108). It is in connection with this collaborative effort that he quotes his stepfather's compliment: "It's glorious to have the ground ploughed, and to sit back in luxury for the real fun of writing—which is rewriting" (108). Stevenson's own reports on this experience are more qualified.

As early as spring 1889, Stevenson set Osbourne to work on the novel that eventually became *The Ebb-Tide*, which occupied them intermittently over the next five years. Conceived and drafted before *The Wrecker*, it was rewritten and published afterward (Osbourne 99). Like *The Wrecker*, it is a tale of South Seas skulduggery, though unrelievedly harsher and bleaker. Its principal characters are unscrupulous and unattractive, described by Stevenson as "barrats, insurance frauds, thieves and would-be murderers" (*Letters* 8: 29). Eventually they encounter a vicious, prosperous, tyrant-trader named Attwater, whom one of them intends to kill with vitriol (sulfuric acid), but Attwater prevails. A grim story, it offers a fascinating portrait of the unattractive sides of human nature, displayed in a colonial setting. Once again Osbourne was commissioned by Stevenson to start the project. Their accounts suggest that Osbourne's principal contribution to the actual writing appears in the first three or four chapters of the twelve-chapter book, though the two apparently also discussed the later parts (Osbourne's claims are inconsistent: 94, 98; Balfour 2: 40–42; see also Swearingen, *Prose Writings* 187; and Hinchcliffe and Kerrigan xviii–xix, 156). In a letter to Sidney Colvin, Stevenson pondered whether Osbourne's name should be deleted as coauthor:

> He has nothing to do with the last half. The first we wrote together, as the beginning of a long yarn [which never materialized]. The second is entirely mine; and I think it rather unfair on the young man to couple his name with so infamous a work. . . . Up to the discovery of the champagne the tale was all planned between us and drafted by Lloyd; from that moment he has had nothing to do with it except talking it over.
> (*Letters* 8: 155–56, 158; cf. Osbourne's account in Balfour 2: 40–42)

Over the period of these last two collaborations, it is clear that Stevenson was growing restive. In a letter to Colvin of 9 May 1889, he wrote:

> Lloyd is learning to make a rude shot at story telling; he will get on. . . . I shall put him on to do and to elaborate all by himself short stories; there he must learn his art. But I doubt if he will ever be very much of a stylist; it is, as yet, rather the root of the matter that he shows: a great knack at certain characters, some sound comedy, and an eye for the picturesque.
> (*Letters* 6: 293)

In a letter to his cousin Bob three months before his death, Stevenson wrote about *The Wrecker*, "it is in the matter [plot] of the book, of course, that collaboration shows." He reports here that "Lloyd is an impressionist, pure and simple"; Osbourne can render characters he has met and known in real life, but he cannot be taught manner or style, "what kind of effect I mean a character to give. . . . These are the impossibilities of collaboration" (8: 364). In *An Intimate Portrait*, Osbourne notes that after Stevenson's "unstinted praise" for his draft of the first three chapters of *The Ebb-Tide*, "the commendation ceased; try as I would I could not please RLS; I wrote and rewrote, and rewrote again, but always to have him shake his head" (95, 98). Still, Osbourne felt that after this collaboration Stevenson "regarded me seriously as a fellow-craftsman; sought my judgment and often took it" (99; cf. 136–37).

Students debating the results of Stevenson's collaborations with Osbourne will find relevant material in Paul Maixner's *Robert Louis Stevenson: The Critical Heritage*. Contemporary responses to the three collaborative novels were varied but often disapproving. Though Rudyard Kipling was amused by *The Wrong Box*, Mrs. Oliphant, writing in *Blackwood's*, called it a "silly and vulgar story," and others found its narrative of a corpse gone astray tasteless and repellent (335–37). Through the years it became something of a cult novel—not widely appreciated but cherished by initiates (see Mehew, Introduction xxxiv–xxxvi). Divided receptions were also accorded the other two collaborations. *The Wrecker* was perceived as fanciful and intriguing but also jumbled and sprawling (Maixner 403–07). A number of contemporary reviewers found *The Ebb-Tide* fierce and even savage and pointed to an uneven and disjointed quality in the work (458, 450). The *Saturday Review* raised the question of whether collaboration had weakened the book, though the reviewer determined in the end that "[t]here are few pages . . . which do not clearly reveal the creative genius and literary craftsmanship of Mr. Stevenson," thus finessing the question (454). Israel Zangwill praised *The Ebb-Tide* for its interweaving of character and adventure and for its depiction of villains and "the abnormal" (462).

Recent criticism can redirect students' questions, for it has been less interested in trying to separate out the often inseparable results of literary collaboration and more concerned with other aspects of the relationship. Students might ask in this context: What did each collaborator offer the other? What motives lay behind Stevenson's desire to collaborate? What sorts of books were produced—in what genres and with what qualities—and how do they relate to the fiction each author produced on his own? Given that an older, established author was collaborating with his junior, a novice, a stepson, how much control over the final product was exercised by the senior author and with what results? (Compare Lillian Nayder's assessment of Charles Dickens's collaboration with Wilkie Collins in her study *Unequal Partners*.) Did it produce work superior or inferior to the established author's other publications? Did Osbourne bring any specific literary talents to these collaborations? Although Stevenson undoubtedly remained the final authority, can one make the case that interactions between the collaborators resulted in a text that was dialogic, hybrid, and multiple rather than imposed by one of the authors in a hierarchical mode of production? (See the general endorsement of collaboration on these grounds by Ede and Lunsford 67, 133, 134.) Even if one granted the assertions of some of

Stevenson's critics and biographers that Osbourne's contributions to these three novels were limited, is it not possible that Stevenson's (perhaps oppositional) responses to Osbourne's drafts and ideas moved Stevenson into new areas of creativity and risk?

Recent critics have suggested that nineteenth-century literary collaborations may reflect a homoerotic interest, and college students will likely be interested in reading and discussing Wayne Koestenbaum's arguments about the relationship between Stevenson and Osbourne ("Shadow" and *Double Talk*; see also Ehnenn). Koestenbaum focuses on such matters as the male friendships in Stevenson's life; his authorship of boys' books with relatively few women in them; his interest in doubleness; and the tendency in his culture toward severe punishment for male homosexual acts, exemplified by the passage in 1885 of the Labouchere Amendment. One might add to this list the growing prominence of Oscar Wilde on the contemporary literary scene and the publication of such significant studies as Richard von Krafft-Ebbing's *Psychopathia Sexualis* (1876) and Havelock Ellis's *Sexual Inversion* (1897). Koestenbaum calls attention to words such as "queer," "cruise," "fag," and "gay" in Stevenson and Osbourne's writing. His readings are intriguing, though students may want to scrutinize the quoted passages to consider how convincing these associations with homosexuality are. They will probably also want to discuss what limitations on behavior, expression, and perhaps even awareness were imposed by Stevenson's Victorian culture.

An interesting facet of all three collaborations with Osbourne is that each represents a departure for Stevenson. *The Wrong Box* employs humor and burlesque in a fantastic absurdist comedy. *The Wrecker* represents perhaps his most sprawling, experimental, almost postmodern plot. *The Ebb-Tide* is remarkable for its colonial, naturalistic bleakness. Because of their idiosyncrasies, these collaborative novels fit not only into surveys of the novel but also into topics courses on noncanonical, experimental, absurdist, problem, or cult fiction. For each formal experiment, students can debate what influences, including Osbourne's, were at work. Certainly Stevenson's travel to the United States and ultimately to the South Seas contributed to his adventuresome, in some respects metafictional and exotic, late fiction. Still, each collaboration resulted in an odd and unconventional work of fiction, attractive to twenty-first-century readers, and asking students to account for these books' accessibility and appeal today usually provokes a lively response.

Classroom teachers will also find it fruitful to ask students to compare one or two of the South Seas stories Stevenson wrote entirely himself (such as *The Beach of Falesá* or "The Bottle Imp") with one or two of Osbourne's South Seas tales written after Stevenson's death (such as "The Phantom City," "Old Dibs," "The Devil's White Man," "A Son of Empire," "The Happiest Day of His Life," "Captain Elijah Coe," and "Professor No No"). How do the two authors represent the clash of European-American and indigenous cultures that occurred in the South Seas? How is Pacific folklore represented? Are indigenous perspectives accorded a voice? How are imperialism and sexuality in the islands depicted? Although much of Osbourne's later fiction—for example, his plots that rely on romance and adventure or his fiction involving motormania (characters' infatuation with their first motorcars)—isn't likely to hold most modern readers' interest, answers to such comparative questions about Stevenson and Osbourne's South Seas tales are likely to suggest that Osbourne learned quite a lot from collaborating with his illustrious stepfather and likely made significant contributions as well. Sometimes even a junior collaborator adds savor to a broth.

COURSE CONTEXTS

Stevenson's Poetry in the Victorian Survey

Abigail Burnham Bloom

Each semester I teach poems from Robert Louis Stevenson's *A Child's Garden of Verses* (1885; *Collected Poems* 21–65) as part of a period spent on poems and literature written for children, in my Victorian literature course, an upper-division survey for undergraduates. At the end of the semester, students frequently remark that the poems were their favorite reading of the semester and this class period the most fun. That the poems were written for children and purport to express the thoughts of children makes them popular with students, who all feel that they can understand them, even students who say they "do not get poetry." The poems have the advantages of being short, easy to read, and often familiar, because many students remember them from their childhood. Yet the meaning of the poems is not as simple as students usually assume. Much discussion is spent on eliciting alternative readings from students and examining the difference between our first responses and our later, critical determinations. The poems also work well in the classroom because they provide a point of comparison with other poems for children as well as with the novels we have read during the semester. In addition, our discussion prepares students to read Stevenson's *Strange Case of Dr Jekyll and Mr Hyde*, which I teach later in the semester.

To contextualize the poems, I ask students what they know about the author, and often they mention works such as *Treasure Island* and *Kidnapped*. I ask if there is any relation between the poems and those works. Students observe that the novels are about children or adolescents in danger and that they are works of imagination rather than realistic works. I tell students that in his childhood Stevenson was sick much of the time and confined to his bed. I ask what the title of the collection of verses implies. They mention that a garden is part of a yard and a safe and beautiful place, a place for growing things and for imagining (see Webb). Typically a student will mention *A Secret Garden*, by Frances Hodgson Burnett, or even the Garden of Eden. I then complicate things by asking about the voice of a poem and what we can tell about the narrator. I ask who the poems were written for. Would they be enjoyed by children or more by the adults who read them to children? The question of Stevenson's voice has been discussed (see Hunt). Does Stevenson evoke the authentic voice of a child, or is it the voice of an adult looking back on childhood? Does Stevenson capture what it feels like to be a child, or is he creating instead a romanticized adult view of childhood?

Stevenson's poems are excellent for metrical and rhythmic analysis and easily read aloud. Since reading to others was a favorite Victorian activity, I use the occasion both to encourage student participation and to suggest Victorian experience. We discuss meters and rhyme schemes. I am surprised when students say that they know nothing about prosody, but luckily Stevenson's poems constitute an excellent primer on how to scan a poem. We look at the first poem, "Bed in Summer," which is written in iambic tetrameter with a rhyme scheme of *aabb* (23). Why, students invariably ask, is this important? They begin to see that the meaning of the poem is reflected in its rhyme and meter. Their regularity underlines the regularity of the child's life—that he needs to go to bed at the same time and get up at the same time, whatever the season or the weather. This routine comes from the belief that children learn through repetition, structure, and consistency. I follow that discussion by looking at a poem that is more complicated in the way its meter reflects its meaning. "Shadow March" has varying lines: the first and third have four beats, the second and fourth have three (46–47). Meter now challenges with spondees, anapests, and dactyls. The four-beat lines tend to be read quickly, the three-beat lines more slowly. The *abab* rhyming emphasizes the difference. The last quatrain reads:

> The shadow of the balusters, the shadow of the lamp,
> The shadow of the child that goes to bed—
> All the wicked shadows coming tramp, tramp, tramp,
> With the black night overhead.

The shadows intrude and approach the child menacingly; he becomes a shadow himself and can find no succor in his bed.

We come to a bigger question: the situation of the child in the family during the late-Victorian period. The reality was that many children died young, and sickness and death were common in Victorian homes. Children might spend more time with their nurse than with their parents. Children's literature was first written for upper- and middle-class children, whose parents had the time, money, and opportunity to buy books and read them to their children. (Students wishing to pursue these themes might consult Ginger S. Frost's *Victorian Childhoods* and Troy Boone's *Youth of Darkest England*.) Stevenson's poems provide a limited but telling view of the world, showing how late-Victorian, middle-class children see their society. The well-heeled child in "The Lamplighter" wants to grow up to be a lamplighter; the narrator of "Looking Forward" longs to have control of his toys "[w]hen [he is] grown to man's estate" (39, 29). A middle-class child will not grow up to be a lamplighter (the streets will be lighted by electricity by the time he is grown). Children believe that when they are adults, they can do as they want, yet adulthood brings a whole different set of concerns. In the poem "Happy Thought," Stevenson hints at the problem:

> The world is so full of a number of things,
> I'm sure we should all be as happy as kings. (36)

This poem contrasts with the common view that children are happy all the time. Yes, they should be, and so should we all—but we aren't. Stevenson acknowledges this truth when he writes that we "should" be as happy as someone with money and power, things children do not have.

Looking at selections from *A Child's Garden of Verses* alongside other poetry written for or about children offers an excellent springboard for discussing the Victorian treatment of children. Many Victorians advocated a strict approach to child rearing. Eliza Cook's poem "The Mouse and the Cake" relates the tale of a mouse that dies because he greedily eats an entire cake without sharing with his siblings. The intent of the poem is to frighten a child into good behavior. Verses such as the anonymous, and frequently reprinted, "Table Rules for Little Folks" give children a long, poetic, and consequently easily memorized guide on how to behave properly. It begins:

> In silence I must take my seat,
> And give God thanks before I eat;
> Must for my food in patience wait,
> Till I am asked to hand my plate;
> I must not scold, nor whine, nor pout,
> Nor move my chair or plate about;
> With knife, or fork, or napkin ring,
> I must not play, nor must I sing.

Stevenson's "Whole Duty of Children" sums up the major advice but manages simultaneously to tone it down and parody it:

> A child should always say what's true
> And speak when he is spoken to,
> And behave mannerly at table:
> At least as far as he is able.
> (*Collected Poems* 26)

Manners become fun and easy to remember. Stevenson's poem makes a reasonable demand on a child by emphasizing that a child should behave not perfectly but "as far as he is able"—and it accomplishes a secular reinterpretation of Ecclesiastes 12.13 while mocking its seventeenth-century reformulations for English Protestants (a point already made in Sheridan's *The Rivals*, when Lydia instructs, "[P]ut *The Innocent Adultery* into *The Whole Duty of Man*" [30]).

The narrator of Stevenson's poem "System" relates his satisfaction with the regularity of his life and with his reward of an orange for being good (34). Those who don't get oranges must be scruffy, "naughty," or—interestingly given as an afterthought—"poor." The narrator's life is visibly different from the children's lives described by Henry Mayhew in *London Labor and the London Poor* (1851), where young children must work for a living. In his poem "The Watercress Seller," based on Mayhew's work, Thomas Miller depicts the life of a young girl who, even during the freezing weather, walks the street selling watercress. Such a graphic contrast between comfortably off and poor children can lead students to a better understanding of class differences and the effect of poverty on children. Yet Stevenson's poems, inviting us to critique their speakers and those speakers' limitations, are also a far cry from the cheerful nonsense verse of Edward Lear and Lewis Carroll.

Stevenson's "Foreign Children" introduces discussions of nineteenth-century attitudes toward other lands, travel, imperialism, colonialism, and the exotic:

> You have curious things to eat,
> I am fed on proper meat;
> You must dwell beyond the foam,
> But I am safe and live at home.
>
> Little Indian, Sioux or Crow,
> Little frosty Eskimo,
> Little Turk or Japanee,
> O! don't you wish that you were me? (38)

This poem appears to condescend to the people of other countries, but Stevenson's poetry is more multifaceted than might appear on the surface. My students have a good time debating the meaning of this poem in the classroom. Many begin by saying that Stevenson's attitude is typical of Victorians who believe their way of life is superior to any other. We encounter this attitude commonly in our readings. A little explanation of Stevenson's history and some digging into the meaning of the poem, however, cause students to doubt their first response. Again, the naive child's voice allows a space for adult irony.

The narrator's point of view in the poems is surprisingly complex and can be compared with that of such young narrators of nineteenth-century prose as Jane Eyre in Charlotte Brontë's novel or Pip in Charles Dickens's *Great Expectations*. Such works reveal the imagination of the child. In Stevenson's poems, however, a middle-class child looks out on the world from the warmth of his bed. He is taken care of by his nurse, to whom the volume is dedicated. Jane and Pip are both orphans, and the novels' early scenes show the children in their beds. Jane, after her experience in the red room, recovers in her bed, where she is looked after by the maid, Bessie, for whom she develops an attachment. Pip huddles in his bed after meeting the convict on the marshes. The voice of the adult Pip tells his fears, "I have often thought that few people know what secrecy there is in the young, under terror. No matter how unreasonable the terror, so that it be terror" (18). In each of these works, childhood hurts and fears are experienced by the narrators. The children are alone in the world, even when in their own beds. Stevenson's narrator is a vulnerable, sickly, and naively judgmental child. The reader feels the anxieties of the young and the presence of troubling shadows in a world that should be safe for children.

Stevenson's poetry provides good preparation for teaching and reading *Strange Case of Dr Jekyll and Mr Hyde*. The novel, students may be surprised to learn, was written just a year later than the poems. Although the only child mentioned in the novel is the girl trampled by Mr. Hyde, the poems and the novel share several themes. In both, the laws of the world are not comprehensible: the child narrator of the poetry fears the unknown, and Dr. Jekyll delves into the supernatural. Both the poems and the novel make frequent use of opposites—night and day, good and bad—that turn out to be intimately connected. One poem, "Good and Bad Children" (*Collected Poems* 37–38), suggests that children who are cruel or who cry too much grow up to be hated, and of course the idea of keeping his reputation intact is the driving force behind Dr. Jekyll' s creation of Mr. Hyde. Fearing that his base desires will become known, Dr. Jekyll enters into deep deception to hide his activities. Stevenson takes advantage of the complex role of the narrator in both works, allowing the meaning to be revealed slowly and subtly. Together, the poems and the novel open their meaning to students after study and discussion.

Stevenson's "Requiem" (from *Underwoods*, in *Collected Poems* 67–123), which provided his epitaph, provides a fitting end for the class period. This poem combines the best of Victorian nostalgia with preparation for death:

> Under the wide and starry sky,
> Dig the grave and let me lie.
> Glad did I live and gladly die,
> And I laid me down with a will.
>
> This be the verse you grave for me:
> *Here he lies where he longed to be;*
> *Home is the sailor, home from sea,*
> *And the hunter home from the hill.* (88)

Questions I ask to help my students discover the meaning of the poem are: Who is the narrator of this poem? Why is he glad to die? Does he long to be in the grave? How does the rhyme scheme and meter enrich the meaning of the poem? Why does the narrator use the imagery of a sailor and hunter? Who is the "you" in the first line of the second quatrain? What does the word "grave" mean? Why are the last three lines in italics? And do you see any similarities between this poem and those we have looked at in *A Child's Garden of Verses*?

The American Journeys in the English Survey: Breaking Down the Binaries

Caroline McCracken-Flesher

> Any one who had come aboard might have supposed we were all absconding from the law.
>
> —"From the Clyde to Sandy Hook," *The Amateur Emigrant*

In 1879 Robert Louis Stevenson, aged twenty-nine, ran away from home. Sentimental biographers and American students alike love the idea of a sickly author racing by boat and train across an ocean and a continent to the object of his affection. Crabbed age (the Stevenson parents) is set against youth (the free-spirited author and Fanny Osbourne), conservative Britain against liberal America (Fanny was an artist and still married). Not surprisingly, the author and this moment appeal to American teenagers sitting within the confines of a literary survey. Such an attraction provides a pedagogical opportunity.

Certainly, Stevenson was a wanderer. In *Edinburgh: Picturesque Notes* (published, interestingly, in 1879), he described those who

> aspire angrily after that Somewhere-else of the imagination, where all troubles are supposed to end. They lean over the great bridge which joins the New Town with the Old—that windiest spot, or high altar, in this northern temple of the winds—and watch the trains smoking out from under them and vanishing into the tunnel on a voyage to brighter skies. Happy the passengers who shake off the dust of Edinburgh, and have heard for the last time the cry of the east wind among her chimney tops! (*Works* 26: 135–36)

This Stevenson was clearly ready to "light out for the territory," in Huckleberry Finn's parlance.

In literary surveys (particularly the one I teach, which brings together "literatures in English"), however, Stevenson's American memoirs offer an unusual chance to break down the binaries of travel writing. Here, we can unpack travel as a discourse and a strategy, the ideas of here and there, self and other, author and editor. The author learned early about travel as a means of escape. He had gone with his mother on her various trips to spas for her health, and as he got older, he used illness as a way to evade his parents. In 1873, Stevenson quarreled with his family, having declared himself agnostic. A few months later, in London to pursue his father's plans for him as a lawyer, the aspiring author consulted a doctor, who advised him to pass right through and on to Europe for his health. Mrs. Stevenson reported, "[Dr. Clark] tells us that Lou's nervous system has quite broken down, that his lungs are delicate and just in the state when disease might very easily set in. When I ask if I ought to go [abroad] with him, [Dr. Clark] said: 'No, he wants a complete change of everything'" (*Letters* 1: 350). Indeed Stevenson's letters, and the rather doubtful responses from his parents, very helpfully convey to students that the traveler's gaze is never disinterested or unencumbered. As Mrs. Stevenson put it: Clark's diagnosis was "a put-up thing" (2: 3). So the Stevenson who fled to America was already wise in the strategies and tactics of travel, already connecting travel and telling stories.

As an interested writer of travel narrative, Stevenson was a canny explorer in the interstices of canonical literature. At the same time, he was often caught in the shoals of parental expectation, or forced into harbor by his readers' views of him and by publishing demands and schedules. With student assumptions, biographical realities, and Stevenson's publishing mandates in mind, I teach the author's American travel writings for these contradictions. Sentimental readings stand beside Stevenson's own, often jaundiced opinions; authoritative editions go cheek by jowl with bowdlerlized versions produced by the interferences of family, editors, and publishers.

Finding usable materials is the challenge of this approach. Here is the problem: on the one hand, Stevenson left Britain in a hurry; on the other, he had long been planning to meet up with Fanny again. In the days before he embarked from Greenock (on the west coast of Scotland, just seaward of Glasgow), he was in London, perhaps hoping for a newspaper assignment to support his travels, and in New York he tried to drum up business. While he journeyed, he worked steadily at *The Amateur Emigrant* and other travel writings as experience provided material (J. Hart, Introduction xix, xx, xxv). Because Stevenson traveled with writing in mind, we have quite a paper trail for his physical and mental journeying. But because his family and his friends (acting as editors) disliked what he wrote, it appeared in snippets, and large chunks were excised. Sidney Colvin wrote to the author that he found Stevenson's account of his ocean voyage "a spiritless record of squalid experiences" that would not help an "only half-established reputation," and when it was published, Thomas Stevenson, Stevenson's father, promptly paid £100 to buy up the edition and take it out of circulation (J. Hart, Introduction xxix, xlii). Until the New Edinburgh Edition produces its volumes of *The Amateur Emigrant*, including "From Clyde to Sandy Hook," *Across the Plains*, and *The Silverado Squatters*, it will remain difficult to peel back the layers of parental and editorial interference and open these texts to student debate. However two magisterial volumes are available through libraries: James D. Hart's *Robert Louis Stevenson: From Scotland to Silverado* and Roger D. Swearingen's *The Amateur Emigrant*. Both assemble Stevenson's preferred text from manuscripts at the Beinecke Library and provide crucial accounts of the volumes' textual history. (These and other less-published Stevenson volumes are slated for release under the Kennedy and Boyd imprint—it is to be hoped in Hart's or Swearingen's recuperated version.)

So what can students learn from Stevenson's American travel writings—especially when they are available in such haphazard form? All editions of *The Amateur Emigrant* open with his description of joining the ship's company in Glasgow. Here, Stevenson makes a literary and cultural passage: "[W]e descended the Clyde in no familiar spirit, but looking askance on each other as on possible enemies. A few Scandinavians, who had already grown acquainted on the North Sea, were friendly and voluble over their long pipes; but among English speakers distance and suspicion reigned supreme" (*Works* 18: 1). This theme develops across the voyage by land and sea. Stevenson ships out intending to absorb the romance of emigrant travel but at a careful distance: "Although anxious to see the worst of emigrant life, I had some work to finish on the voyage, and was advised to go by the second cabin" (1). Soon he learns from a sign that steerage passengers are "males and females; in the second cabin ladies and gentlemen. . . . [W]hen I felt out of spirits I could go down and refresh myself with a look of that brass plate" (3–4). These perceptions are soon challenged by experience. Stevenson describes the variety of passengers—a list of types, to begin with, that includes the Norseman "Johnny," the "universal favorite"; a Scots mason "known from his favorite dish as 'Irish Stew'"; "a fine young Irishman, O'Reilly"; and "an old lady. . . . We had to take her own word that she was married; for it was sorely contradicted by the testimony of her appearance. . . . [E]ven the colour of her hair was incompatible with matrimony" (4–5). But soon he admits "there is a free or common accent among English-speaking men who follow the sea. They catch a twang in a New England Port; from a cockney skipper even a Scotsman sometimes learns to drop an *h*" (6). Distinction fades the farther the boat sails from shore; the discriminating author finds that he belongs to "one small iron country on the deep" (8).

On board, Stevenson's art shifts according to experience. Not only does he lose the distance of the leisured and privileged observer, he also begins to see beyond his narrow artistic expectations: "The more I saw of my fellow-passengers, the less I was tempted to the lyric note" (9). This is a perception that students can track through his (less bowdlerized) *Across the Plains*. Stevenson's trip across the continent both manifests nineteenth-century narratives of westward expansion and shows how they fall into question under pressure of events. Students are fascinated to see the author encounter their country through the lens of the gothic, of manifest destiny, of the dime novel, and of liberal sentiment in sequence:

> As we drew near to New York I was at first amused, and then somewhat staggered, by the cautious and grisly tales that went the round. You would have thought we were to land upon a cannibal island. You must speak to no one in the streets, as they would not leave you till you were rooked and beaten. You must enter a hotel with military precautions; for the least you had to apprehend was to awake next morning without money or bag-

> gage, or necessary raiment, a lone forked radish in a bed; and if the worst befell, you would instantly and mysteriously disappear from the ranks of mankind. (66)

The knowing author mocks, "I have usually found such stories correspond to the least modicum of fact" (66). Yet students can compare with this version of America his later acknowledgment that "[for] many years America was to me a sort of promised land. 'Westward the march of empire holds its way'; the race is for the moment to the young . . . to these States . . . like another Eve, from the rib out of the side of their own old land, the minds of young men in England turn naturally" (69). Before long, Stevenson is traveling west, through "a favorite home of my imagination," the American Midwest, where he had "played at being in Ohio by the week, and enjoyed some capital sport there with a dummy gun" (*Works* 18: 88). Yet here, students find, as on ship, his expectations tumble: "I had come to pity the poor negro, to put him at his ease, to prove in a thousand condescensions that I was no sharer in the prejudice of race; but I assure you I put my patronage away for another occasion"—faced with a waiter who "with every word, look, and gesture marched me farther into the country of surprise. . . . [E]very inch a man of the world" (87). The author's journey, students quickly see, is not so much in space as in sensibility.

As a result, Stevenson's prose, too, shifts. Students will find examples from his previous travel writing and from reviews of these pieces when they were originally published enlightening. By this point in his career, Stevenson enjoyed a reputation as a stylish and entertaining travel writer. The vagaries of *An Inland Voyage* and *Travels with a Donkey* notwithstanding—leisure does not always betoken pleasure—his public expected from him the readable and amusing prose of the flaneur or languid man about town. The *Athenaeum* anticipated a "third set of [Stevenson's] *charming impressions de voyage*" (J. Hart, Introduction xxxix). The *Scottish Leader*, perhaps biased by national sentiment, doggedly focused on this Stevenson: "To make a literary effect—that is Mr Stevenson's object, and he avows it in the most un-English fashion, and utterly without shame" (Maixner 381). If we read the critic sympathetically, perhaps he is pointing to Stevenson's protomodernist tendencies that will come into view in the abstract, musical structures of *The Ebb-Tide*. But at the same time the critic disturbingly reduces Stevenson's physical and mental journeying to a matter of style and finds Stevenson "merely ingenious and graceful" (382).

This is where materials from Hart and Swearingen are helpful, for the passages culled by Colvin and the text bought up by Stevenson's father point away from style—or at least they demonstrate how substance can alter style and that style and substance are importantly intertwined. Passages I find particularly productive here include Stevenson's description of his encounter with a sick passenger on the *Devonia*. The early published version, laudable for its incisiveness, is nonetheless notable for two types of excisions: phrases that paint

Stevenson as that louche, casual wanderer and those that point to the repulsiveness of assisting a man sick at sea. (Angle brackets are used for material reinserted in the text.)

> For some time we observed something lying black and huddled in the scuppers, <not far from where I was wakened by the fireman. At first we made light of it; but as we passed again and again, it began insensibly to occupy our minds; and as we reached the spot, the talk would languish, the pace would halt, and our three heads would all be inclined to that side. Almost unconsciously, we were beginning to grow interested in the black bundle; and before long by a natural process, we should have stopped of our own accord to satisfy our curiosity. But the matter was taken out of our hands; for the bundle> heaved a little and moaned aloud. . . . <He had been sick and his head was in the vomit.> ("Sick Man" 46)

Such passages invite students to think about how the author who flees home gets boxed in by audience expectation—whether the boxing is imposed by friends, family, editors, or reviewers—and about the value of letting him out again in new editions.

Most important, perhaps, students can see how an author of whom *they* have specific expectations, bred out of *Jekyll and Hyde* or *A Child's Garden*, wrestles with his own cultural and literary conventions, sometimes succeeding, sometimes failing, but always bringing to the fore the ethics of authorship—and the ethics of our role as academic readers.

Young Adult Novels for English Secondary Education Students

Leslie S. Rush

Preservice English teachers in my courses can be pictured as travelers crossing bridges: between content and pedagogy, between college student and professional educator, between methods semester and student-teaching semester. As an English teacher educator, I work to escort them across these bridges on their way to becoming professionals.

The first goal for my English methods course is to help preservice teachers make connections between the literature courses they have taken and their upcoming student teaching. In addition, I seek to prepare them to be independent instructors for grade 6–12 students; to choose appropriate, motivating texts for their students; and to understand the theory and pedagogy that will enable them to develop their students' skills in literary analysis, reading, and writing.

In this essay, I describe how I use Stevenson's novels commonly taught with young adults, such as *Kidnapped* and *Treasure Island*, to model texts and methods in my English–language arts pedagogy course. I discuss the use of text sets in a workshop format with concomitant reading and writing strategies. Using these techniques, providing opportunities for preservice teachers to experience them as students, and then asking them to step back and reconsider these techniques as teachers, I help them to navigate their way into their work as professional educators.

Stevenson's young adult novels are particularly well suited to use as models for students who will be junior high school and high school teachers, because these classics contain intriguing and engaging elements of today's young adult literature, such as young heroes, adventure, realistic problems, and far-flung locales. Like many other classics, however, these novels present problems for adolescent readers: vocabulary, syntax, and dialect can interfere with comprehension. They therefore provide an opportunity for preservice teachers, many of whom are anxious about ensuring the interest and motivation of their future students, to experience instruction that blends classic literature with modern texts, collaborative learning, and instruction strategies. Reading and working with Stevenson's young adult novels with an eye to instruction can demonstrate potential problems with literary works and provide preservice teachers with tools for their future classrooms. Prior experience with these novels in junior high or high school classes makes possible a layered approach, such that past, present, and imagined future teaching practices can be explored.

Modeling is a practice used in public schools to teach reading comprehension and writing processes; it has also been used to improve preservice English teachers' implementation and development of classroom language and literacy strategies (O'Neill 613). I devote one class per week to modeling a literature workshop in order to give preservice teachers experience with workshop formats.

This experience should show them how to implement modeling once they reach their student teaching classrooms.

Modeling Theme Sets Using Stevenson's Texts as a Central Focus

One staple assignment in the methods course is the development of a unit plan, a three- to six-week plan of instruction. It centers on a text and includes lesson plans, materials, assessment tools, and a discussion of underlying theory and research. Preservice teachers first develop a theme set related to a central text. Jeannine Richison, Anita Hernandez, and Marcia Carton describe theme sets as "collections of books from a variety of reading levels and genres that introduce the major theme (or themes) of a piece of literature commonly found in the high school canon" (x). Theme sets provide multiple entryways into the central text; present diversity in genres, authorship, cultures, style, and perspective; and offer engaging opportunities for students to connect with the themes and ideas raised by all the texts.

To model the development and use of a theme set for preservice teachers, I developed one with Stevenson's young adult novels as the central texts. The first step in this process is to establish a set of curricular goals. Curricular goals address both a thematic perspective on a piece of literature and the skills and knowledge students should master by the end of the unit. I focused on piracy and the question of ownership. Here is a sample curricular goal for this theme set:

> Through investigation of *Kidnapped* and *Treasure Island,* by Robert Louis Stevenson, students will explore questions of ownership (What does it mean to own something? What can and cannot be owned? What is intellectual property?) and of piracy (What roles have pirates played in cultures historically? in the present day?).

I ask the preservice teachers to provide goals and questions that could be used to direct the texts and teaching techniques in their unit plans. With curricular goals in place, they develop theme sets that contain short texts representing diversity in genre, authorship, and perspective. This exercise is particularly important for public school teachers of English and language arts, who are frequently required to teach classic texts and who may be looking for a more culturally relevant pedagogy (Ladson-Billings).

To broaden their conceptions of piracy—shaped as those are by both Stevenson's tales and the prevalence of the *Pirates of the Caribbean* franchise—I ask the preservice teachers to read texts that shed differing lights on piracy:

> a chapter from David Cordingly's *Under the Black Flag: The Romance and the Reality of Life among the Pirates*, which explores the roles women have played in piracy, particularly during the eighteenth century

a series of maps (2005–09) displaying data related to piracy and armed robbery incidents, as provided by the International Maritime Bureau (www.icc-ccs.org/index.php)

a statement on piracy by the Recording Industry Association of America (www.riaa.com/physicalpiracy.php)

Supplemental texts such as these are used throughout our reading of the central texts. As preservice teachers interact with the readings in this theme set, they also work on developing their own theme sets and teaching techniques to accompany them.

Modeling a Workshop Format

What I call a workshop format comes from a reader-response theoretical and pedagogical perspective (Rosenblatt). Use of this perspective encourages preservice teachers to engage with texts directly, before they form a critical perspective on those texts. Reader response derives from readers' life experiences and their readings of other texts. Readers construct, for texts, meanings that have relevance for them personally. When teachers base their instruction on students' internal connections to texts instead of on what may be construed as an external critique, they have an opportunity to encourage students to be both lifelong readers and critical analysts (Probst 18).

The techniques I typically use in a workshop format are reading logs, gallery walks, small and whole-class discussions, and other forms of teaching that involve students in collaborative and individual investigation of questions developed around many texts. My workshop-based strategies have several purposes: they provide students with avenues to make connections between the central text and the supplemental texts; they serve as models of interactive, engaging instruction; and they give preservice teachers opportunities with the instructional techniques that I model while they are still students. As students read the central texts, they keep reading logs, which require them to track their responses using a two-column note-taking system. On each page of their notes, they write quotations from the text (along with page numbers) in the left-hand column and their responses, questions, or connections to them in the right-hand column. Preservice teachers are expected to bring their reading logs to the workshop and to be prepared to engage with classmates in discussion and work around both the central text and whatever supplemental text I provide.

Gallery walk requires my students to develop written material, to post that material on the classroom wall, and then to interact (as if in a museum gallery) with the written material of others. For example, I might ask them to read silently Cordingly's chapter on women as pirates and make a list of the differences in tone, plot, and style Stevenson would have used if he adopted one of the historical female pirates as his central character in place of Long John Silver. Once these materials are created and posted, my students walk around the classroom, read their classmates' lists, and write their own comments. The whole-class discussion that ensues is based on the lists that receive the largest number of comments.

Modeling the Use of Reading and Writing Strategy Instruction

I require preservice teachers to investigate and use reading and writing strategies as part of their unit plans. Strategy instruction has been shown to improve the reading comprehension of junior high and high school students (Nokes and Dole). The idea is to teach students who are struggling with reading comprehension to use the strategies that good readers have already developed and use without conscious thought. I ask my preservice teachers to concentrate their strategy instruction in three areas. Before-reading strategies are designed to build background knowledge, to develop interest in a text, and to preteach vocabulary and concepts that may prove difficult. During-reading strategies are designed to help student readers stay engaged with a text while they read and to develop rereading skills. After-reading strategies are designed to build on understanding. They encourage students to connect ideas in a text to those in other texts and to their background knowledge, so that they continue to be engaged and move to larger tasks. The preservice teachers should also provide opportunities for their future students to think reflectively about their use of these reading strategies and to implement a metacognitive focus (Underwood and Pearson 144).

To help preservice teachers build their understanding of strategy instruction, I model strategy use with supplemental texts. Before reading the Recording Industry Association of America statement on piracy, I engage them in a before-reading brainstorming activity called list-group-label (J. Allen). In this strategy, students individually brainstorm lists of words that they associate with a word or concept—in this instance, I use *piracy*—and then work in groups to develop categories that will encompass all the terms on their lists. The categories and lists are then used to support class reading and writing, to guide class discussion, and to clarify and extend understandings of the central concept of piracy.

We move on to the reading of the text, using a during-reading strategy such as reciprocal teaching (Rosenshine and Meister). In reciprocal teaching, students are asked to read a portion of the text and create discussion or knowledge questions from it. They then work with a partner or small group to polish their questions and eventually put their questions to the teacher or one another. Students are encouraged to turn to the text in order to check or find answers to the questions asked. After all questions are answered, they do the same with the remaining portions of the text.

I engage my preservice teachers in an after-reading strategy called RAFT writing (J. Allen). RAFT writing engages students in a creative exercise designed to solidify and build on the concepts read in the text. The acronym stands for "role, audience, format, and topic." Students may be assigned a certain role to play in their writing, an audience, a format, or a topic. With the text on music piracy from the Recording Industry Association of America, I might ask class participants to write a letter (format) to a friend who is making money to pay his or her college tuition by selling pirated music files online (audience). In the letter, they must make their position on music piracy clear (role) and use the information from the text to do so (topic).

When working with classroom students to improve reading comprehension skills, a teacher should provide opportunities for them to think metacognitively and answer questions about their use of these strategies, such as:

> What did using this strategy help me do?
> How might I apply it to my reading in other courses? to my reading at home or online?

This metacognitive activity enables students to take ownership of their own reading processes and to transfer the strategies to other reading contexts.

By utilizing these instructional techniques, I model a collaborative classroom community in which students can feel safe in trying out new learning approaches, in hazarding educated guesses, and in working together toward a common goal.

It is important to provide preservice teachers with opportunities, after they experience these techniques as students, to step back and reconsider them as teachers. To facilitate this process, I ask them to consider what issues might arise in their secondary school classrooms as they try various approaches. For example, after we work with the RAFT writing exercise, I ask them to consider how they might need to change this instructional strategy to meet the needs of a sixth-grade class or of a group of English-language learners or when using a fictional instead of a nonfictional text. The opportunity to think reflectively about refining the use of instructional techniques to meet the needs of students is a crucial aspect of this learning.

I have found that using Stevenson's classic young adult texts, with all their challenges, in my English–language arts methods courses has provided me with an excellent opportunity to model for preservice teachers the instructional techniques that will be most useful for them in their future educational settings. Specifically, Stevenson adds to the usual workshop mix a text that combines with the comprehension impediments often encountered in classic texts the engaging qualities of young adult literature.

The Pacific Story and the Indigenous Student: "The Bottle Imp" and "The Isle of Voices"

Richard J. Hill

Postcolonial studies have caught up with Stevenson's project of humanizing the Pacific savage, critiquing the haoles ("whites") and their effects on indigenous cultures, and discovering commonalities between races and between cultures that erode racial preconceptions and imperial discourse. Western attitudes to Pacific cultures were indelibly shaped by the death of Captain Cook in 1779 on the Island of Hawai'i (the largest island of the chain), a highly controversial and misunderstood event. It is on this island that Stevenson locates his compassionate Hawaiian heroes of "The Bottle Imp," Keawe and Kokua. For students in Pacific communities, and perhaps for students from other indigenous cultures, Stevenson represents a refreshing voice of empathy and humanity that is conspicuously absent from most nineteenth-century colonial writing. His empathy for the indigenous cultures he stayed among and his channeling of their modes of narration, motifs, and humanity offer an early example of a member of an imperial culture integrating into, and cautiously speaking for, Pacific communities. This essay concentrates on "The Bottle Imp" (1891; *Works* 13: 77–110) and "The Isle of Voices" (1893; 111–33), stories that help students connect with, analyze, and critique colonialism.

The first thing to emphasize to students is the range of Stevenson's intended audience. "The Bottle Imp," first published in the *New York Herald* and in *Black and White* (London), was also translated into Samoan by Reverend Arthur E. Claxton in a missionary publication, *O Le Sulu Samoa* (Swearingen, *Prose Writings* 144). Although "The Isle of Voices" did not receive the same treatment after it was published in the *National Observer* and *Island Nights' Entertainments*, its style, subject matter, and theme all serve as strong reminders that this story was written in the South Pacific and dealt with problems facing Pacific communities. A good question to ask students, either for class discussion or as a writing assignment, is how different these stories might have been if Stevenson was writing solely for a white American and European audience.

The two narratives echo oral and biblical modes of storytelling, but they are also modern parables or fairy tales that address multiple audiences. "The Bottle Imp" is a variation of the genie-in-the-bottle paradigm, interweaving Arabic, European, and Polynesian motifs and symbolism. Roger Swearingen traces the story back to an 1828 melodrama of the same name by Richard Brinsley Peake (*Prose Writings* 144); but given Stevenson's childhood fascination with *Arabian Nights*, it can also be linked to "Aladdin and the Wonderful Lamp" and to the Grimm Brothers' "The Spirit in the Bottle." "The Isle of Voices" also subtly references the *Arabian Nights*, as the evil chief Kalamake transports himself on a magic carpet. Just as parables and fables often do, these stories work as metaphors dealing with the perpetual problem of good and evil as they relate to personal choice.

Stevenson weaves his biographical knowledge of the South Seas across Hawaiian expectation, binding Western narrative and local story in a way accessible to many different audiences. Stories of magic and superstition are performed in the context of actual topography, people, and events. Stevenson weaves places he visited, like Molokai, Maui, and Hookena and Honaunau on the Big Island of Hawai'i, and the people he stayed with, like Judge Nahinu, into the fabric of the stories, grounding them in a recognizable, tangible environment, thus suspending disbelief. The ships that Keawe travels on in "The Bottle Imp" are named after ships Stevenson took between the islands: the *Hall*, the *Tropic Bird*, and the *Umatilla*. More important, Molokai, notorious for its leper colony on Kalaupapa, is accurately portrayed in "The Isle of Voices" as a location connected in Hawaiian tradition with dark magic and kahunas ("priests" or "doctors"); its dual connection with sickness, physical and spiritual, translates across native and white cultures, grounding a metaphoric narrative in a real location.

Stevenson's use of native language also rewards consideration in class. There is much literature discussing his mastery of various forms of pidgin English. Students might well debate whether this mastery amounts to colonial appropriation. To tease out the complexities, class discussion can focus on two Hawaiian words that Stevenson uses judiciously: *kanaka* and *haole*. Both have mutated in meaning dramatically since Cook's arrival in Hawai'i. The literal interpretation of *kanaka* is "man" or "person"; this word was used by white colonials to denote a person from the islands, but subsequently it became a racist pejorative. Stevenson, however, puts this word into good use: when uttered by a Hawaiian character, it is a term of identification and endearment; when uttered by white characters, it becomes offensive. *Haole* literally is "without breath," denoting the foreigners who refused to greet each other in the traditional Polynesian manner by rubbing noses and thereby sharing a breath. This term gradually transformed into a pejorative, applied especially to Caucasian people (it is still used widely today). With both words, Stevenson demonstrates the power of language to establish or undermine colonial authority, depending on the speaker. In "The Bottle Imp" and "The Isle of Voices," the narrative perspective is Hawaiian (though not first-person); in the context of this voice, *haole* is a term of exclusion and differentiation, while *kanaka* connects readers directly to the Hawaiian heroes. These words and their use thus can lead into a broader classroom discussion of racist terms and how they change in the mouths of different speakers.

Students can go on to review Stevenson's use of Hawaiian names, which are also chosen for their meanings. In "The Bottle Imp," Keawe is a name associated with the traditional ruling family of the island of Hawai'i, alluded to at the beginning of the story, while Kokua is a Hawaiian word for "help" or "helper." In "The Isle of Voices," Kalamake is a name made up of two Hawaiian words: *kala*, which means "money," and *make* (ma-keh), which means "dead" or "death." Loosely translated, Kalamake is "dead money," which identifies the theme of the story. Kalamake's daughter's name, Lehua, means "blossom of the 'ohia tree" (endemic to Hawai'i), a symbol of beauty or something that is highly prized. Finally, Keola, from the Hawaiian *ke ola*, means "the life," "living," or "health" and therefore becomes a highly ironic term for a character whose life is constantly threatened by his greed. I encourage students to discover the definitions of these names once they have read either story to see if this knowledge helps them comprehend the themes and how the author negotiates between his Western and indigenous audiences.

Crucial to that negotiation is the way Stevenson innovates with Polynesian point-of-view narration. His use of a third-person narrator has a specifically Polynesian inflection. Hawaiian students identify immediately with his short, declamatory sentences and simple sentence structures. The Polynesian tone is supported by sympathetic plots: Keawe is a true Polynesian hero; as a Hawaiian, he is rooted in the philosophy of aloha, a complex concept that encapsulates love, mercy, compassion, pity, greeting, and friendship. Aloha helps him resist the temptation of the magic bottle. Keawe, tempted by the bright houses of San Francisco, builds his own, but when the house is completed, he sells the bottle, having fulfilled his modest ambition; he reacquires it only to cure himself of the leprosy that will taint Kokua's future with him. He demonstrates a restraint and balance conspicuously lacking in the haole owners of the bottle.

These stories are marked by their portrayal of strong Hawaiian female characters. It can be argued that Kokua is the true hero of "The Bottle Imp." She buys the bottle to save her husband and suffers in silence, even under his selfish taunts. Similarly, Lehua in "The Isle of Voices" saves her lazy, greedy (and bigamist) husband from the isle, in defiance of her father. Stevenson's narrative voice, with its familiar sentencing, makes these stories accessible to native Hawaiian students, and at the same time it helps American and European students connect to a Polynesian perspective on unattractive colonial behavior. The white characters—sailors, missionaries, traders—are marginal in these two stories and not positive. They are domineering, drunk, lecherous, or dirty. It is the native Hawaiian characters and the Hawaiian voice that provide the point of identification for all readers. This fact is reassuring to Hawaiian students, who have become accustomed to being marginalized by history.

When Stevenson aims for a colonial critique, he achieves it in island terms. Both stories deal with the malicious and invisible influence of capitalism on native cultures—but they do so through the discourse of magic. When teaching these stories, particularly "The Isle of Voices," it is useful from the outset to equate magic and the economy or Adam Smith's "invisible hand" of the market (351). Kalamake makes money by transporting himself on a magic carpet to the Isle of Voices, picking shells off the beach, and returning to his Hawaiian home of Molokai, where the shells turn into coin. His magic is secret and dark, producing material wealth much as the magic of the haole does. This whole operation, to a nineteenth-century native Polynesian, would naturally (and perhaps accurately) seem like black magic, and it is embodied in Kalamake's colonial-style house, which ironically references Stevenson's own house at Vailima. This house represents Kalamake's power and success through his use of black magic, and this black magic is a metaphor for white commercial exploitation of the natural resources of the Pacific Islands.

This point resonates with a Hawaiian classroom, as Hawai'i suffered at the hands of ambitious capitalists keen to exploit the land. Students may understand better the symbolism of the shells if they are asked what natural resources on their particular island the shells might represent. In Hawai'i, answers invariably include sugar, pineapples, salt, and the land itself (used for enormous tourist hotels, condos, and government buildings). The voices Keola hears on the island as he's trying to escape are colonial voices, all extracting the island's resources to produce coin: "All tongues of the earth were spoken there; the French, the Dutch, the Russian, the Tamil, the Chinese," and, crucially, "whatever land knew sorcery, there were some of its people whispering in Keola's ear" (*Works* 13: 130). The natives are forced to fight invisible invaders to their lands—much as the Samoans and Hawaiians, who were losing their lands to unseen monarchs and oligarchs.

"The Bottle Imp" offers a different take on this theme. For both a Polynesian and nonindigenous audience, the imp (which we never really see) conforms to a shared preconception of evil, whether it assumes the form of a Christian devil or Samoan *aitu* (as used in *The Beach of Falesá* [49]). Indeed, nonspecificity is an important technique used in both these stories, as Stevenson does not want to anchor any imagery or symbol to a specific cultural belief. If the imp identifiably belongs to Christian theology, the story loses its hold on a native Samoan imagination, and any overtly pagan, Polynesian imagery will alienate the story from its European audience. Just as the Hawaiian characters attempt to navigate a way of life between their inherited culture and the encroaching commercialism of the colonial one, so Stevenson's story attempts to navigate between different cultural modes of storytelling. It should be emphasized in the classroom that Stevenson was consciously seeking to create a new kind of narrative, one that would include local oral modes while employing traditional techniques of the West. The imp represents the temptations of the material world: You can own the bottle, and any physical object you want, but at the cost of your soul. This essentially Christian morality tale resonates beyond Christianity.

Students will realize, from a strong classroom reading, that a major difference between the Hawaiian heroes of "The Bottle Imp" and those of "The Isle of Voices" is that the first resist temptation and are willing to sacrifice their souls for others, while the second fail in Western terms. "The Bottle Imp" offers a solution, a middle way, between the dying native culture that its protagonists come from and the culture of colonial commercialism, but "The Isle of Voices" takes a bleaker view. Keola barely survives, having not heeded the wise advice of his wife, and the natives of the Low Archipelago are slaughtered by their invisible assailants. Keola and Lehua are advised by the white missionary, who represents the ultimate authority in this universe, what to do with their ill-gotten gains, as they are clearly incapable of handling those gains themselves. "The Isle of Voices" therefore warns of the dangers of natives' competing with colonials at their own game. Kalamake, although he is descended from "the best blood in Molokai and Maui," cannot compete successfully with the white man. It is heavily ironic that the one native Hawaiian character who possesses the secret of the haole is himself albino: "more white to look upon than any foreigner," with "hair the colour of dry grass, and his eyes red and very blind" (13: 113). A classroom analysis of Kalamake's appearance and behavior as haole can generate informative and passionate discussion on the nature of indigenous cultural integrity. Both Stevenson's stories sound a warning about the dangers of the colonial subject's behaving like the colonizer. Kalamake looks and acts haole, but his betrayal of his cultural heritage leads to his downfall. Keawe and Kokua, by contrast, engage with the magic of the bottle but ultimately remain true to their cultural values and do not allow the capitalist instinct to corrupt them. In a contemporary classroom, it should be asked: How should indigenous cultures protect their traditions and heritage while still engaging in a modern global capitalist society? Should a Hawaiian, for example, adopt a capitalist mind-set to survive, like Kalamake or Keola, or can a middle ground be found, as for Keawe or Kokua?

Stevenson's Pacific stories turn colonial discourses against the colonizers but in such a way as to avoid alienating his nonindigenous readership. It is literature designed to bridge, not divide, cultures. For a teacher in a Pacific college, this bridging is valuable in addressing many social and cultural gaps. Yet the themes raised by a consideration of Stevenson's stories should be applicable to any multicultural classroom, because they emphasize and prioritize marginalized hero figures and narrative voices. They are also helpful to any class that examines postcolonial themes of race and ethnicity, economic imperialism, and oral cultures.

Stevenson's Short Stories in the Creative Writing Classroom

Alan Riach

Teaching creative writing classes, I often begin by saying that in contrast to literature courses, where we try to provide as much context for a work as possible, today we are going to read the material as far as we can without reference to the historical period or national traditions in which it was written or the biography of the writer. Instead, we are going to read the material to see how the writing itself works on our imaginations, what techniques we can spot and learn from, what its effects are, how its narrative develops, how its characters are created, how its dialogue works, how its humor is conveyed, and, most especially, how its tension is initiated, sustained, and resolved in the language.

Two questions give the best beginning. First: Do we like the piece of writing?

There are a number of things we can say about what it is we like or don't and how we respond to aspects of the writing. To what extent is our liking generated by associations we bring to the material? (Are we so familiar with narrative techniques in film and television that we become impatient with techniques in writing, which seem slow and predictable? Are there things that writing can do that cannot be done onscreen? What are they?) To what extent is our liking generated by the material in its own terms? What are those terms, and when do they appear in the text?

Second question: Is the writing good?

Even if we like it, it might not be good. There might be things we don't like so much but know they are good, in the sense of technically proficient, exemplary in one way or another. Can we say why they are good, what makes them good, whether we like them or not? When Henry James writes not, "He had shaved that morning," but rather, "His eye was of a clear, cold grey, and save for the abundant droop of his moustache he spoke, as to cheek and chin, of the dry matutinal steel," we know that there is something impressive going on, but some of us will like it more than others (*American* 4).

When we turn to Stevenson's short stories, we bear these questions in mind, reading them first as samples of creative work with a perennial appeal, then as works that show us things we can learn from. What we can gain in this way, I usually advise students, is going to be helpful whether we wish to write prose, poems, or plays and bring the creative imagination into alignment with our critical abilities.

One aspect of his stories links Stevenson to the Scottish tradition (from Henryson's *Fables* to Irvine Welsh) and, through his Calvinist inheritance, to Nathaniel Hawthorne and Herman Melville: this is the unreliable narrator. Iain Banks begins *Transition* with the sentence, "Apparently I am what is known as an Unreliable Narrator, though of course if you believe everything you're told you deserve whatever you get" (1). When we consider Stevenson's stories, there is a specific historical moment that invites consideration. James Hogg, Walter Scott, and Stevenson grew up in a Scotland where oral storytelling was a common currency. Hogg and Scott were pioneers recording and writing oral stories, songs, and ballads. Something very particular in written narrative is happening in this transitional overlap between the literary artifice of these writers—preeminently Stevenson—and the oral traditions they experienced. Walter Benjamin's "The Storyteller" deals with this overlap. In Hogg's *Private Memoirs and Confessions of a Justified Sinner*, the ambivalence between a rational and a supernatural explanation of events sustains a tension as the narratives—plural—of the novel reveal themselves. In *Jekyll and Hyde*, the multiple narrative perspectives delivered in different forms of written address help create an equally effective tension. What seems credible and rational in *The Master of Ballantrae* is highly questionable as we go deeper into that novel. In Stevenson's shorter fiction, this consideration presents itself most forcefully in the way the narratives are disclosed and in the palpable physicality of the language—or languages—in which they are written.

"Thrawn Janet" is a good place to begin. A minister who thinks he knows what's what is confronted with inexplicable realities. In terms of language and style, the story opens in English and apparent objectivity. Yet place-names are already creating atmosphere and portent: "Dule" suggests gloom, "the Hanging Shaw" creates a literally suspenseful picture of trees (a shaw) overhanging the minister's house (*Works* 8: 109). These Scots words taint the English language unobtrusively. The section ends with a vague reference to "the older folk," one of whom might tell the story after drinking "his third tumbler" (110). The writing evokes the anonymity of oral transmission, while it emphasizes particular people, places, events. But after the third tumbler, you might be wary of believing everything that follows.

The story now immerses the reader in Scots, close enough to English to be readable but different enough to be strange. Try reading parts of the English and then the Scots out loud, for contrast. Even if it's difficult to pronounce the Scots, it's worth students' having a go, for two reasons. It should demonstrate the gulf that opens up between writing and speech, and it should draw attention to how Scots works as a language in writing. It seems to be a fluent vernacular idiom, natural and easily spoken. Yet to many students it may be difficult to speak and will slow down their reading. It's worth comparing passages of "Thrawn Janet" with those from *Huckleberry Finn* and looking at the prefatory paragraph where Twain talks about the different dialects he has used deliberately. Twain is making a point about the validity of different spoken idioms and implying a vital point about racism: that a black man's language is as valid as a white man's. What does that statement suggest about the ways in which we think of the people who use English and those who use Scots?

Janet, we are told, was thought to be "sib [related] to the de'il" and, a footnote informs us, "it was a common belief in Scotland that the devil appeared as a black man" (111, 114). Compare the information this purports to deliver soberly with the dramatic relish of the description that prompts it: a man "of a great stature, an' black as hell, and his e'en were singular to see." Then Reverend Mr. Soulis sees Janet turn to him, "an' it was borne in upon him what folk said, that Janet was deid lang syne, an' this was a bogle in her clay-cauld flesh." So the crux of the story settles on an agony of interpretation: is she just "a puir, auld afflicted wife that hadna a freend forbye himsel" or is her "fearsome face" that of a devil possessed (116)? The story's resolution comes as the minister finds Janet "hangin' frae a single nail an' by a single wursted thread for darnin' hose," and this discovery sends him to his bed, where "lang, lang he lay ravin' . . . an' frae that hour to this, he was the man ye ken the day" (118, 120).

Besides the twists and turns of the story's narrative and language, the representations of race, gender, and authorial objectivity that are all put into question, there is macabre or black humor here. That single thread used "for darnin' hose" is a lovely detail. *Thrawn* in the title is an old Scots word meaning "twisted, crotchety, carnaptious, oppositional, difficult, feisty." Hugh MacDiarmid's short poem "The Sauchs in the Reuch Heuch Hauch" provides an illustration of this quality (trees blown out of shape by prevailing winds are said to be as twisted as the Devil's heart: "As the deil's ain hert are thrawn"). The poet Norman MacCaig in his poem "Space Travel" once referred to "the homicidal hilarity / of a laugh in a ballad" (197). Something gruesome, horrible, and yet horribly funny is at work. The unknown, the violent and distorted, the devilish parts of the world are wreaking revenge on the minister's self-righteous sense of order and the justness of things in what he believes is God's universe. In the creative writing class, I ask how seriousness and black humor work together to convey this revenge. Who or what does the reader rely on?

In "Markheim," the essential catalyst of the story is a mysterious object acquired in a strange place: a mirror in a London antiques shop. The classic model is Aladdin's lamp, but the same idea opens the popular film *Gremlins*. A simple classroom application is to make this plot device the opening of a story, poem, or short play, offering a range of possible locations: a shop, a beach, a market, a farm, or a lecture in which a vital piece of information is (perhaps unwittingly) transmitted. As in "Thrawn Janet," secure coordinates are shifted in "Markheim": the mysterious visitor, Markheim, seems to be a thief, and when the dealer suggests he purchase a mirror, Markheim murders him. The opening dialogue and action are mysterious, unexplained, unfolding with theatrical poise. Then the central section of the story—in which Markheim moves around the apparently deserted shop, hears noises, and meets a strange figure who may be the devil and who prompts a Dostoevskian discussion about good and evil—leads us deeper into uncertainty: how is this story to be resolved? The climax, as Markheim goes out, leaves the question open: Does his confession of evil begin his repentance?

The class should look at how dialogue establishes atmosphere and propulsion in the narrative. What is unsaid or only hinted at creates uncertainty. The theatrical poise creates tension. Silences are thick with tension. How do the encounters in the story—between Markheim and the dealer, the satanic visitor, and the maid—provide structure? As in *Jekyll and Hyde*, the human question at the heart of the story questions orthodox Christian morality. Markheim tells us, "Evil and good run strong in me, haling me both ways. I do not love the one thing, I love all" (*Works* 8: 104). Stevenson seems to be saying that what we know as good and evil are both entwined in human character and cannot be separated. At the end of the tale, the "visitant" is transformed from a satanic to an almost angelic character. This ambiguity prompts the question, How can serious and deep issues be addressed and explored in popular fiction? The resultant discussion can drive the creative writing class toward a piece of work that sets out to do exactly that.

In "A Lodging for the Night: A Story of Francis Villon," Stevenson evokes medieval winter in Paris, where the cold strangeness and historical distance of the location lead the reader to sympathize with the poet, "only a poor Master of Arts," who will be seen to be cynical, attractive, and criminal (*Works* 1: 219). Characterization is lurid, heightened by descriptions of his companions and physical acts: food, drink, writing, the portentous hanged man in the gibbet nearby—everything is heavily accentuated. Once these features have been savored, the class might be asked how the work of the writer is figured in a context of criminality and bourgeois priorities. There is wry humor here too. The story balances between the observation, "In many ways an artistic nature unfits a man for practical existence," and Villon's final throwaway line, "Many thanks for the cold mutton" (225, 240). In the character of Villon, how do material needs and physical reality balance against the urgencies of imagination and invention?

"A Fable: The Persons of the Tale" poses questions about authorial process. It offers a surreal or protopostmodernist interruption to *Treasure Island*, ostensibly taking place between chapters 32 and 33: "[T]wo of the puppets strolled out to have a pipe before business should begin again, and met in an open place not far from the story" (*Works* 2: 223). These are Captain Trelawney and Long John Silver, and their dialogue is a delightful revelation, discussing where they are in the story ("You're in a bad way, Silver," says the captain) and debating the relative attractiveness each has for his author (223). When the upstanding, self-righteous captain reprimands Silver for feeling comfortable in his villainy, reminding him, "Don't you know there's such a thing as an Author?" Silver responds, "[I]f there is sich a thing as a Author, I'm his favourite chara'ter. He does me fathoms better'n he does you—fathoms, he does. And he likes doing me. . . . [H]e's on my side, and you may lay to it!" (224). A discussion question: What makes a character attractive, dynamic, worth writing about? A writing exercise: Declare an intermission in any great novel and write a similar short dialogue between characters. Or take a couple of characters from any story and put them in a different context, either in a different narrative or in a nonliteral situation. A related exercise might follow readings of "Stevenson's Companion to the Cook Book," where brief sketches describe dialogues of characters from history and literature: "Fielding and Richardson," "Laurence Sterne," or "Robert Burns," for example (*Works* 5: 201–16). These sketches are highly suggestive. Students might be encouraged to write equally succinct pieces presenting characters from history or literature in a revealing moment, in conversation with a questioner, about to do or just having done something for which they are famous but offering an unexpected explanation for it.

Other fables that work well in creative writing classes are "The Sinking Ship," which might prompt students to start writing a story with a spectacular catastrophic end in view (5: 79–81), and "The House of Eld," in which a hideous allegorical world of chains and oppression is described. In "House," one tiny detail supplies an unforgettable moment. When the oppressive sorcerer is finally knocked to the ground, "a little bloodless white thing fled from the room" (90). The creation of an entire dramatic theater in a few pages is exemplary here. Indeed the *Fables* generally offer a valuable lesson in writing in a condition of restraint. This is the Stevenson who insisted that the essential self-discipline of the writer lay in deleting unnecessary words: "Jesus, there is but one art: to omit!" (*Letters* 4: 169; students might also read 168–71 and 180–82 for Stevenson's extended musings on authorship).

"For Success," one of the "Prayers Written for Family Use at Vailima," raises a different question (*Works* 21: 5). A beautiful, brief example of humility and sincerity in writing from someone who notoriously broke with his father over religion, it challenges students to think about how to write without irony. What problems arise when you are attempting to write something that expresses directly things that you believe in and hope for? Discuss responses to this prayer in class: can you concur with its hope in a secular world? Are the references to "Thee" and "Christ" acceptable even to a non-Christian? What do they mean for Stevenson? What is the meaning of the word *success*? Compare "For Success" with the last paragraph of George Eliot's *Middlemarch*. What are we trying to say about common humanity and human value?

Of course, the essential exercise in a creative writing class is for students to produce their own work. This is mine—written in response to my particular assignment for this volume:

Revenge

It's not that you would ever recommend it,
Or ever think of doing it yourself, but
When you're stuck in the house with your leg in plaster,
Your arms in crutches and hopping around, it helps
To reread *Treasure Island*, and get to Chapter XIV. You remember it?
Long John Silver's plot has come adrift, and the sailor Tom
Is asking him to give it up, to come back in and do his rightful duty.
Tom gets nowhere, turns around, and starts to walk away . . .
(And young Jim Hawkins, looking from the bushes,

Sees it all in wonder through the leaves, as fear and understanding grow.)
Long John holds a tree branch with one hand, lifts his wooden crutch up
With the other hand, and with almighty strength, he throws it like a spear
To strike poor Tom with terrifying accuracy, square in the middle of his spine.
And finishes him off with a big sharp knife.
It's good to have that power, in imagination.
That's what stories help with, at such times.
Thank heaven for fiction and pieces of eight.

Creative work is frequently prompted by the writing of major authors. Shakespeare is perhaps the most common example: Disney's *The Lion King* is *Hamlet* with a happy ending, Ivan Turgenev's "A Lear of the Steppes" redeploys *King Lear* in prose fiction in Russia, while Zbigniew Herbert's "Elegy of Fortinbras" arises frighteningly from *Hamlet*, and Rainer Maria Rilke's "The Spirit Ariel" and Edwin Morgan's "Caliban Falls Asleep in the Isle Full of Noises" and "Ariel Freed" are prompted by *The Tempest*. After Shakespeare, Stevenson has prepared some of the most fertile fields for further writing, not only in fiction. *Jekyll and Hyde* has entered popular imagination through innumerable texts in literary and screen media, and the *Pirates of the Caribbean* franchise surely owes something to him. If my poem has its own integrity, it might also offer three useful examples for teachers and students. It illustrates a key element in the relationship of adult and child, a crucial perception in *Treasure Island*; it demonstrates the way in which dramatic immediacy and reflective thought can be balanced, showing how the imagination works beyond and through literalism; and more generally it describes how literature might help in the apprehension of reality. Each can be applied in the practices of creative writing.

Stevenson's Essays in the Composition Classroom

Emily A. Bernhard Jackson

At first glance, Robert Louis Stevenson's essays may not seem ideal for use in the composition classroom. Consider the opening sentences of "A Plea for Gas Lamps":

> Cities given, the problem was to light them. How to conduct individual citizens about the burgess-warren, when once heaven had withdrawn its leading luminary? Or—since we live in a scientific age—when once our spinning planet has turned its back on the sun? The moon, from time to time, was doubtless very helpful; the stars had a cheery look among the chimney pots; and a cresset here and there, on church or citadel, produced a fine pictorial effect. (*Works* 25: 129)

Leaving aside the old-fashioned language, there is much here to puzzle even an advanced essayist: the abrupt opening, the apparently easy immediacy of tone, the humor that teeters on the verge of arch without ever quite falling off the ledge of charming. What, then, can essays such as this offer to beginning and higher-level writers in the classroom?

For one thing, Stevenson can be a good writing model simply because he is already famous to students, although they may not know it. The plot of *Strange Case of Dr Jekyll and Mr Hyde* is firmly placed in the cultural unconscious, and when students learn that their essay writer is the same man who produced the story they have seen countless times on TV and in the movies, they become exponentially more interested. Moreover, Stevenson also makes a good writing model precisely because he seems so little like one. His manner and voice are so approachable, and his style so relaxed and conversational, that it is easy to lose sight of the fact that he follows through with his ideas and points tenaciously. His conversational mode often appeals to beginning writers, who enter a writing classroom with the attitude that the straightforward essay (thesis, argument, conclusion) is tedious or even counterproductive. For them, Stevenson's ability to develop a subject to the end, making his points subtly along the way, offers an alternative. Moreover, Stevenson makes a good addition to the writing classroom simply because he is both readable and enjoyable. Beginning students in particular are typically given dry or sententious essays in their readers and rhetorics; Stevenson's lively essays, in contrast, cover topics guaranteed to interest college students: selecting a partner and fostering a relationship, the value of travel and adventure, the benefits of idling. For these reasons, his essays provide composition instructors with a chance to introduce students to the importance of tone, style, and voice by using texts that entertain as well as teach.

Indeed, one of the best uses of Stevenson in the writing classroom is to highlight the metaprocess of writing: the essay as a tool to question what precisely an essay should do. There is often a sense, especially in writing programs that focus on producing academic prose, that essays are meant only to communicate information as efficiently as possible. Stevenson follows William Hazlitt in seeing the essay as a space in which to converse, to muse, to consider, and even (here not following Hazlitt) to laugh. He thus prompts discussion about whether and how essays should do this. That the nineteenth century placed a different value on the essay and gave it a different purpose opens up a conversation about the history of essay writing, the past and current uses of the essay, and its innovative possibilities in academia. In programs that allow students to focus on personal as well as academic prose, and in courses on advanced essay writing or creative nonfiction, Stevenson gives writers an opportunity to consider not only what topics can work to advantage but also what difference the treatment of a topic can make. What is gained by laughing over a subject? by casting a cool and amused eye, as Stevenson often does? by hiding sensible thinking under puckishness, as he also often does? These and other questions raise the issue of essay production and construction in fruitful ways.

Most beginning writing courses seek to teach students how to write in many genres—indeed, it seems that one of the greatest challenges in composition teaching is how to serve students who may go on to major in fields other than English literature: archaeology, biology, social science. Because Stevenson draws from a wide range of subject matter, he can be used as an exemplar of how to introduce fine prose into all areas: "Child's Play" is an unexpected example of the sociology or anthropology essay; "Walking Tours" can be read as an acute psychological study (*Works* 25: 106–16, 117–24 [*Virginibus Puerisque*]). Students will almost certainly object that these essays do not deal with sociology or psychology in the strictest sense of the word, that the writing is not clinical or straightforward, and they will be right. But because much of excellent writing consists in recognizing the way in which even a single word can change the feel of a sentence, reading these essays from the perspective of different academic disciplines can make students consider how they might shape their own discipline-specific prose to increase involvement and pleasure. It is therefore useful for the teacher to ask students to examine how Stevenson's language works—in other words, to break down his sentences as minutely as possible.

But Stevenson works best with more advanced students, even if "more advanced" simply means a beginning writing classroom toward the end of the course. Because his prose is highly polished, he serves as a better example for those writers who have passed the stage of worrying about basic construction and reached the level at which they can focus on style. Perhaps the simplest way to use him at this level is as a prompt for an exercise in modeling: students are presented with a paragraph out of context (like the one quoted above, "Cities given . . .") and asked to write one of their own that imitates it. This exercise is illuminating, both because it shows how elegant writing can transform even the most banal topic—after all, street lamps are scarcely a subject to set the blood racing—and because it demonstrates how difficult such elegance is to produce.

It takes work to sound as off-the-cuff, casual, and whimsical as Stevenson does and even more work to get to the heart of a writing matter immediately, as he does. This exercise encourages students to think very carefully about how to construct their own writing for maximum effect and achieve that effect with the appearance of minimal effort. Indeed, one result of this exercise is that students unconsciously begin to focus on the sound of their prose: on word choice, on sentence-by-sentence rhythm, on the precise ways in which language creates tone and thus on how even a very small change can alter tone. They may not produce faithful models of Stevenson, but the very act of attempting to do so increases their feel for their own prose.

Another exercise, which works precisely in reverse, is somewhat more difficult. Students take an excerpt from a Stevenson essay (or, time permitting, even a whole essay) and "translate" it into a more modern idiom. This task creates a number of opportunities. If students follow the suggestion to translate the excerpt into slack modern prose, as a way of showing them the difference between writing that is thought about and writing that is not, it becomes apparent how much is lost when prose is unthinking. If students try instead to capture Stevenson's zest in modern language, it becomes clear both (again) how much effort is involved in producing that zest and to what extent focusing on the nuts and bolts of tone and style can pay off. In either case, the exercise emphasizes the degree to which good writing is created through concentration and care.

Finally, Stevenson can be a guide for those in creative nonfiction courses because of the way he employs form in the guise of formlessness. I select a specific essay: *Virginibus Puerisque*, especially its early parts, works well because it is amusing and because its topic is accessible (*Works* 25: 1–38). A careful reading reveals that although the voice is extremely relaxed and Stevenson appears simply to be musing, the piece is quite sensible, even stern, and offers some practical advice: be coolheaded when choosing a mate, look to the long-term, don't be fooled by immediate, obvious charms. The essay traces clearly the outcome of successful and unsuccessful matches, with the result that under the wit a good deal of wisdom soaks in. Because lightness of touch is so difficult an aspect of writing to parse, the instructor can lead students in a very close reading of the text, analyzing it to determine precisely how, technically, Stevenson achieves the result he does. Does he begin with a serious theme, then decorate it whimsically, or are the seriousness and whimsy interdependent? What kind of balance is struck between them, and is such a balance advisable in every topic? Are there topics that would be destroyed by such treatment? After this dissection, students should apply what they've learned to a piece of writing of their own, thus testing their theories in the realm of the actual.

Admittedly, Stevenson's essays can be tough nuts to crack. They sometimes seem to promote humor at the expense of impact or weight; they sometimes appear self-indulgent. What's more, simply because they are less studied they can appear less worthy of study. But for these very reasons they are valuable tools in the writing classroom. Stevenson forces essayists to consider the value and practice of lightness of touch and of deploying that lightness in concert with seriousness of subject in such a way that an essay becomes thought-provoking without hectoring or being dull. In addition, he spurs student writers to think how reflective writing avoids self-indulgence and thereby invites an uninvolved readership to become involved. Finally, Stevenson reminds students that essays—reading and writing them—can be a pleasure, and it is for this reason above all that he repays serious study and imitation in the writing classroom.

Classroom and Courtroom across the Curriculum: *The Strange Case of Dr Jekyll and Mr Hyde*

Jason Goldsmith

The Strange Case of Dr Jekyll and Mr Hyde draws on Robert Louis Stevenson's intimate knowledge of Victorian legal culture, knowledge Stevenson acquired while studying law at the University of Edinburgh. (Although he was called to the Scottish bar in 1875, he abandoned the legal profession and never practiced it.) Its trace can be found in the work's title, main characters, and narrative structure: the title suggests a legal action; Mr. Utterson is the legal representative of Henry Jekyll, who is himself both a doctor of law (LLD) and a doctor of civil laws (DCL); and the final two chapters function as depositions. So powerful is this aspect of the novel that it has led at least one criminal defense to cite Dr. Jekyll's plight in court (see Stern). This legal context provides me the occasion to engage students in a collective act of close reading and reasoned argumentation. Turning the classroom into a courtroom, the students place Henry Jekyll on trial for the crimes committed by Edward Hyde.

The Writing Class

Although the legal approach to the novel can be applied to classes at various levels of the curriculum, I have utilized it most frequently in the first-year seminar, a general humanities course that introduces all incoming students to critical thinking and academic writing. In the version of the class I offer, which takes drug culture as its theme, a large number of pharmacy and business majors enroll. Taking the course to satisfy a requirement, these students are often uncomfortable interpreting literary texts. I schedule *Jekyll and Hyde* early in the semester, as they get ready for their first essay assignment, which inevitably elicits worry. Before our scheduled discussion of the text, I prepare the students for the exercise by asking them to consider, as they read, to what extent Jekyll is guilty of the crimes committed by Hyde. On the day of our class discussion, I divide the students into three groups: prosecution, defense, and grand jury. Prosecution and defense are tasked with combing the text to gather evidence that supports their argument for Jekyll's innocence or guilt. The grand jury has access to all the evidence and will question each team, so it too needs to examine the "case file." The teams have fifteen minutes to prepare and four minutes to present their case. After both sides have made their initial arguments, the grand jury poses questions for two minutes. Following this phase of the trial, each team has five minutes to prepare a two-minute rebuttal in which students respond to the opposing argument and offer a summation. Although the work is collective, each team elects one student to present its case.

The trial format brings the argumentative process to life. There is an immediate and obvious goal in sight—exonerating or incriminating Henry Jekyll—so the students feel invested in the outcome. The exercise excites them about the novel as they pool their resources and try to outmaneuver opposing counsel. At the same time, they are thinking critically, questioning the nature and limits of both accountability and personal identity. What is more relevant to my immediate pedagogical aims, the exercise forces the students to argue a position, to build their case through a logical presentation of reasons, and to draw on specific textual evidence to substantiate their claims.

As the teams begin to prepare their case, I visit each to offer encouragement. I urge students to locate places in the text that support their case and suggest how they might begin to organize their evidence into a compelling argument. Charged with convincing the jury that Jekyll is accountable for the crimes committed by Hyde, the prosecuting students are quick to point out that Jekyll confesses to the murder of Sir Danvers Carew in the first person: "I mauled the unresisting body" (*Works* 5: 67). This admission of guilt is a fine place to begin. However, I suggest that they should not rely on the confession alone—the letter is not signed—and push them to consider other evidence as well. As the students point out, Jekyll not only confesses to the crime but also admits both explicitly and implicitly that he and Hyde are one and the same. Recalling his transformations, for instance, Jekyll maintains, "I was once more Edward Hyde" (69–70). Someone might point out that Hyde, too, collapses the distinction between himself and Jekyll. Before he drinks the transforming draft prepared by Lanyon, Hyde invokes the professional bonds that Lanyon and Jekyll, both doctors, share: "[W]hat follows is under the seal of our profession" (55). Although Hyde is physically present, this is Jekyll speaking.

When the students note that the walking stick used to beat Sir Danvers and found in Hyde's apartment belongs to Jekyll, I ask them to identify other moments in the tale that corroborate Jekyll's assertions. For example, in order to confirm Jekyll's claim that "[his] two natures had memory in common" (66), one of the students will point to Hyde's behavior when first accosted by Mr. Utterson. "[H]ow did you know me?" Hyde inquires of the lawyer (12). When Utterson claims that Jekyll described him, Hyde cries out, "He never told you . . . I did not think you would have lied." The boldness of Hyde's reply, delivered "with a flush of anger," is telling, and his accusation suggests he knows that Jekyll did not provide such a description (13).

Given Jekyll's confession and the preponderance of evidence linking Jekyll to Hyde, the defense has a more difficult case to make. Nevertheless, the novel provides a wealth of information that can be used to distance Jekyll from the criminal acts of Hyde. The students might, for example, dismiss the confession as the product of a diseased imagination. Indeed, Jekyll's two oldest friends repeatedly question his sanity: Utterson thinks Jekyll's behavior "pointed to madness" (32), while Lanyon is convinced that he "was dealing with a case of cerebral disease" (52). Or students might suggest that Jekyll is at most an accessory to Hyde's crimes. Although Jekyll prepares the apartment in Soho, tells his servants that Hyde is to have full liberty of his house, and establishes a will to transfer his assets to Hyde, eyewitnesses identify Hyde, not Jekyll, as the perpetrator.

The existence of the will, a legally binding document, implies that the two men are distinct entities, at least in the eyes of the law. At this point, the defense might demonstrate that Jekyll and Hyde are physically dissimilar. Hyde is "smaller, slighter and younger than Henry Jekyll" (61). His footsteps "fell lightly and oddly, with a certain swing," in contrast to the "heavy creaking tread of Henry Jekyll" (43). Even two symbolic markers of personal identity—the hand, associated with writing, and the voice, associated with speech—differ. Jekyll's hand is "large, firm, white and comely," while Hyde's is "lean, corded, knuckly, of a dusky pallor, and thickly shaded with a swart growth of hair" (64). When Hyde locks himself in the lab and tries to pass himself off as Jekyll, Poole declares, "[W]as that my master's voice? . . . Have I been twenty years in this man's house, to be deceived about his voice?" (39). The only evidence linking Jekyll to the crimes beyond an association, which in itself is no crime, is his confession.

In fact, the defense will often open its case by trying to undermine the legitimacy of the confession. They will suggest, for example, how in the very act of his confession Jekyll wishes to distinguish himself as a knowing, active agent from Hyde. "It was Hyde, after all, and Hyde alone, that was guilty," asserts Jekyll, who would attempt to "undo the evil done by Hyde" (63). The confession concludes in a similar vein, as Jekyll declares, "[T]his is my true hour of death, and what is to follow concerns another than myself" (74). A particularly astute student may observe that throughout the confession Jekyll syntactically resists conflating himself with Hyde: "he sat," "he dined," "he set forth," "He, I say—I cannot say, I" (71). Such examples are doubly significant, because they demonstrate that the students are attending closely to the novel's language.

Having presented its case, each group has five minutes to prepare a response to their opposition. The rebuttal is an important phase of the exercise, because it asks students to consider the argument presented by opposing counsel and to respond to it in such a way as to minimize its effect on their own. If the prosecution enters into evidence Mr. Guest's testimony that Jekyll's handwriting bore "a rather singular resemblance" to Hyde's "murderer's autograph" (29, 28), the defense might argue that this evidence does not prove that Jekyll and Hyde are the same individual. Although Mr. Guest is "a great student and critic of handwriting" (28), it could be argued that Jekyll wrote the note for Hyde out of fear, loyalty, or some other motive, as Utterson argues. Throughout the novel, handwriting is presented as an unreliable indicator of personal identity. Pursuing this line, the defense could cast doubt on the authenticity of the confession by reminding the jury how Hyde scrawled blasphemies in Jekyll's own hand in Jekyll's books (73). If Hyde can forge Jekyll's handwriting, the authority of the confession is in doubt. It may be one more of Hyde's tricks intended to blame an innocent party.

While I am happy to let this debate unfold for most of the class, I set aside fifteen or twenty minutes to reflect on the nature of the arguments the students have put forth. First we outline the two opposing cases on the board. Then I suggest to the students that what they have done in class resembles what they need to do in their upcoming essay assignment. Using the outlined cases, I identify the various elements of an effective argument: a debatable thesis that takes a stand on an issue, reasons that inform the reader why the thesis is valid, analysis of evidence to support that validity, and responses to potential objections to the main points. Backing into a discussion of academic argument from this lively exercise demystifies the writing process and allays the students' anxiety. In addition, the trial makes students comfortable using specific textual evidence to underwrite their assertions, a skill that challenges many students who pass through my first-year writing courses.

Science and Society

The courtroom exercise can easily be adapted to classes in which writing is not the primary focus. In an upper-division course titled Technology and the Body in Literature and Film, which enrolls both English majors and science, technology, and society majors, I use the courtroom exercise to generate discussion about the limits of the human subject. As the debate unfolds, students consider moral agency and the vexed nature of personal identity. Does identity reside in memory, which is notoriously unreliable? Is it somehow linked to the body, although the body can be modified and augmented? Is identity situated beyond the individual, interpellated through webs of social, legal, and legislative networks? To what extent are our identities mediated by new technologies? In what ways are our technologies already interior to and an essential part of us, legally, morally, biologically? The specific parameters of the exercise, set by time limits and the need to respond formally to opposing arguments, are less important here than the discussion it generates about what it means to be human.

The Undergraduate Research Seminar

One final course example suggests how the exercise may be used to develop specific disciplinary skills. In their junior year, English majors are required to take a seminar that introduces them to the research skills required for advanced study in literature. I offer a seminar on Victorian sensation fiction in which we approach literary works as cultural documents, situating them in the social milieu of the 1860s. Although published some two decades after the vogue for sensation fiction, Stevenson's novel builds on that tradition and allows students to consider the lasting effects of one particular genre. By the time we turn our attention to *Jekyll and Hyde*, they have read novels such as Wilkie Collins's *The Woman in White* and Mary Elizabeth Braddon's *Lady Audley's Secret* and have learned to identify, locate, and access Victorian-era documents such as public health records, critical reviews, lithographs, periodicals and newspapers, diaries, and government records.

We devote two sessions to Stevenson's novel. In the first, we discuss *Jekyll and Hyde* in relation to the tradition of sensation fiction. Our conversation generally revolves around such issues as gender, evolution and degeneration, insanity, criminality, class, immigration, and nationalism, which have occupied us throughout the semester. At the end of this session I introduce a variation of the courtroom exercise described above. I ask students to supplement the evidence presented in the novel with "expert testimony" by tracking down other cultural documents of the time period to support their case. My goal in adapting the courtroom exercise in this manner is to deepen their investigative abilities.

Because the course deals with sensation fiction, we have spent much of the semester discussing the status of women in Victorian Britain. Not surprisingly, the students want to bring this knowledge to bear on the case at hand. Recalling that Hyde "was knit to [Jekyll] closer than a wife" (73), the prosecution might consider the relevance of the common-law doctrine of coverture, whereby a woman's independent legal existence was incorporated into that of her husband upon marriage. The defense might argue that changes in matrimonial law through which married women achieved greater legal status, such as the Divorce and Matrimonial Causes Act of 1857 and the Married Women's Property Acts of 1870 and 1882, suggest that a single legal identity for two distinct individuals was becoming increasingly untenable.

To cinch the relationship between Jekyll and Hyde, the prosecution might draw on the testimony of Victorian psychologists. Exploring pathological indications of personality, Frederic Myers's "Multiplex Personality" (1886) and Henry Maudsley's "The Double Brain" (1889) point to the duality of identity. The defense might find the Italian criminologist Cesare Lombroso a useful witness. Adapting Darwin's biological theory to help explain criminal behavior, Lombroso's *Criminal Man* (1876) identifies the criminal as a distinct physiological type akin to primitive human beings. Calling attention to Hyde's "bestial avidity" (63) and "ape-like fury" (21), the defense could distinguish the civilized Dr. Jekyll from the atavistic criminal.

Although these expert testimonies often fail to convince, the trial encourages students to apply the literary research skills they have been learning throughout the course (Danahay's Broadview edition provides a starting point that whets students' appetite for more). In this respect, the trial is a success. Although we don't always come to a unanimous verdict, the exercise provides a satisfying sense of closure to our discussion of the text.

Jekyll and Heidegger: Stevenson in the Theory Classroom

Matthew Wickman

> [M]an is not truly one, but truly two. I say two, because the state of my own knowledge does not pass beyond that point. . . . [O]thers will outstrip me on the same lines; and I hazard the guess that man will be ultimately known for a mere polity of multifarious, incongruous and independent denizens. (*Works* 5: 58)

Thus proclaims Henry Jekyll in perhaps the most famous passage from Robert Louis Stevenson's most famous novel. Today, more than a century after its publication, and in the wake of psychoanalytic and postmodern theories of fragmented selfhood, Jekyll's speculation appears prophetic, if not clichéd *avant la lettre*. Indeed, the schizoid nature of modern subjectivity has become so axiomatic, so widely assumed, that one feels grateful that Jekyll's declaration is false, at least on its own terms. I call it false, because Jekyll himself qualifies it when he reflects on how it is "the curse of mankind that [such] incongruous" facets of being should be "bound together" (58). This qualification spawns a set of interesting reflections on the ephemeral nature of corporeal materiality and immateriality (which makes it possible for Jekyll to slip into the figure of Hyde and back again), but Jekyll's "Full Statement of the Case" reconciles these facets of being into a single point of view. In doing so, his "statement" essentially mimics Stevenson's narrative, which lends similar coherence to its multiple threads (Utterson's and Enfield's first-person accounts, Lanyon's letter, etc.). For Jekyll, as for the overall narrative, the act of writing shapes the diversity of selves and voices into a kind of compendium, a single mathematical "set" of disparate components.

Such self-reflexivity, as the narrative reproduces both the complexity and coherence of what it describes, is a hallmark of Stevenson's work. It is a trait, moreover, that he believed to be requisite to literature as a work of art rather than nature. In "A Humble Remonstrance," he writes:

> For the welter of impressions . . . which life presents, [literature] substitutes a certain artificial series of impressions . . . all aiming at the same effect, all eloquent of the same ideas, all chiming together like consonant notes in music or like the graduated tints in a good picture. From all its chapters, from all its pages, from all its sentences, the well-written novel echoes and re-echoes its one creative and controlling thought. (*Works* 29: 136)

This principled reconciliation of multiplicity is a provocative topic in its own right, but its relevance to an MLA Approaches to World Literature volume may be that it provides a model for good analytic writing, especially when that writing involves theory. I would go so far as to say, somewhat cheekily, that theoretical discourse has essentially become the esoteric corollary to sophomore-level writing in the English major. Theory and sophomore-level writing are the Jekyll and Hyde—or, if you prefer, the Hyde and Jekyll—of the English major.

Let me hasten to add that by likening theory and sophomore-level writing, I'm not labeling theory sophomoric. In many ways, reading and writing theory and about theory are more sophisticated exercises today, some two decades after theory's perceived apex in literary studies, than they were when engagements of theory broadly meant the straightforward application of predigested paradigms to literary texts (the dreadful "critical approaches" model that treated texts as repositories of deconstructive, psychoanalytic, feminist, Marxist, or what-have-you symptoms). Call that the "freshman composition" era of theory instruction—the era when students were taught to craft and defend a single (theoretical) position. Today, by contrast, theory represents a more complex negotiation of discourses. Perusing any top theory journal, one is less likely to find direct applications of theoretical models than critical discussions of intersecting topics—like the religious iconography of Joan of Arc alongside the French government of Nicolas Sarkozy (Françoise Meltzer), or climate change and historicism (Dipesh Chakrabarty), or biopolitics and posthumanism (Cary Wolfe), or literature and globalization (Ralph Cohen). And this is to say nothing of the dynamic theory arguments linking literature with mathematics, physics, genetics, sociology, cinema, art history, and so on. Indeed, theory today often (even usually) involves lateral thinking, across disciplines and topics. On that score, what this new phase of theory has in common with writing at the sophomore level, when most students enter the English major, is that each emphasizes the building of bridges—between texts and contexts, arguments and critical implications, literature and other disciplines. Writing at this level emphasizes content as much as or more than the basics of voice, style, and argument. Hence, even when sophomore-level writing doesn't explicitly involve theory, and even though it does not attain the same level of sophistication, its intellectual processes aren't necessarily different in kind.

My essay is about Stevenson and theory, not Stevenson and student writing. However, I introduce Stevenson's work here in this way to help explain why I find his fiction not only intellectually stimulating but also pedagogically useful. His horror at the divisions rending modern life, especially his home nation of Scotland, inspired him to build wonderfully intricate literary bridges—bridges that, in the courses I teach, serve as models of conceptual creativity. So while Stevenson fits neatly into a variety of literary history courses, I prefer to teach his work in topically driven literature seminars. These are courses in which we not only read literary texts alongside theory but also use literary texts themselves to frame, articulate, and provisionally solve theoretical problems.

A few years ago, Stevenson figured prominently in a senior-level seminar I titled An Enlightenment History of Trauma: Pathways from the Scottish Highlands to Auschwitz. The aim of the course was to introduce students to trauma theory and also to situate this theory, widely understood as a twentieth-century innovation, in a longer historical context. We read works on trauma theory by Sigmund Freud, Geoffrey Hartman, Cathy Caruth, and Dominick LaCapra alongside literary texts by writers like James "Ossian" Macpherson, Walter Scott, and Stevenson. When we turned to Stevenson's *Kidnapped*, his 1886 novel designed around the famous Appin Murder of 1752 (whose subsequent trial narrative our class also read), we focused on Stevenson's engagement of material, legal, and literary history, discussing ways in which the novel called attention to the chasms it tenuously bridged—emphasizing, for example, the transference between fact and fiction during a time when the authority accruing to science increasingly drove a wedge between fact and fiction. At novel's end, David Balfour, the novel's callow and coming-of-age narrator, finds justice only after participating in a kind of legal charade. As Stevenson would make clear in *Catriona*, his sequel to *Kidnapped*, David thus achieves his wishes at the cost of a deeper disillusionment, which reconciles him to social reality even as it separates him from his childhood ideals. The novel thus underscores the fragile state of reconciliation—between person and person, between present and past—in a complex world. But this principle too functions as a bridge in *Kidnapped*, one that imparts to its readers an understanding of what its characters and, by extension, the readers experience but never fully grasp. The novel, that is, installs representation as a simulacrum of the understanding to which David aspires (this argument is fully developed in my *Ruins of Experience*).

Having representation serve as a simulacrum of understanding is a principle of literary fiction but also one of trauma theory. More broadly, in speaking to the anxiety that tinctures a sense of perpetual uncertainty, Stevenson's novel puts its finger on the pulse of modern being. This was the premise of a second seminar I built around Stevenson, this time in a course titled Hard-Boiled Heidegger. The seminar juxtaposed the philosophy and theoretical legacy of Martin Heidegger with crime fiction—specifically, Scottish crime fiction. The aim here was not to engage in Heideggerian readings of this literary genre but rather to elucidate an uncanny set of motifs connecting the two, from the commission of a terrible misdeed (i.e., murder or, for Heidegger, the forgetting of Being) and the sense of conspiracy (i.e., criminality or, for Heidegger, the ubiquity of metaphysics) to noirish atmospherics (for Heidegger, in the feelings of anxiety that function as a precursor to ontological awareness). Interpreting crime fiction in the context of Heidegger, we hypothesized, would reinforce the degree to which pulp fiction is part of the culture that also produces high theory; at the same time, reading Heidegger through the lens of crime fiction would reveal the kitschy element inscribed into modern thought. Taking this approach, we believed, would enable us to get a different purchase on the nature of the theoretical debates that multiplied in Heidegger's wake and through his influence.

We directed most of our attention to so-called Tartan Noir, Scottish crime fiction published since the late 1970s, but began by reading *Jekyll and Hyde*, because Jekyll's nominally split identity resembles a rupture that Heidegger identified between traditional metaphysics and the forgotten philosophy of being. The imputation that such rifts are widespread—the rule rather than the exception (Hyde being the garish allegory of Victorian hypocrisy)—means that, in both *Jekyll and Hyde* and Heidegger's *Being and Time*, divisiveness is a general condition. This divisiveness in turn implies that the category of being itself is "not truly one, but truly two" (58). There is the Being that Heidegger claims is all but lost to us, and then there is the category of modern being, which, in Heidegger's own terms, itself constitutes a state of being lost. To be in the one ontological mode is thus not to be in the other—a Jekyll and Hyde dynamic. Hence those forces of modernity that Heidegger criticizes across the body of his work (science, technology, mathematics, etc.) function as his monstrous double, his Hyde—a condition for which Stevenson's novella and not Heidegger's philosophy provides the hermeneutic key. So at least we contended in the seminar.

Jekyll and Hyde provided a template for our subsequent reading of the doppelgängers of modern thought—those theories, from deconstruction to ecocriticism, that grow out of Heideggerian philosophy but bear legacies uncannily different from the ones they project at face value. This assertion, I admit, is irreverent. Heidegger's brief but intense affiliation with the Nazi Party in 1933, coupled with his subsequent refusal to apologize for that involvement, has inspired an aura of pathos, scandal, and residual fascism around his work and the theories associated with it—Heidegger is consequently associated with scandal more than with kitsch (see Derrida, *Of Spirit*; Philippe Lacoue-Labarthe, *Heidegger, Art, and Politics*; Jean-François Lyotard, *Heidegger and "The Jews"*). But interpreting Heidegger alongside crime fiction reveals the kitschy quality of that same aura, as though Hamlet went to sleep and awoke as Sam Spade if not Inspector Clouseau. Our interpretive practice in class revealed the absurdity, the unbearable lightness of Being, that dwells at the edges of horror. This revelation proved to be pedagogically valuable, because it raised ethical as well as intellectual questions. A key to our discussions was to replicate the paradox I mentioned at the outset: Stevenson's novella may assert a bifurcated human condition, but its narrative fosters a kind of coherence. By the same token, a hard-boiled Heidegger may point to an uncanny trajectory in the history of theory, but that trajectory must remain in contact with theory in its more conventional terms. In following this line of thought, we aimed to enrich our understanding of Heidegger's legacy, not trivialize it.

I have likened this type of intellectual engagement to sophomore-level writing. My department at Brigham Young University makes explicit the curricular connection between the senior seminar and the sophomore-level writing class: it envisions the senior course as a capstone of the major, with writing as the major's most fundamental and sophisticated form of expression. The main course requirement was therefore a research paper, and students chose to write on a variety of subjects: Heidegger, Ian Rankin (of Inspector Rebus fame), the relation between deconstruction and police procedurals, and Stevenson. We led up to this final project with two preliminary but substantial assignments. The first was a take-home essay exam of two questions, distributed piecemeal. The questions were designed to elicit reflection on like with unlike or, if you will, Jekyll with Hyde; that is, they encouraged bridge building. One question reminded students of instances in which Heidegger describes philosophical awareness as a momentary epiphany into the entire conceptual network in which Being operates. It then asked students to compare one such instance with the modality of vision in one of three novels we had read to that point in the term (*Jekyll and Hyde*, Arthur Conan Doyle's *The Hound of the Baskervilles*, and John Buchan's *The Thirty-Nine Steps*). The other lead-in assignment was to be a presentation, both oral and written (replete with an annotated bibliography), in which students were to "sleuth out" Heidegger's influence in some specified area, whether phenomenology or deconstruction, posthumanism or biopolitics, theories of information (e.g., network theory), cultural studies, and so on. Together, these preliminary assignments set a high bar for the research papers by demanding original thinking and meaningful conceptual connections. The students, it turns out, were up to the challenge.

Stevenson's novella set an important precedent for all that followed in this seminar, as his work has done for my courses in the past. The material in this most recent theory seminar was occasionally abstruse, especially for members of the group without much background in theory. The crime fiction angle was crucial, as it framed the theory in a way that made it more accessible and often a great deal of fun. (We laughed often, and sometimes loudly.) *Jekyll and Hyde,* the first piece of fiction that we read, created an important historical backdrop for the subsequent novels. The concept of the double, after all, is ubiquitous in Scottish crime fiction. *Jekyll and Hyde* was even more crucial to our engagement of theory, perhaps precisely because our aim was not simply to digest central (Heideggerian) concepts but also to think creatively and critically about those concepts' legacy. Stevenson helped us do this less because he articulates a radically divided existence or bifurcated state of being than because he is a master at tying together loose threads. This ability makes him an exemplar for anybody teaching—or hoping that his or her students will generate—serious ideas.

NOTES ON CONTRIBUTORS

Emily A. Bernhard Jackson is a senior member at Robinson College, Cambridge University. She has published on Byron, Tennyson, Spenser, and composition. She is the author of *The Development of Byron's Philosophy of Knowledge: Certain in Uncertainty*.

Abigail Burnham Bloom teaches Victorian literature at Hunter College. She is the author of *The Literary Monster on Film: Five Nineteenth-Century British Novels and Their Cinematic Adaptations*, editor of *Personal Moments in the Lives of Victorian Women: Selections from Their Autobiographies*, and coeditor of *Victorian Literature and Film Adaptation*.

Oliver S. Buckton is professor of English at Florida Atlantic University, where he teaches Victorian literature, critical theory, and film. He is the author of *Cruising with Robert Louis Stevenson: Travel, Narrative, and the Colonial Body* and *Secret Selves: Confession and Same-Sex Desire in Victorian Autobiography*.

Jenni Calder is the author of *Robert Louis Stevenson: A Life Study*, *Stevenson and Victorian Scotland*, *Lost in the Backwoods: Scots in the North American Wilderness*, *Frontier Scots: The Scots Who Won the West*, the poem cycle *Smoke*, and the autobiography *Not Nebuchadnezzar*.

Robert L. Caserio is professor of English at Penn State University. His *The English Novel, 1900–1950: History and Theory* won the Perkins Prize in 2000. He is the editor of *The Cambridge Companion to the Twentieth-Century English Novel* and coeditor of *The Cambridge History of the English Novel*.

Barbara Chatton is professor emerita of education at the University of Wyoming. She is the author of *Using Poetry across the Curriculum: Learning to Love Language*, *Blurring the Edges: Writing and Children's Literature across the Curriculum*, and *Using Poetry across the Curriculum: A Whole Language Approach*.

Ann C. Colley is SUNY distinguished professor at the State University College of New York, Buffalo. She is the author of *Victorians in the Mountains: Sinking the Sublime*, *Robert Louis Stevenson and the Colonial Imagination*, *Nostalgia in Victorian Culture*, *The Search for Synthesis in Literature and Art*, and *Tennyson and Madness*.

Martin Danahay is professor of English at Brock University. He is the author of *Gender at Work in Victorian Culture* and has produced an edition of *Jekyll and Hyde* as well as the essay collection *Victorian Animal Dreams*.

Dennis Denisoff is chair of English at Ryerson University. He is the author of *Sexual Visuality from Literature to Film* and *Aestheticism and Sexual Parody* and the editor of *The Nineteenth-Century Child and Consumer Culture*. He is working on the monograph "Decadence, Animality, and Natural Dissidence."

Linda Dryden is professor of literature and director of the Centre for Literature and Writing at Edinburgh Napier University. She is the author of *The Modern Gothic* and *Literary Doubles: Stevenson, Wilde and Wells* and the editor of *Stevenson and Conrad: Writers in Transition*.

Ian Duncan is professor of English at the University of California, Berkeley. He is the author of *Modern Romance and Transformations of the Novel: The Gothic, Scott, Dickens* and *Scott's Shadow: The Novel in Romantic Edinburgh*, which won the Saltire Society and National Library of Scotland Research Book of the Year.

Penny Fielding teaches English and Scottish literature at Edinburgh University and is codirector of Edinburgh's Centre for Scottish Writing in the Nineteenth Century. She is the author of *Scotland and the Fictions of Geography: North Britain, 1760–1830* and *Writing and Orality: Nationality, Culture, and Nineteenth-Century Scottish Fiction*.

Jason Goldsmith is associate professor at Butler University, where he offers courses on Romanticism, visual art, and modern critical theory. He has published articles on a range of nineteenth-century topics and is completing a monograph titled "Cult Figures: The Spectacle of Romantic Nationalism, 1802–52."

Scott Hames lectures at the University of Stirling. He is the coeditor of the *International Journal of Scottish Literature* and editor of the *Edinburgh Companion to James Kelman*. His work on Stevenson includes "A Box of Toys: Robert Louis Stevenson and Andrew O'Hagan."

Richard J. Hill teaches English at Chaminade University, Honolulu. He is the author of *Picturing Scotland through the Waverley Novels: Sir Walter Scott and the Origins of the Victorian Illustrated Novel* and is working on a book on the illustrations of Robert Louis Stevenson.

Gordon Hirsch is professor of English at the University of Minnesota. With William Veeder, he edited *Dr. Jekyll and Mr. Hyde after One Hundred Years*. He publishes widely on Stevenson and other nineteenth-century authors.

Wendy R. Katz is professor emerita of English at Saint Mary's University in Halifax. She is the author of *Rider Haggard and the Fiction of Empire: A Critical Study of British Imperial Fiction* and *The Emblems of Margaret Gatty: A Study of Allegory in Nineteenth-Century Children's Literature* and an editor of *Treasure Island*.

J. Derrick McClure recently retired from the University of Aberdeen. He is the author of *Doric: The Dialect of North-East Scotland*, *Language, Poetry and Nationhood: Scots as a Poetic Language from 1878 to the Present*, and *Why Scots Matters*.

Caroline McCracken-Flesher is professor of English at the University of Wyoming. She is the author of *Possible Scotlands: Walter Scott and the Story of Tomorrow* and *The Doctor Dissected: A Cultural Autopsy of the Burke and Hare Murders* and the editor of *Culture, Nation, and the New Scottish Parliament* and *Scotland as Science Fiction*.

Glenda Norquay is professor of Scottish literary studies at Liverpool John Moores University. She is the author of *Robert Louis Stevenson and Theories of Reading: The Reader as Vagabond* and the editor of *R. L. Stevenson on Fiction: An Anthology of Literary and Critical Essays*.

Susan Oliver teaches at the University of Essex. Her *Scott, Byron and the Poetics of Cultural Encounter* won the British Academy's Rose Mary Crawshay Prize. She is a bibliographer for the MLA.

Alan Riach is a poet and professor of Scottish literature at Glasgow University. He is the author of *Arts of Resistance: Poets, Portraits and Landscapes of Modern Scotland* (with

Alexander Moffat), *Representing Scotland in Literature, Popular Culture and Iconography*, *The Poetry of Hugh MacDiarmid*, and *Homecoming*, a collection of poetry.

Thomas Richardson is Eudora Welty Professor of English and dean of the College of Arts and Sciences at Mississippi University for Women. He is the editor of *James Hogg: Contributions to Blackwood's* Edinburgh Magazine, *Volume 1, 1817–1828* and *Contributions to Blackwood's* Edinburgh Magazine, *Volume 2, 1829–1835*.

Leslie S. Rush is associate professor of English education at the University of Wyoming and the coeditor of the NCTE journal *English Education*. Her *Secondary School Literacy: What Research Reveals for Classroom Practice* was nominated for the Literacy Research Association's Edward Frye Award.

Anne Stiles is assistant professor of English at Saint Louis University. She is the author of *Popular Fiction and Brain Science in the Late Nineteenth Century* and the editor of *Neurology and Literature, 1860–1920*. Her articles have appeared in the *Journal of the History of Ideas*, *SEL*, and the *Journal of the History of Neurosciences*.

Graham Tulloch is professor of English at Flinders University. He is the author of *The Language of Walter Scott* and an editor of Walter Scott's *Ivanhoe*, *The Siege of Malta*, and *Bizarro*; Marcus Clarke's *His Natural Life*; Catherine Martin's *An Australian Girl*; and James Hogg's *The Three Perils of Man*.

H. Aram Veeser is professor at the City College of New York. He is the author of *Edward Said: The Charisma of Criticism*, the coauthor of *Painting between the Lines*, and the editor of *The New Historicism*, *The New Historicism Reader*, *Confessions of the Critics*, and *The Stanley Fish Reader*.

Roderick Watson is a poet and critic, recently retired from his professorship at the University of Stirling. He is the author of *The Literature of Scotland*, *The Poetry of Norman MacCaig*, and *Hugh MacDiarmid*. His poetry books include *Into the Blue Wavelengths* and *True History on the Walls*.

Matthew Wickman is associate professor of English and director of the Humanities Center at Brigham Young University. He is the author of *The Ruins of Experience: Scotland's "Romantick" Highlands and the Birth of the Modern Witness*.

Fiona Wilson teaches at Sarah Lawrence College. Her scholarly articles have appeared in *Romanticism's Debatable Lands*, *Keats-Shelley Journal*, *The Edinburgh Companion to Contemporary Scottish Literature*, and *The Edinburgh Companion to Contemporary Scottish Poetry*. Her poetry has appeared in *Best Scottish Poems*, *Poetry Review*, *Grand Street*, and *Literary Review*.

SURVEY PARTICIPANTS

Antje Anderson, *Hastings College*
Martin Axford, *Verkmenntaskoli a Akureyri Iceland*
Emily A. Bernhard Jackson, *University of Arkansas*
Abigail Burnham Bloom, *The New School*
Oliver S. Buckton, *Florida Atlantic University*
Ian Campbell, *University of Edinburgh*
Gerard Carruthers, *University of Glasgow*
Robert L. Caserio, *Penn State University*
Ann C. Colley, *State University College of New York, Buffalo*
John Corbett, *University of Macau*
Ian Duncan, *University of California, Berkeley*
Christofer Foss, *University of Mary Washington*
Nancy Gish, *University of Southern Maine*
Jason Goldsmith, *Butler University*
Evan Gottlieb, *Oregon State University*
Scott Hames, *University of Stirling*
Sarah Hardy, *Hamden-Sydney College*
Krystal Hart, *University of North Texas*
Anthony Hasler, *Saint Louis University*
Richard J. Hill, *Chaminade University, Honolulu*
Gordon Hirsch, *University of Minnesota*
Rebecca Hogan, *University of Wisconsin, Whitewater*
Katherine Linehan, *Oberlin College*
Manfred Malzahn, *United Arab Emirates University*
J. Derrick McClure, *University of Aberdeen*
Ken McNeil, *Eastern Connecticut State University*
Martin McQuillan, *University of Leeds*
Tim Middleton, *Bath Spa University*
Susan Oliver, *University of Essex*
Carla Saggini, *Universita della Tuscia*
Alex Thomson, *University of Edinburgh*
Roderick Watson, *University of Stirling*
Matthew Wickman, *Brigham Young University*

WORKS CITED

Abrams, M. H. *A Glossary of Literary Terms*. 9th ed. Boston: Wadsworth, 2009. Print.

Aldiss, Brian, and David Wingrove. *Trillion Year Spree: The History of Science Fiction*. New York: Atheneum, 1986. Print.

Allen, Janet. *Tools for Teaching Content Literacy*. Portland: Stenhouse, 2004. Print.

Allen, Walter. *The English Novel*. London: Penguin, 1954. Print.

Alliata, Michela Vanon. "'Markheim' and the Shadow of the Other." Ambrosini and Dury, *Robert Louis Stevenson* 299–314.

Ambrosini, Richard. "The Art of Writing and the Pleasure of Reading: R. L. Stevenson as Theorist and Popular Author." Jones, *Robert Louis Stevenson* 21–36.

Ambrosini, Richard, and Richard Dury. Introduction. Ambrosini and Dury, *Robert Louis Stevenson* xiii–xxviii.

———, eds. *Robert Louis Stevenson, Writer of Boundaries*. Madison: U of Wisconsin P, 2006. Print.

Arata, Stephen. *Fictions of Loss in the Victorian Fin de Siècle*. Cambridge: Cambridge UP, 1996. Print.

———. "Stevenson Reading." *Journal of Stevenson Studies* 1 (2004): 192–200. Print.

Ashton, Susanna. *Collaborators in Literary America, 1870–1920*. New York: Palgrave, 2003. Print.

Athanassiou, Dino, dir. *The Legends of Treasure Island*. Voice perf. Dawn French, Juliet Stevenson, Richard E. Grant, Hugh Laurie, and Robert Powell. ITV, 1993–95. Television. Cartoon. 26 episodes.

Autograph Letters, Original Manuscripts, Books and South Sea Curios from the Library of the Late Robert Louis Stevenson. 3 vols. New York: Anderson Auction, 1914. Print.

Avi. Introduction. *Treasure Island*. By Robert Louis Stevenson. New York: Aladdin, 2000. Print.

———. *The True Confessions of Charlotte Doyle*. New York: Harper, 2004. Print.

Baker, Roy Ward, dir. *Dr. Jekyll and Sister Hyde*. Perf. Ralph Bates and Martine Beswick. Hammer Horror, 1971. Thorn EMI, n.d. Videocassette.

Bal, Mieke. *Narratology*. 3rd ed. Toronto: U of Toronto P, 2009. Print.

———. "Over-writing as Un-writing: Descriptions, World-Making, and Novelistic Time." *The Novel*. Vol. 2. Ed. Franco Moretti. Princeton: Princeton UP, 2006. 571–610. Print.

Balfour, Graham. *The Life of Robert Louis Stevenson*. 2 vols. New York: Scribner's, 1901. Print.

Banks, Iain. *Transition*. London: Little, 2009. Print.

Barab, Seymour. *A Child's Garden of Verses*. 2 vols. London: Boosey, n.d. Print. Score for voice and piano.

Barrie, J. M. "Brought Back from Elysium." *Contemporary Review* 57 (1890): 846–54. Print.

———. Peter Pan *and Other Plays*. Oxford: Oxford UP, 1999. Print. Oxford World's Classics.

———. *Peter Pan in Kensington Gardens* [and] *Peter and Wendy*. Oxford: Oxford UP, 2009. Print. Oxford World's Classics.

Bathhurst, Bella. *The Lighthouse Stevensons*. London: Harper, 2000. Print.

Beattie, Hilary J. "Father and Son: The Origins of *Strange Case of Dr. Jekyll and Mr. Hyde*." *Psychoanalytic Study of the Child* 56 (2001): 317–60. Print.

Beaumont, Matthew, ed. *Adventures in Realism*. Oxford: Blackwell, 2007. Print.

Bell, Gavin. *In Search of Tusitala: Travels in the Pacific after Robert Louis Stevenson*. London: Picador, 1995. Print.

Belson, Jerry, dir. *Jekyll and Hyde Together Again*. Perf. Mark Blankfield and Bess Armstrong. Paramount, 1982. Legend, 2002. DVD.

Benjamin, Walter. "The Storyteller." *Illuminations*. Ed. and introd. Hannah Arendt. Trans. Harry Zorn. London: Pimlico, 1999. 83–107. Print.

Besant, Walter. *All Sorts and Conditions of Men: An Impossible Story*. 1882. Open Library, n.d. Web. 24 Sept. 2012.

———. *The Art of Fiction: A Lecture Delivered at the Royal Institution on Friday Evening, April 25, 1884*. London: Chatto, 1884. Print.

———. "On Literary Collaboration." *New Review* 6 (1892): 200–09. Print.

Bhabha, Homi K. *The Location of Culture*. London: Routledge, 1994. Print.

Blake, Howard. *The Land of Counterpane*. Op. 451. 1993. *Howard Blake*. Blake, n.d. Web. 20 Aug. 2011.

Blanton, Casey. *Picturing Paradise: Colonial Photography of Samoa, 1875 to 1925*. Daytona Beach: Southeast Museum of Photography, 1995. Print.

Block, Ed, Jr. "James Sully, Evolutionary Psychology, and Late Victorian Gothic Fiction." *Victorian Studies* 25 (1982): 443–67. Print.

Boone, Troy. *Youth of Darkest England: Working-Class Children at the Heart of the Victorian Empire*. New York: Routledge, 2005. Print.

Borges, Jorge Luis. *Conversations*. Ed. Richard Burgin. Jackson: UP of Mississippi, 1998. Print.

Bourdieu, Pierre. *Distinction: A Social Critique of the Judgment of Taste*. Cambridge: Harvard UP, 1984. Print.

Bowers, Q. David. *Thanhouser Films: An Encyclopedia and History*. Thanhouser Educ., 1997. CD-ROM.

Brantlinger, Patrick. "The Gothic Origins of Science Fiction." *Novel: A Forum on Fiction* 14.1 (1980): 30–43. Print.

Bricusse, Leslie. *Jekyll and Hyde*. Music by Frank Wildhorn. Alley Theatre. May, 1990. Plymouth Theatre. 28 Apr. 1997. Performance.

Brontë, Charlotte. *Jane Eyre*. Ed. Richard Dunn. 3rd ed. New York: Norton, 2001. Print.

Buchan, John. *Greenmantle*. London: Hodder, 1916. Print.

Buckton, Oliver S. *Cruising with Robert Louis Stevenson: Travel, Narrative, and the Colonial Body*. Athens: Ohio UP, 2007. Print.

Buell, Lawrence. *The Future of Environmental Criticism*. Malden: Blackwell, 2005. Print.

Bunge, Nancy. "The Calvinistic Romance: Nathaniel Hawthorne and Robert Louis Stevenson's *Dr Jekyll and Mr* Hyde." *Journal of Stevenson Studies* 6 (2009): 167–80. Print.

Burns, Robert. *Poems and Songs*. Ed. James Kinsley. Oxford: Oxford UP, 1969. Print.

Burton, Richard. *The Book of the Thousand Nights and a Night*. N.p.: Burton Club, 1885–88. *Sir Richard Francis Burton*. Burtoniana.org., n.d. Web. 3 Oct. 2012.

Buzard, James. *The Beaten Track: European Tourism, Literature, and the Ways to "Culture," 1800–1918*. New York: Oxford UP, 1993. Print.

Calder, Jenni. "Figures in a Landscape: Scott, Stevenson, and Routes to the Past." Ambrosini and Dury, *Robert Louis Stevenson* 121–32.

———. *Robert Louis Stevenson: A Life Study*. New York: Oxford UP, 1980. Print.

———, ed. *Stevenson and Victorian Scotland*. Edinburgh: Edinburgh UP, 1981. Print.

Campbell Pearson, Tracey, illus. *The Moon*. By Robert Louis Stevenson. New York: Farrar, 2006. Print.

Carpenter, Angelica Shirley. *Robert Louis Stevenson: Finding Treasure Island*. Minneapolis: Lerner, 1997. Print.

Caruth, Cathy. *Unclaimed Experience: Trauma, Narrative, and History*. Baltimore: Johns Hopkins UP, 1996. Print.

Caserio, Robert L. "Story, Discourse, and Anglo-American Philosophy of Action." *Journal of Narrative Technique* 17.1 (1987): 1–11. Print.

Catalogue of Books and Manuscripts of Robert Louis Stevenson in the Library of the Late Harry Elkins Widener. Philadelphia: privately printed, 1913. Print.

Caveney, Philip. *Sebastian Darke: Prince of Pirates*. New York: Delacorte, 2009. Print.

Chakrabarty, Dipesh. "The Climate of History: Four Theses." *Critical Inquiry* 35.2 (2009): 197–222. Print.

Chalmers, Stephen. *The Penny Piper of Saranac: An Episode in Stevenson's Life*. Boston: Houghton, 1916. Print.

Champagne, Andre, dir. *The Dr. Jekyll and Mr. Hyde Rock 'n' Roll Musical*. Perf. Alan Bernhoft. Andre Champagne Productions. Elite Entertainment, 2008. DVD.

"Christmas Extra." *Pall Mall Gazette*. 5 Dec. 1884: 16. Print.

Clements, Ron, and John Musker, dirs. *Treasure Planet*. Disney, 2003. DVD. Cartoon.

Cohen, Ralph. Introduction. *New Literary History* 39.3 (2008): vii–xx. Print.

Colley, Ann C. *Robert Louis Stevenson and the Colonial Imagination*. Aldershot: Ashgate, 2004. Print.

———. "Robert Louis Stevenson's South Sea Crossings." *Studies in English Literature, 1500–1900* 48.4 (2008): 871–84. Print.

———. "'Writing towards Home': The Landscape of *A Child's Garden of Verses*." *Victorian Poetry* 35.3 (1997): 303–18. Print.

Collins, Wilkie. "The Unknown Public." *Household Words* 18 (1858): 217–22. Print.

Colvin, Sidney, ed. *Letters of Robert Louis Stevenson*. 4 vols. New York: Scribner's, 1911. Print.

———, ed. *Vailima Letters: Being Correspondence Addressed by Robert Louis Stevenson to Sidney Colvin, November 1890–October 1894*. New York: Scribner's, 1986. Print.

Conrad, Joseph. *Heart of Darkness*. New York: Penguin, 1999. Print.

Cook, Eliza. "The Mouse and the Cake." Henderson and Sharpe 1713.

Coote, Stephen. *The Penguin Short History of English Literature*. London: Penguin, 1993. Print.

Cordingly, David. *Under the Black Flag: The Romance and the Reality of Life among the Pirates*. New York: Random, 2006. Print.

Cornwell, Tim. "Read More Books, Kids—but Not This One." *Scotsman.com*. Johnston Publishing, 9 Jan. 2008. Web. 12 Jan. 2008.

Craig, Cairns. "Beyond Reason: Hume, Seth, Macmurray and Scotland's Postmodernity." *Scotland in Theory: Reflections on Culture and Literature*. Ed. Eleanor Bell and Gavin Miller. Amsterdam: Rodopi, 2004. 249–83. Print.

———. *The Modern Scottish Novel: Narrative and the National Imagination*. Edinburgh: Edinburgh UP, 1999. Print.

———. *Out of History: Narrative Paradigms in Scottish and British Culture*. Edinburgh: Polygon, 1996. Print.

Crain, William, dir. *Dr. Black, Mr. Hyde*. By Robert Louis Stevenson. Perf. Bernie Casey. Dimension, 1976. VCI Home Video, 1992. Videocassette. In the United States, *Decision for Doom* and *The Watts Monster*.

Crane, Stephen. *The Red Badge of Courage*. New York: Appleton, 1895. Print.

Crosland, Alan. *Kidnapped*. Perf. Raymond McKee, Robert Cain, and Franklin Hanna. Forum; Edison, 1917. Film.

Culler, Jonathan. "Structuralism and Literature." *Contemporary Approaches to English Studies*. Ed. Hilda Schiff. London: Heinemann, 1977. 59–76. Print.

Cumming, Fiona, dir. *The Master of Ballantrae*. By Robert Louis Stevenson. Perf. Brian Cox and Brigit Forsyth. BBC, 1975. Television. 6 episodes.

Daiches, David. *Robert Louis Stevenson and His World*. London: Thames, 1973. Print.

Danahay, Martin A., ed. *The Strange Case of Dr Jekyll and Mr Hyde*. 2nd ed. Toronto: Broadview, 2005. Print.

Danahay, Martin, and Alex Chisholm. *Jekyll and Hyde Dramatized: The 1887 Richard Mansfield Script and the Evolution of the Story on Stage*. Jefferson: McFarland, 2004. Print.

Davis, Michael. "Incongruous Compounds: Re-reading *Jekyll and Hyde* and Late-Victorian Psychology." *Journal of Victorian Culture* 11.2 (2006): 207–25. Print.

Degas, Edgar. "From Notebooks 1867–83." *Art in Theory, 1815–1900: An Anthology of Changing Ideas*. Ed. Charles Harrison, Paul Wood, and Jason Gaiger. Oxford: Blackwell, 1998. 565–67. Print.

Denisoff, Dennis. "Consumerism and Stevenson's Misfit Masculinities." Ambrosini and Dury, *Robert Louis Stevenson* 286–98.

Derrida, Jacques. *Of Spirit: Heidgger and the Question*. Trans. Geoffrey Bennington and Rachel Bowlby. Chicago: U of Chicago P, 1989. Print.

Devine, Tom. *Scotland's Empire, 1600–1815*. London: Lane, 2003. Print.

Dick, Philip K. *A Scanner Darkly*. Garden City: Doubleday, 1977. Print.

Dickens, Charles. *Great Expectations*. Ed. Edgar Rosenberg. New York: Norton, 1999. Print.

Dimock, Wai Chee. *Through Other Continents: American Literature across Deep Time*. Princeton: Princeton UP, 2006. Print.

Doane, Janice, and Devon Hodges. "Demonic Disturbances of Sexual Identity: The Strange Case of Dr. Jekyll and Mr/s Hyde." *Novel* 23.1 (1989): 63–74. Print.

Douglas, Gordon, dir. *The Black Arrow*. Perf. Louis Hayward, Janet Blair, George Macready, and Lowell Gilmore. Edward Small; Columbia, 1948. Film.

Doyle, Arthur Conan. *The Coming of the Fairies*. New York: Hodder, 1922. Print.

Dryden, Linda. "Robert Louis Stevenson and Popular Culture." *Nordic Journal of English Studies* 9.3 (2010): 11–24. Print.

Dryden, Linda, Stephen Arata, and Eric Massie, eds. *Robert Louis Stevenson and Joseph Conrad: Writers of Transition*. Lubbock: Texas Tech UP, 2009. Print.

Duncan, Ian. *Modern Romance and Transformations of the Novel: The Gothic, Scott, Dickens*. Cambridge: Cambridge UP, 1992. Print.

———. "Stevenson and Fiction." Fielding 11–26.

Dury, Richard. "Crossing the Boundaries of Single Identity: *Dr. Jekyll and Mr. Hyde* and a Paper in a French Scientific Journal." Ambrosini and Dury, *Robert Louis Stevenson* 237–52.

———, ed. *Strange Case of Dr Jekyll and Mr Hyde*. By Robert Louis Stevenson. Edinburgh: Edinburgh UP, 2004. Print.

Ede, Lisa S., and Andrea Lunsford. *Singular Texts / Plural Authors: Perspectives on Collaborative Writing*. Carbondale: Southern Illinois UP, 1990. Print.

Edwards, Owen Dudley. *The Quest for Sherlock Holmes*. Edinburgh: Mainstream, 1983. Print.

Ehnenn, Jill R. *Women's Literary Collaboration, Queerness, and Late-Victorian Culture*. Aldershot: Ashgate, 2008. Print.

Fanon, Frantz. *The Wretched of the Earth*. Trans. Richard Philcox. 1963. New York: Grove, 2004. Print.

Fernandes, Kim, illus. *The Little Land*. By Robert Louis Stevenson. Tonawanda: Kids Can, 2002. Print.

Fielding, Penny, ed. *The Edinburgh Companion to Robert Louis Stevenson*. Edinburgh: Edinburgh UP, 2010. Print.

Finger, Stanley. *Origins of Neuroscience: A History of Explorations into Brain Function*. Oxford: Oxford UP, 1994. Print.

Fisher, Terence, dir. *The Two Faces of Dr. Jekyll*. Perf. Paul Massie. Hammer, 1960. Sony, 1997. Videocassette. In the United States, *House of Fright*.

Fitt, Matthew, trans. *Kidnappit*. By Robert Louis Stevenson. Illus. Alan Grant. Edinburgh: Itchy Coo, 2007. Print.

Fleischman, Sid. *The Giant Rat of Sumatra; or, Pirates Galore*. New York: Greenwillow, 2006. Print.

Fleming, Victor, dir. *Dr. Jekyll and Mr. Hyde*. Perf. Spencer Tracy, Ingrid Bergman, and Lana Turner. MGM, 1941. MGM/UA, 1985. Videocassette.

Forbes, Bryan, dir. *The Wrong Box.* Perf. John Mills, Ralph Richardson, Michael Caine, Dudley Moore, Peter Cook, and Peter Sellers. Salamander; Columbia, 1966. DVD.

Foucault, Michel. *Discipline and Punish: The Birth of the Prison*. New York: Random, 1975. Print.

———. *The History of Sexuality*. 1978. New York: Vintage, 1996. Print.

Fox, Mem. *Tough Boris*. New York: Harcourt, 1994. Print.

Frost, Ginger Suzanne. *Victorian Childhoods*. Westport: Praeger, 2009. Print.

Furnas, J. C. *Voyage to Windward: The Life of Robert Louis Stevenson*. London: Faber, 1952. Print.

Gherman, Beverly. *Robert Louis Stevenson, Teller of Tales.* New York: Atheneum, 1996. Print.

Gilman, Charlotte Perkins. "The Yellow Wallpaper." *Charlotte Perkins Gilman Reader: "The Yellow Wallpaper" and Other Fiction*. Ed. Ann J. Lane. New York: Pantheon, 1980. 3–19. Print.

Goode, Diane, illus. *A Child's Garden of Verses*. By Robert Louis Stevenson. New York: Morrow, 1998. Print.

Gosse, Edmund. *The Life and Letters of Sir Edmund Gosse*. Ed. Evan Charteris. New York: Harper, 1932. Print.

Gramsci, Antonio. *Selections from the Prison Notebooks*. Trans. and ed. Quintin Hoare and Geoffrey Nowell Smith. New York: Intl., 1971. Print.

Grant, Alan, adapt. *Kidnapped.* By Robert Louis Stevenson. Illus. Cam Kennedy. Modern Text Ed. Edinburgh: Barrington, 2007. Print.

Gray, William. *Death and Fantasy: Essays on Philip Pullman, C. S. Lewis, George MacDonald and R. L. Stevenson*. Cambridge: Cambridge Scholars, 2009. Print.

———. *Robert Louis Stevenson: A Literary Life*. London: Palgrave-Macmillan, 2004. Print.

Greenaway, Kate. *Kate Greenaway's Birthday Book*. 1880. London: Warne, 1963. Print.

Greene, Carol. *Robert Louis Stevenson: Author of* A Child's Garden of Verses. Chicago: Children's, 1995. Print.

Greenslade, William. *Degeneration, Culture, and the Novel, 1880–1940*. Cambridge: Cambridge UP, 2010. Print.

Greven, David. *Manhood in Hollywood from Bush to Bush*. Austin: U of Texas P, 2009. Print.

Grover, Max, illus. *Where Go the Boats? Play Poems of Robert Louis Stevenson*. New York: Harcourt, 1998. Print.

Guillory, John. *Cultural Capital: The Problem of Literary Canon Formation*. Chicago: U of Chicago P, 1994. Print.

Hacking, Ian. *Rewriting the Soul: Multiple Personality and the Sciences of Memory.* Princeton: Princeton UP, 1995. Print.

Haggard, H. Rider. *King Solomon's Mines*. Oxford: Oxford UP, 1989. Print.

Haggard, Lilias Rider. *The Cloak That I Left: A Biography of the Author Henry Rider Haggard K.B.E.* London: Hodder, 1951. Print.

Halberstam, Judith. “An Introduction to Gothic Monstrosity.” Linehan, *Strange Case* 128–31.

Hamilton, Tim, illus. Treasure Island*: The Graphic Novel*. London: Puffin, 2005. Print.

Hammond, J. R. *A Robert Louis Stevenson Chronology*. London: Macmillan, 1997. Print.

Harman, Claire. *Myself and the Other Fellow: A Life of Robert Louis Stevenson*. London: Harper, 2005. Print.

———. *Robert Louis Stevenson: A Biography*. London: Harper, 2005. Print.

Harrington, Anne. *Medicine, Mind, and the Double Brain.* Princeton: Princeton UP, 1987. Print.

Hart, F. R. *The Scottish Novel: From Smollett to Spark*. Cambridge: Harvard, 1978. Print.

Hart, James D., ed. *From Scotland to Silverado*. By Robert Louis Stevenson. Cambridge: Harvard UP, 1966. Print.

———. Introduction. Hart, *From Scotland* xiii–li.

Haskin, Byron, dir. *Treasure Island*. Perf. Robert Newton. RKO-Disney, 1950. Disney, 2003. DVD.

Hatcher, Jeffrey. *Dr. Jekyll and Mr. Hyde*. New York: Dramatists Play Service, 2008. Print.

Hawthorne, Nathaniel. *The Scarlet Letter*. 1846. London: Dent, 1971. Print.

Heath, Stephen. “Psychopathia Sexualis: Stevenson’s *Strange Case*.” *Critical Quarterly* 28.1-2 (1986): 93–108. Print.

Heidegger, Martin. *Being and Time*. Trans. John Macquarrie and Edward Robinson. San Francisco: Harper, 1962. Print.

Henderson, Heather, and William Sharpe, eds. *The Victorian Age*. 2nd ed. New York: Longman, 2003. Print. Vol. 2B of *The Longman Anthology: British Literature*.

Henderson, Lucius, dir. *Dr. Jekyll and Mr. Hyde*. Perf. James Cruze, Marguerite Snow, and Marie Eline. Thanhouser, 1912. DVD.

Hennessy, James Pope. *Robert Louis Stevenson*. New York: Simon, 1974. Print.

Henson, Brian, dir. *Muppet Treasure Island*. Disney, 1996. Disney, 2005. DVD.

Herbert, Zbigniew. “Elegy of Fortinbras.” Trans. Czesław Miłosz. *Encounter* 17.2 (1961): 32. Print.

Heston, Fraser Clarke, dir. *Treasure Island*. Perf. Charlton Heston, Christian Bale, and Oliver Reed. Turner Home Entertainment, 1990. Videocassette.

Hickox, Douglas, dir. *The Master of Ballantrae.* Perf. Michael York, Timothy Dalton, John Gielgud, Brian Blessed, and Finola Hughes. Columbia, 1984. Videocassette.

Hillier, Robert Irwin. *The South Seas Fiction of Robert Louis Stevenson*. Frankfurt: Lang, 1989. Print.

Hinchcliffe, Peter, and Catherine Kerrigan. Introduction and textual notes. *The Ebb-Tide: A Trio and Quartette*. By Robert Louis Stevenson and Lloyd Osbourne. Ed. Hinchcliffe and Kerrigan. Edinburgh: Edinburgh UP, 1995. xvii–xxxi, 133–72. Print.

Hirsch, Gordon. "*Frankenstein*, Detective Fiction, and *Jekyll and Hyde*." Veeder and Hirsch 223–46.

Hogg, James. *The Private Memoirs and Confessions of a Justified Sinner*. Oxford: Oxford UP, 2010. Print.

Holmes, Richard. *Footsteps: Adventures of a Romantic Biographer*. New York: Vintage, 1996. Print.

Honaker, Lisa. "'One Man to Rely On': Long John Silver and the Shifting Character of Victorian Boys' Fiction." *Journal of Narrative Theory* 34.1 (2004): 27–53. Print.

Hough, John, dir. *The Black Arrow*. Perf. Oliver Reed, Benedict Taylor, and Georgia Stowe. Disney Cable Network, 1985. Film.

———, dir. *Treasure Island*. Perf. Orson Welles. Central Cinema Company, 1972. DVD.

Howells, William Dean. "Editor's Study." *Harper's New Monthly Magazine* 74.443 (1887): 824–29. Print.

Hunt, Peter. *Children's Literature*. Oxford: Blackwell, 2001. Print.

Irvine, Robert P. "Romance and Social Class." Fielding 27–40.

Jacques, Brian. *The Angel's Command*. New York: Philomel, 2003. Print.

James, Henry. *The American*. New York: Signet, 2005. Print.

———. "The Art of Fiction." *Longman's Magazine* 4 (1884): 502–21. Rpt. in J. Smith 53–85.

Jarrott, Charles, dir. *The Strange Case of Dr. Jekyll and Mr. Hyde*. Perf. Jack Palance. Canadian Broadcasting, 1968. MPI, 2002. DVD.

Jefford, Andrew. "Dr. Jekyll and Professor Nabokov: Reading a Reading." Noble, *Robert Louis Stevenson* 47–73.

Jeffords, Susan. *Hard Bodies: Hollywood Masculinity in the Reagan Era*. New Brunswick: Rutgers UP, 1994. Print.

Jeffrey, Francis. "*The Excursion*." *Edinburgh Review* 24 (1814): 1–30. Print.

Jetton, Tamara L., and Janice Dole, eds. *Adolescent Literacy Research and Practice*. New York: Guilford, 2004. Print.

Johnstone, Arthur. *Recollections of Robert Louis Stevenson in the Pacific*. London: Chatto, 1905. Print.

Jolly, Roslyn. *Robert Louis Stevenson in the Pacific: Travel, Empire, and the Author's Profession*. Farnham: Ashgate, 2009. Print.

———. "Stevenson's 'Sterling Domestic Fiction,' 'The Beach of Falesá.'" *Review of English Studies* 50.200 (1999): 463–82. Print.

Jones, William B., Jr. *Classics Illustrated: A Cultural History*. Jefferson: McFarland, 2001. Print.

———, ed. *Robert Louis Stevenson Reconsidered: New Critical Perspectives*. Jefferson: McFarland, 2003. Print.

Kaplan, Justin. *Mr Clemens and Mark Twain*. London: Cape, 1967. Print.

Katz, Wendy W. "Whitman and Thoreau as Literary Stowaways in Stevenson's American Writings." Ambrosini and Dury, *Robert Louis Stevenson* 327–37.

Keach, William. "A Transatlantic Romantic Century." *European Romantic Review* 11.1 (2000): 31–34. Print.

Keating, Peter. *The Haunted Study: A Social History of the English Novel, 1875–1914.* London: Fontana, 1991. Print.

Keighley, William, dir. *The Master of Ballantrae.* Perf. Errol Flynn, Roger Livesey, Anthony Steel, and Beatrice Campbell. Warner Bros., 1953. Warner, 2003. DVD.

King, Stephen. *The Dark Half.* New York: Viking, 1989. Print.

Kirk, Daniel, illus. *Block City.* By Robert Louis Stevenson. New York: Simon, 2005. Print.

Klaper, Steve, and Caitlin M. G. Klaper. *I Have a Little Shadow: A Child's Garden of Songs Inspired by the Poems of Robert Louis Stevenson.* Klaper and Klaper, 2005. Web. 20 Aug. 2011.

Koestenbaum, Wayne. *Double Talk: The Erotics of Male Literary Collaboration.* New York: Routledge, 1989. Print.

———. "The Shadow on the Bed: Dr. Jekyll, Mr. Hyde, and the Labouchère Amendment." Spec. issue of *Critical Matrix* 1 (1988): 31–55. Print.

Kucich, John. "Melancholy Magic: Masochism, Stevenson, Anti-Imperialism." *Nineteenth-Century Literature* 56.3 (2001): 364–400. Print.

Lacoue-Labarthe, Philippe. *Heidegger, Art and Politics: The Fiction of the Political.* Trans. Chris Turner. Oxford: Blackwell, 1990. Print.

Ladson-Billings, Gloria. "Toward a Theory of Culturally Relevant Pedagogy." *American Educational Research Journal* 21.3 (1995): 465–91. Print.

Lamont, Charles. *Abbott and Costello Meet Dr. Jekyll and Mr. Hyde.* Perf. Bud Abbott, Lou Costello, and Boris Karloff. Universal, 1953. MCA, 1983. Videocassette.

Landon, Brooks. *Science Fiction after 1900: From Steam Man to the Stars.* New York: Twayne, 1997. Print.

Lang, Glenna, illus. *My Shadow.* By Robert Louis Stevenson. Boston: Godine, 1989. Print.

Laplanche, Jean, and J.-B. Pontalis. *The Language of Psycho-analysis.* Trans. Donald Nicholson-Smith. New York: Norton, 1974. Print.

Lawler, Donald. "Reframing Jekyll and Hyde: Robert Louis Stevenson and the Strange Case of Gothic Science Fiction." Veeder and Hirsch 247–61.

Leask, Nigel. *Curiosity and the Aesthetics of Travel Writing, 1770–1840.* Oxford: Oxford UP, 2004. Print.

Lee, Stan. *The Incredible Hulk 1.* Illus. Jack Kirby. New York: Marvel Comics, 1962. Print.

Le Guin, Ursula K., and Brian Attebery, eds. *The Norton Book of Science Fiction.* New York: Norton, 1997. Print.

Lenman, Bruce. *The Jacobite Risings in Britain, 1689–1746.* London: Methuen, 1980. Print.

Levin, Harry. *The Power of Blackness: Hawthorne, Poe, Melville.* London: Faber, 1958. Print.

Lewis, Jerry, dir. *The Nutty Professor.* Perf. Jerry Lewis. Paramount, 1963. Paramount, 2004. DVD.

Linehan, Katherine Bailey. "'Closer Than a Wife': The Strange Case of Dr. Jekyll's Significant Other." Jones, *Robert Louis Stevenson* 85–100.

———, ed. *Strange Case of Dr. Jekyll and Mr. Hyde*. By Robert Louis Stevenson. New York: Norton, 2003. Print. Norton Critical Ed.

Luckhurst, Roger, ed. Strange Case of Dr Jekyll and Mr Hyde *and Other Tales*. Oxford: Oxford UP, 2008. Print.

Lukács, Georg. *The Historical Novel*. Trans. Hannah Mitchell and Stanley Mitchell. New York: Humanities, 1965.

———. *The Meaning of Contemporary Realism*. Trans. John Mander and Necke Mander. London: Merlin, 1962. Print.

Lumsden, Alison. "Stevenson, Scott, and Scottish History." Fielding 70–85.

Lyotard, Jean François. *Heidegger and "The Jews."* Trans. Andreas Michel and Mark Roberts. Minneapolis: U of Minnesota P, 1990. Print.

MacCaig, Norman. "Space Travel." *The Poems of Norman MacCaig*. Ed. Ewen McCaig. Edinburgh: Polygon, 2005. 196–97. Print.

MacDhomhnaill, Iain, trans. *Fo Bhruid*. Adapt. Alan Grant. Illus. Cam Kennedy. Lanark: Waverley, 2007. Print. Trans. of *Kidnapped*, by Robert Louis Stevenson.

MacDiarmid, Hugh. "The Sauchs in the Reuch Heuch Hauch." *Selected Poetry*. Ed. Alan Riach and Michael Grieve. Introd. Eliot Weinberger. New York: New Directions, 1993. 10. Print.

MacDuffie, Allen. "Irreversible Transformations: Robert Louis Stevenson's *Dr. Jekyll and Mr. Hyde* and Scottish Energy Science." *Representations* 96 (2006): 1–20. Print.

Machen, Arthur. *Things Near and Far*. New York: Knopf, 1923. Print.

———. The Three Impostors *and Other Stories*. Hayward: Chaosium, 2007. Print.

Mackay, Margaret. *The Violent Friend: The Story of Mrs. Robert Louis Stevenson, 1840–1914*. London: Dent, 1969. Print.

Mackinnon, Douglas, and Matt Lipsey, dirs. *Jekyll*. Perf. James Nesbitt. BBC, 2007. BBC Video, 2007. DVD.

Maclaren, Ian. *Beside the Bonnie Brier Bush*. London: Hodder and Stoughton, 1894. Print.

Maclaren, Pharic, dir. *The Master of Ballantrae*. Perf. John Breslin and John Cairney. BBC, 1962. Television. 6 episodes.

Maclean, Fitzroy. *Scotland: A Concise History*. 2nd ed. London: Thames, 2000. Print.

Maixner, Paul, ed. *Robert Louis Stevenson: The Critical Heritage*. London: Routledge, 1981. Print.

Mamoulian, Rouben, dir. *Dr. Jekyll and Mr. Hyde*. Perf. Frederic March and Miriam Hopkins. Paramount, 1931. MGM, 1989. DVD.

Mann, Delbert, dir. *Kidnapped*. Perf. Michael Caine. Omnibus, 1971. DVD.

Manning, Susan. *Fragments of Union: Making Connections in Scottish and American Writing*. Houndmills: Palgrave, 2002. Print.

Manning, Susan, and Andrew Taylor, eds. *Transatlantic Literary Studies: A Reader*. Baltimore: Johns Hopkins UP, 2007. Print.

Martin, Valerie. *Mary Reilly*. New York: Doubleday, 1990. Print.

Marx, Karl. *A Contribution to the Critique of Political Economy*. 1859. Trans. S. W. Ryazanskaya. Moscow: Progress, 1977. Print.

Masson, Rosaline, ed. *I Can Remember Robert Louis Stevenson*. New York: Stokes, 1923. Print.

Matthews, Brander. "The Art and Mystery of Collaboration." *Longman's Magazine* 15 (1890): 157–70. Print.

McCracken-Flesher, Caroline. "Cultural Projections: The 'Strange Case' of Dr. Jekyll, Mr. Hyde, and Cinematic Response." *Narrative and Culture*. Ed. Janice Carlisle and Daniel R. Schwarz. Athens: U of Georgia P, 1994. 179–99. Print.

———. Introduction. *Scotland as Science Fiction*. Ed. McCracken-Flesher. Lewisburg: Bucknell UP, 2011. 1–14. Print.

———. "Mapping David Balfour: Scotland, Scots, Sequels, and Scenery." Stevenson Textual Workshop. 11 July 2008. U of Edinburgh. Lecture.

———. "Thinking Nationally / Writing Colonially? Scott, Stevenson, and England." *NOVEL: A Forum on Fiction* 24.3 (1991): 296–318. Print.

McCrone, David, Angela Morris, and Richard Kiely. *Scotland—the Brand: The Making of Scottish Heritage*. Edinburgh: Edinburgh UP, 1995. Print.

McKay, George L. *A Stevenson Library: Catalogue of a Collection of Writings by and about Robert Louis Stevenson Formed by Edwin J. Beinecke*. 6 vols. New Haven: Yale UP, 1951–54. Print.

McLynn, Frank. *Robert Louis Stevenson: A Biography*. New York: Random, 1993. Print.

Mehew, Ernest. Introduction and notes. *The Wrong Box*. By Robert Louis Stevenson and Lloyd Osbourne. Ed. Mehew. London: Nonesuch, 1989. vii–xxxix, 183–218. Print.

———, ed. *Selected Letters of Robert Louis Stevenson*. 1997. New Haven: Yale UP, 2001. Print.

Meier, Sid. *Pirates!* Micro Prose, 1987. Video game.

Meltzer, Françoise. "Reviving the Fairy Tree: Tales of European Sanctity." *Critical Inquiry* 35.3 (2009): 493–520. Print.

Melville, Herman. "Hawthorne and His Mosses." *Literary World* 17–24 Aug. 1850. *Nathaniel Hawthorne, 1804–1864*. Ibiblio.org, n.d. Web. 13 Jan. 2012.

———. *Typee: A Peep at Polynesian Life*. 1846. Harmondsworth: Penguin, 1972. Print.

Menikoff, Barry, ed. *The Beach of Falesá*. Stanford: Stanford UP, 1987. Print.

———. Introduction. *Kidnapped; or, The Lad with the Silver Button*. San Marino: Huntington Lib., 1999. xi–lxvi. Print.

———. *Narrating Scotland: The Imagination of Robert Louis Stevenson*. Columbia: U of South Carolina P, 2005. Print.

———. "'These Problematic Shores': Robert Louis Stevenson in the South Seas." *The Ends of the Earth, 1876–1918*. Ed. Simon Gatrell. London: Ashfield, 1992. 141–46. Print.

Mighall, Robert. *A Geography of Victorian Gothic Fiction: Mapping History's Nightmares*. New York: Oxford, 1999. Print.

Miller, Thomas. "The Watercress Seller." Henderson and Sharpe 1714–15.

Moore, Alan. *The League of Extraordinary Gentlemen 1*. Illus. Kevin O'Neill. New York: DC Comics, 2002. Print.

———. *The League of Extraordinary Gentlemen 2*. Illus. Kevin O'Neill. New York: DC Comics, 2004. Print.

Moretti, Franco. *Signs Taken for Wonders: Essays in the Sociology of Literary Forms*. Trans. Susan Fischer, David Forgacs, and David Miller. London: Verso, 1983. Print.

Morgan, Edwin. "Ariel Freed." *Virtual and Other Realities*. Manchester: Carcanet, 1997. 101. Print.

———. "Caliban Falls Asleep in the Isle Full of Noises." *Poems of Thirty Years*. Manchester: Carcanet, 1982. 427. Print.

Mulholland, Honor. "Robert Louis Stevenson and the Romance Form." Noble, *Robert Louis Stevenson* 96–118.

Mulvey, Laura. "Visual Pleasure and Narrative Cinema." *Screen* 16.3 (1975): 6–18. Print.

Murphy, Jim. *Across America on the Emigrant Train*. New York: Clarion, 1993. Print.

Nabokov, Vladimir. "*The Strange Case of Dr. Jekyll and Mr. Hyde*." *Lectures on Literature*. New York: Harcourt, 1980. 179–206. Print.

Nabokov, Vladimir, and Edmund Wilson. *Dear Bunny, Dear Volodya: The Nabokov-Wilson Letters, 1940–1971*. Ed. Simon Karlinsky. Berkeley: U of California P, 2001. Print.

Nash, Andrew. *Kailyard and Scottish Literature*. Amsterdam: Rodopi, 2007. Print.

Naugrette, Jean-Pierre. *R. L. Stevenson [et] A. Conan Doyle: Aventures de la fiction*. Rennes: Terre de Brume, 2003. Print.

Nayder, Lillian. *Unequal Partners: Charles Dickens, Wilkie Collins, and Victorian Authorship*. Ithaca: Cornell UP, 2002. Print.

Neilan, Marshall, dir. *The Bottle Imp*. Perf. Sessue Hayakawa. 1917. Film.

Newman, Lance, ed. *Sullen Fires across the Atlantic: Essays in Transatlantic Romanticism*. U of Maryland, Nov. 2006. Web. 26 Feb. 2012. Romantic Circles Praxis Ser.

Noble, Andrew. Introduction. *From the Clyde to California, Robert Louis Stevenson's Emigrant Journey*. Ed. Noble. Aberdeen: Aberdeen UP, 1985. 3–33. Print.

———, ed. *Robert Louis Stevenson*. Totowa: Vision; Barnes, 1983. Print.

Nokes, Jeffery, and Janice Dole. "Helping Adolescent Readers through Explicit Strategy Instruction." Jetton and Dole 162–81.

Norquay, Glenda, ed. *R. L. Stevenson on Fiction: An Anthology of Literary and Critical Essays*. Edinburgh: Edinburgh UP, 1999. Print.

———. *Robert Louis Stevenson and Theories of Reading: The Reader as Vagabond*. Manchester: Manchester UP, 2007. Print.

Norrington, Stephen, dir. *The League of Extraordinary Gentlemen*. Perf. Sean Connery, Stuart Townsend, and Peta Wilson. Twentieth Century–Fox, 2003. DVD.

Ó'Donghaile, Deaglán. "Conrad, the Stevensons, and the Imagination of Urban Chaos." Dryden, Arata, and Massie 159–74.

O'Neill, Marnie. "Language, Literacy, and Learning: Modelling Integration and Reflective Practices in Preservice Teacher Education." *Teaching and Teacher Education* 16.5-6 (2000): 613–33. *ERIC*. Web. 30 Apr. 2012.

Osbourne, Lloyd. *An Intimate Portrait of R. L. S.* New York: Scribner's, 1924. Print.

Pace, Joel. "Towards a Taxonomy of Transatlantic Romanticism(s)." *Literature Compass* 5.2 (2008): 228–91.

Palahniuk, Chuck. *Fight Club*. New York: Norton, 1996. Print.

Passer, Ivan, dir. *Kidnapped*. Perf. Armand Assante. American Zoetrope, 1995. Allumination, 2004. DVD.

Paterson, Stuart. *Treasure Island*. Play. London: Hern, 2007. Print.

Pearson, Ridley, and Dave Barry. *Peter and the Starcatchers*. New York: Disney, 2004. Print.

Pembroke, Scott, dir. *Dr. Pyckle and Mr. Pryde*. Perf. Stan Laurel. Joe Rock Comedies, 1925. Videocassette.

Pick, Daniel. *Faces of Degeneration: A European Disorder, c. 1848–1918*. Cambridge: Cambridge UP, 1993. Print.

Pratt, Mary Louise. *Imperial Eyes: Travel Writing and Transculturation*. London: Routledge, 1992. Print.

Prideaux, W. F. *A Bibliography of the Works of Robert Louis Stevenson*. Ithaca: Cornell UP, 2009. Print.

Priestley, J. B. *The English Novel*. London: Benn, 1931. Print.

Probst, Robert. *Response and Analysis: Teaching Literature in Secondary School*. 2nd ed. Portsmouth: Heinemann, 2004. Print.

Proctor, Richard. "Dual Consciousness." *Cornhill* 35 (1877): 86–105. Print.

———. "Have We Two Brains?" *Cornhill* 31 (1875): 146–66. Print.

Punter, David. *The Literature of Terror*. New York: Longman, 1996. Print.

Rand, Ted, illus. *My Shadow*. By Robert Louis Stevenson. New York: Putnam, 1990. Print.

Rankin, Nicholas. *Dead Man's Chest: Travels after Robert Louis Stevenson*. London: Faber, 1987. Print.

Reed, Thomas L., Jr. *The Transforming Draught:* Jekyll and Hyde, *Robert Louis Stevenson and the Victorian Alcohol Debate*. Jefferson: McFarland, 2006. Print.

Reid, Alastair, dir. *Dr. Jekyll and Mr. Hyde*. BBC. 20 Nov. 1986. Television.

Reid, Julia. "Childhood and Psychology." Fielding 41–52.

———. *Robert Louis Stevenson, Science, and the Fin de Siècle*. Basingstoke: Palgrave-Macmillan, 2006. Print.

Rennie, Neil. *Far-Fetched Facts: The Literature of Travel and the Idea of the South Seas*. Oxford: Oxford UP, 1999. Print.

Renton, Nicholas, dir. *The Ebb Tide*. By Robert Louis Stevenson. Koch Vision, 1997. DVD.

Richison, Jeannine, Anita Hernandez, and Marcia Carter. *Theme-Sets for Secondary Students: How to Scaffold Core Literature*. Portsmouth: Heinemann, 2006. Print.

Riddell, Chris, and Paul Stewart. *The Last of the Sky Pirates*. Oxford: Fickling, 2005. Print. Book 5 of the Edge Chronicles.

Rilke, Rainer Maria. "The Spirit Ariel (after reading Shakespeare's *Tempest*)." *Selected Poems*. Trans. J. B. Leishman. Harmondsworth: Penguin, 1972. 73–74. Print.

Robert Louis Stevenson, 1850–1894. U Libs. Rare Book and Special Collections, U of

South Carolina, n.d. Web. 9 Apr. 2012. <http://library.sc.edu/spcoll/britlit/rls/rls.html>.

Robertson, J. Logie. "On the Decadence of the Scots Language, Manners and Customs." *Poems*. Dundee: John Lang, 1878. 42–62. Print.

Robertson, John Stuart, dir. *Dr. Jekyll and Mr. Hyde*. Perf. John Barrymore, Martha Mansfield, and Nita Naldi. Famous Players–Lasky/Paramount, 1920. Viking Entertainment, 1986. Videocassette.

Robinson, Charles, illus. *A Child's Garden of Verses*. By Robert Louis Stevenson. 1895. New York: Robinson, 1898. Print.

Rohde, David. "Army Enlists Anthropology in War Zones." *New York Times*. New York Times, 5 Oct. 2007. Web. 26 Feb. 2012.

Rose, Brian A. *Jekyll and Hyde Adapted: Dramatizations of Cultural Anxiety*. Westport: Greenwood, 1996. Print.

Rosenblatt, Louise M. *The Reader, the Text, the Poem: The Transactional Theory of the Literary Work*. Carbondale: Southern Illinois UP, 1978. Print.

Rosenshine, Barak, and Carla Meister. "Reciprocal Teaching." *Review of Educational Research* 64.4 (1994): 479–530. Print.

Said, Edward. *Orientalism*. New York: Vintage, 1979. Print.

———. *Yeats and Decolonization*. Derry: Field Day Theatre, 1988. Print. Field Day Pamphlet 15.

Samuels, Rachel, dir. *The Suicide Club*. Perf. David Morrissey, Paul Bettany, and Jonathan Pryce. New Concorde, 2001. DVD. Also titled *The Game of Death*.

Sandison, Alan. *Robert Louis Stevenson and the Appearance of Modernism: A Future Feeling*. Basingstoke: Macmillan, 1996. Print.

Scott, Walter. *The Bride of Lammermoor*. 1819. Ed. J. H. Alexander. Edinburgh: Edinburgh UP, 1995. Print.

———. *The Tale of Old Morality*. 1816. Ed. Douglas S. Mack. Edinburgh: Edinburgh UP, 1993. Print.

———. *Waverley*. 1814. Ed. Peter Garside. Edinburgh: Edinburgh UP, 2007. Print.

Sedgwick, Eve Kosofsky. *Between Men: English Literature and Male Homosocial Desire*. New York: Columbia UP, 1985. Print. Gender and Culture.

Shakespeare, William. *Hamlet*. New York: Signet, 1963. Print.

———. *King Lear*. New York: Signet, 1963. Print.

———. *The Tempest*. New York: Signet, 1964. Print.

———. *The Tragedy of Julius Caesar*. New York: Signet, 2000. Print.

———. *The Tragical History of Hamlet Prince of Denmark*. New York: Signet, 1998. Print.

Shand, Alexander Innes. "Contemporary Literature: VII: Readers." *Blackwood's Magazine* 126 (1879): 235–56. Print.

Sheridan, Richard Brinsley. *The Rivals*. 1775. Ed. G. A. Aitken. London: J. M. Dent, 1897. Print.

Showalter, Elaine. *Sexual Anarchy: Gender and Culture at the Fin de Siècle*. New York: Viking, 1990. Print.

Skal, David J. *Hollywood Gothic: The Tangled Web of* Dracula *from Novel to Stage to Screen*. New York: Faber, 2004. Print.

Smith, Adam. *An Inquiry into the Nature and Causes of the Wealth of Nations*. 1776. New York: Collier, 1909. Print.

Smith, Janet Adam, ed. *Henry James and Robert Louis Stevenson: A Record of Friendship and Criticism*. London: Hart-Davis, 1948. Print.

Smith, Vanessa. *Literary Culture and the Pacific: Nineteenth-Century Textual Encounters*. Cambridge: Cambridge UP, 1998. Print.

Sontag, Susan. *I, Etcetera*. New York: Farrar, 1978. Print.

———. *On Photography*. New York: Farrar, 1973. Print.

Stableford, Brian. *Scientific Romance in Britain, 1890–1950*. New York: St. Martin's, 1985. Print.

Steer, Dugald A. *Pirateology: The Pirate Hunter's Companion*. Somerville: Candlewick, 2006. Print.

Stern, Simon. Rev. of *The Strange Case of Dr. Jekyll and Mr. Hyde*, by Robert Louis Stevenson. *Law and Politics Book Review* 18.4 (2008): 356–59. *JSTOR*. Web. 10 Mar. 2009.

Stevenson, Fanny. *The Cruise of the* Janet Nichol *among the South Sea Islands: A Diary by Mrs Robert Louis Stevenson*. New York: Scribner's, 1914. Print.

Stevenson, Randall. "A Postmodern Scotland?" *Beyond Scotland: New Contexts for Twentieth-Century Scottish Literature*. Ed. Gerard Carruthers, David Goldie, and Alastair Renfrew. Amsterdam: Rodopi, 2004. 209–28. Print.

Stevenson, Robert, dir. *Kidnapped*. Perf. James MacArthur, Peter Finch, and Peter O'Toole. Walt Disney, 1960. Disney, 1997. Videocassette.

Stevenson, Robert Louis. *The Collected Poems of Robert Louis Stevenson*. Ed. Roger C. Lewis. Edinburgh: Edinburgh UP, 2003. Print.

———. *The Complete Stories of Robert Louis Stevenson*. Ed. Barry Menikoff. New York: Modern Lib.–Random, 2002. Print.

———. *The Letters of Robert Louis Stevenson*. Ed. Bradford A. Booth and Ernest Mehew. 8 vols. New Haven: Yale UP, 1994–95. Print.

———. "A Pearl Island: Penrhyn." *Sun* (New York) 24 May 1891: 23. Print.

———. *Robert Louis Stevenson's* Kidnapped; or, The Lad with the Silver Button*: The Original Text*. Ed. Barry Menikoff. San Marino: Huntington Lib., 1999. Print.

———. "The Sick Man." J. Hart, *From Scotland* 46–56.

———. *The Works of Robert Louis Stevenson: Tusitala Edition*. 35 vols. London: Heinemann, 1923–24. Print.

Stiles, Anne. "Robert Louis Stevenson's *Jekyll and Hyde* and the Double Brain." *Studies in English Literature, 1500–1900* 46.4 (2006): 879–900. Print.

Stillwell, Nick, dir. *Jekyll and Hyde*. Perf. Bryan Fisher, Bree Turner. Lionsgate, 2005. DVD.

Stowe, Harriet Beecher. *Sunny Memories of Foreign Lands*. 2 vols. Boston: Phillips; Sampson, 1854. Print.

Sullivan, T. R., and Richard Mansfield. *Dr. Jekyll and Mr. Hyde*. Danahay and Chisholm 47–78.

Swearingen, Roger, ed. *The Amateur Emigrant*. 2 vols. Ashland: Osborne, 1976–77. Print.

———. *The Prose Writings of Robert Louis Stevenson: A Guide*. Hamden: Archon, 1980. Print.

"Table Rules for Little Folks." Henderson and Sharpe 1712–13.

Taylor, Jenny Bourne, and Sally Shuttleworth. *Embodied Selves: An Anthology of Psychological Texts, 1830–1890*. Oxford: Oxford UP, 1998. Print.

Thomas, Roy, adapt. *Treasure Island (Marvel Illustrated)*. Illus. Mario Gully. New York: Marvel, 2007. Print.

Treglown, Jeremy, ed. *The Lantern Bearers*. Lanham: Cooper Square, 1999. Print.

Tudor, Tasha, illus. *A Child's Garden of Verses*. By Robert Louis Stevenson. New York: Oxford, 1947. Print.

Turgenev, Ivan. *A Lear of the Steppes*. Trans. Constance Garnett. London: Heinemann, 1920. Print.

Turner, Mark. *The Literary Mind*. Oxford: Oxford UP, 1996. Print.

Twain, Mark. "Explanatory." *The Adventures of Huckleberry Finn*. Harmondsworth: Puffin, 1967. 6. Print.

Underwood, Terry, and P. David Pearson. "Teaching Struggling Adolescent Readers to Comprehend What They Read." Jetton and Dole 135–62.

Veeder, William. "Children of the Night: Stevenson and Patriarchy." Veeder and Hirsch 107–60.

Veeder, William, and Gordon Hirsch, eds. *Dr. Jekyll and Mr. Hyde after One Hundred Years*. Chicago: U of Chicago P, 1988. Print.

Verbinski, Gore, dir. *Pirates of the Caribbean*. Disney, 2003. Film.

Vergil. *The Aeneid*. Trans. John Dryden. Ed. Howard Clarke. University Park: Penn State UP, 1989. Print.

Villa, Luisa. "Quarreling with the Father." Ambrosini and Dury, *Robert Louis Stevenson* 109–20.

Vorpahl, Ben M. "Henry James and Owen Wister." *Pennsylvania Magazine of History and Biography* 95.3 (1971): 291–338. Print.

Wainwright, A. D. *Robert Louis Stevenson: A Catalogue*. Princeton: Princeton U Lib., 1971. Print.

Warren, Austin. *The New England Conscience*. Ann Arbor: U of Michigan P, 1966. Print.

Watson, Roderick. "'The Unrest and Movement of Our Century': The Universe of *The Wrecker*." *Journal of Stevenson Studies* 4 (2007): 114–28. Print.

———. "'You Cannot Fight Me with a Word': *The Master of Ballantrae* and the Wilderness beyond Dualism." *Journal of Stevenson Studies* 1 (2004): 1–23. Print.

Watt, Ian. *The Rise of the Novel: Studies in Defoe, Richardson and Fielding*. 1957. London: Hogarth, 1987. Print.

Webb, Jean. "Conceptualising Childhood: Robert Louis Stevenson's *A Child's Garden of Verses*." *Cambridge Journal of Education* 32.3 (2002): 359–65. Print.

Weeks, Stephen, dir. *I Monster*. Perf. Christopher Lee and Peter Cushing. Amicus Productions, 1971. Image Entertainment, 2005. Videocassette.

Wexman, Virginia Wright. "Horrors of the Body: Hollywood's Discourse on Beauty and Rouben Mamoulian's *Dr. Jekyll and Mr. Hyde*." Veeder and Hirsch 283–307.

White, Jerry. *London in the Nineteenth Century*. London: Cape, 2007. Print.

Wickes, David, dir. *Jekyll and Hyde*. Perf. Michael Caine. Wickes, 1989. Television.

Wickman, Matthew. *The Ruins of Experience: Scotland's "Romantick" Highlands and the Birth of the Modern Witness*. Philadelphia: U of Pennsylvania P, 2007. Print.

Wilde, Oscar. "The Decay of Lying: An Observation." *"The Soul of Man under Socialism" and Selected Critical Prose.* Ed. Linda Dowling. New York: Penguin, 2001. 163–92. Print.

Willard, Nancy. *The Voyage of the Ludgate Hill: Travels with Robert Louis Stevenson.* Illus. Martin and Alice Provensen. New York: Harcourt, 1987. Print.

Wilt, Judith. *Secret Leaves*. Chicago: U of Chicago P, 1985. Print.

Winters, David, dir. *Dr. Jekyll and Mr. Hyde*. TV musical. Perf. Kirk Douglas and Stanley Holloway. NBC, 1972. Sony, n.d. Videocassette.

Wolfe, Cary. "Flesh and Finitude: Thinking Animals in (Post)Humanist Philosophy." *SubStance* 37.3 (2008): 8–36. Print.

Wolff, Ashley, illus. *Block City*. By Robert Louis Stevenson. New York: Dutton, 1988. Print.

Wood, James, dir. *Dr. Jekyll's Dungeon of Death*. Perf. Dawn Carver Kelly and James Mathers. Magnum Video, 1985. Videocassette.

Wood, James. *How Fiction Works.* New York: Farrar, 2008. Print.

Wood, Naomi J. "Gold Standards and Silver Subversions: *Treasure Island* and the Romance of Money." *Children's Literature* 26 (1998): 61–86. Print.

Wright, Daniel. "'The Prisonhouse of My Disposition': A Study of the Psychology of Addiction in *Dr. Jekyll and Mr. Hyde*." *Studies in the Novel* 26.3 (1994): 254–67. Print.

Yeats, William Butler. "Leda and the Swan." *Selected Poems and Two Plays by W. B. Yeats*. Ed. M. L. Rosenthal. New York: Macmillan, 1962. 114. Print.

INDEX

Modern Language Association of America

Approaches to Teaching World Literature

Achebe's Things Fall Apart. Ed. Bernth Lindfors. 1991.
Arthurian Tradition. Ed. Maureen Fries and Jeanie Watson. 1992.
Atwood's The Handmaid's Tale *and Other Works*. Ed. Sharon R. Wilson, Thomas B. Friedman, and Shannon Hengen. 1996.
Austen's Emma. Ed. Marcia McClintock Folsom. 2004.
Austen's Pride and Prejudice. Ed. Marcia McClintock Folsom. 1993.
Balzac's Old Goriot. Ed. Michal Peled Ginsburg. 2000.
Baudelaire's Flowers of Evil. Ed. Laurence M. Porter. 2000.
Beckett's Waiting for Godot. Ed. June Schlueter and Enoch Brater. 1991.
Beowulf. Ed. Jess B. Bessinger, Jr., and Robert F. Yeager. 1984.
Blake's Songs of Innocence and of Experience. Ed. Robert F. Gleckner and Mark L. Greenberg. 1989.
Boccaccio's Decameron. Ed. James H. McGregor. 2000.
British Women Poets of the Romantic Period. Ed. Stephen C. Behrendt and Harriet Kramer Linkin. 1997.
Charlotte Brontë's Jane Eyre. Ed. Diane Long Hoeveler and Beth Lau. 1993.
Emily Brontë's Wuthering Heights. Ed. Sue Lonoff and Terri A. Hasseler. 2006.
Byron's Poetry. Ed. Frederick W. Shilstone. 1991.
Camus's The Plague. Ed. Steven G. Kellman. 1985.
Writings of Bartolomé de Las Casas. Ed. Santa Arias and Eyda M. Merediz. 2008.
Cather's My Ántonia. Ed. Susan J. Rosowski. 1989.
Cervantes' Don Quixote. Ed. Richard Bjornson. 1984.
Chaucer's Canterbury Tales. Ed. Joseph Gibaldi. 1980.
Chaucer's Troilus and Criseyde *and the Shorter Poems*. Ed. Tison Pugh and Angela Jane Weisl. 2006.
Chopin's The Awakening. Ed. Bernard Koloski. 1988.
Coleridge's Poetry and Prose. Ed. Richard E. Matlak. 1991.
Collodi's Pinocchio *and Its Adaptations*. Ed. Michael Sherberg. 2006.
Conrad's "Heart of Darkness" and "The Secret Sharer." Ed. Hunt Hawkins and Brian W. Shaffer. 2002.
Dante's Divine Comedy. Ed. Carole Slade. 1982.
Defoe's Robinson Crusoe. Ed. Maximillian E. Novak and Carl Fisher. 2005.
DeLillo's White Noise. Ed. Tim Engles and John N. Duvall. 2006.
Dickens's Bleak House. Ed. John O. Jordan and Gordon Bigelow. 2009.
Dickens's David Copperfield. Ed. Richard J. Dunn. 1984.
Dickinson's Poetry. Ed. Robin Riley Fast and Christine Mack Gordon. 1989.
Narrative of the Life of Frederick Douglass. Ed. James C. Hall. 1999.
Duras's Ourika. Ed. Mary Ellen Birkett and Christopher Rivers. 2009.
Early Modern Spanish Drama. Ed. Laura R. Bass and Margaret R. Greer. 2006.

Eliot's Middlemarch. Ed. Kathleen Blake. 1990.
Eliot's Poetry and Plays. Ed. Jewel Spears Brooker. 1988.
Shorter Elizabethan Poetry. Ed. Patrick Cheney and Anne Lake Prescott. 2000.
Ellison's Invisible Man. Ed. Susan Resneck Parr and Pancho Savery. 1989.
English Renaissance Drama. Ed. Karen Bamford and Alexander Leggatt. 2002.
Works of Louise Erdrich. Ed. Gregg Sarris, Connie A. Jacobs, and James R. Giles. 2004.
Dramas of Euripides. Ed. Robin Mitchell-Boyask. 2002.
Faulkner's As I Lay Dying. Ed. Patrick O'Donnell and Lynda Zwinger. 2011.
Faulkner's The Sound and the Fury. Ed. Stephen Hahn and Arthur F. Kinney. 1996.
Fitzgerald's The Great Gatsby. Ed. Jackson R. Bryer and Nancy P. VanArsdale. 2009.
Flaubert's Madame Bovary. Ed. Laurence M. Porter and Eugene F. Gray. 1995.
García Márquez's One Hundred Years of Solitude. Ed. María Elena de Valdés and Mario J. Valdés. 1990.
Gilman's "The Yellow Wall-Paper" and Herland. Ed. Denise D. Knight and Cynthia J. Davis. 2003.
Goethe's Faust. Ed. Douglas J. McMillan. 1987.
Gothic Fiction: The British and American Traditions. Ed. Diane Long Hoeveler and Tamar Heller. 2003.
Poetry of John Gower. Ed. R. F. Yeager and Brian W. Gastle. 2011.
Grass's The Tin Drum. Ed. Monika Shafi. 2008.
H.D.'s Poetry and Prose. Ed. Annette Debo and Lara Vetter. 2011.
Hebrew Bible as Literature in Translation. Ed. Barry N. Olshen and Yael S. Feldman. 1989.
Homer's Iliad *and* Odyssey. Ed. Kostas Myrsiades. 1987.
Hurston's Their Eyes Were Watching God *and Other Works*. Ed. John Lowe. 2009.
Ibsen's A Doll House. Ed. Yvonne Shafer. 1985.
Henry James's Daisy Miller *and* The Turn of the Screw. Ed. Kimberly C. Reed and Peter G. Beidler. 2005.
Works of Samuel Johnson. Ed. David R. Anderson and Gwin J. Kolb. 1993.
Joyce's Ulysses. Ed. Kathleen McCormick and Erwin R. Steinberg. 1993.
Works of Sor Juana Inés de la Cruz. Ed. Emilie L. Bergmann and Stacey Schlau. 2007.
Kafka's Short Fiction. Ed. Richard T. Gray. 1995.
Keats's Poetry. Ed. Walter H. Evert and Jack W. Rhodes. 1991.
Kingston's The Woman Warrior. Ed. Shirley Geok-lin Lim. 1991.
Lafayette's The Princess of Clèves. Ed. Faith E. Beasley and Katharine Ann Jensen. 1998.
Works of D. H. Lawrence. Ed. M. Elizabeth Sargent and Garry Watson. 2001.
Lazarillo de Tormes *and the Picaresque Tradition*. Ed. Anne J. Cruz. 2009.
Lessing's The Golden Notebook. Ed. Carey Kaplan and Ellen Cronan Rose. 1989.
Works of Naguib Mahfouz. Ed. Waïl S. Hassan and Susan Muaddi Darraj. 2011.
Mann's Death in Venice *and Other Short Fiction*. Ed. Jeffrey B. Berlin. 1992.

Marguerite de Navarre's Heptameron. Ed. Colette H. Winn. 2007.
Medieval English Drama. Ed. Richard K. Emmerson. 1990.
Melville's Moby-Dick. Ed. Martin Bickman. 1985.
Metaphysical Poets. Ed. Sidney Gottlieb. 1990.
Miller's Death of a Salesman. Ed. Matthew C. Roudané. 1995.
Milton's Paradise Lost. First edition. Ed. Galbraith M. Crump. 1986.
Milton's Paradise Lost. Second edition. Ed. Peter C. Herman. 2012.
Milton's Shorter Poetry and Prose. Ed. Peter C. Herman. 2007.
Molière's Tartuffe *and Other Plays*. Ed. James F. Gaines and Michael S. Koppisch. 1995.
Momaday's The Way to Rainy Mountain. Ed. Kenneth M. Roemer. 1988.
Montaigne's Essays. Ed. Patrick Henry. 1994.
Novels of Toni Morrison. Ed. Nellie Y. McKay and Kathryn Earle. 1997.
Murasaki Shikibu's The Tale of Genji. Ed. Edward Kamens. 1993.
Nabokov's Lolita. Ed. Zoran Kuzmanovich and Galya Diment. 2008.
Works of Ngũgĩ wa Thiong'o. Ed. Oliver Lovesey. 2012.
Works of Tim O'Brien. Ed. Alex Vernon and Catherine Calloway. 2010.
Works of Ovid and the Ovidian Tradition. Ed. Barbara Weiden Boyd and Cora Fox. 2010.
Poe's Prose and Poetry. Ed. Jeffrey Andrew Weinstock and Tony Magistrale. 2008.
Pope's Poetry. Ed. Wallace Jackson and R. Paul Yoder. 1993.
Proust's Fiction and Criticism. Ed. Elyane Dezon-Jones and Inge Crosman Wimmers. 2003.
Puig's Kiss of the Spider Woman. Ed. Daniel Balderston and Francine Masiello. 2007.
Pynchon's The Crying of Lot 49 *and Other Works.* Ed. Thomas H. Schaub. 2008.
Works of François Rabelais. Ed. Todd W. Reeser and Floyd Gray. 2011.
Novels of Samuel Richardson. Ed. Lisa Zunshine and Jocelyn Harris. 2006.
Rousseau's Confessions *and* Reveries of the Solitary Walker. Ed. John C. O'Neal and Ourida Mostefai. 2003.
Scott's Waverley Novels. Ed. Evan Gottlieb and Ian Duncan. 2009.
Shakespeare's Hamlet. Ed. Bernice W. Kliman. 2001.
Shakespeare's King Lear. Ed. Robert H. Ray. 1986.
Shakespeare's Othello. Ed. Peter Erickson and Maurice Hunt. 2005.
Shakespeare's Romeo and Juliet. Ed. Maurice Hunt. 2000.
Shakespeare's The Tempest *and Other Late Romances.* Ed. Maurice Hunt. 1992.
Shelley's Frankenstein. Ed. Stephen C. Behrendt. 1990.
Shelley's Poetry. Ed. Spencer Hall. 1990.
Sir Gawain and the Green Knight. Ed. Miriam Youngerman Miller and Jane Chance. 1986.
Song of Roland. Ed. William W. Kibler and Leslie Zarker Morgan. 2006.
Spenser's Faerie Queene. Ed. David Lee Miller and Alexander Dunlop. 1994.
Stendhal's The Red and the Black. Ed. Dean de la Motte and Stirling Haig. 1999.

Sterne's Tristram Shandy. Ed. Melvyn New. 1989.
Works of Robert Louis Stevenson. Ed. Caroline McCracken-Flesher. 2013.
The Story of the Stone (Dream of the Red Chamber). Ed. Andrew Schonebaum and Tina Lu. 2012.
Stowe's Uncle Tom's Cabin. Ed. Elizabeth Ammons and Susan Belasco. 2000.
Swift's Gulliver's Travels. Ed. Edward J. Rielly. 1988.
Teresa of Ávila and the Spanish Mystics. Ed. Alison Weber. 2009.
Thoreau's Walden *and Other Works*. Ed. Richard J. Schneider. 1996.
Tolstoy's Anna Karenina. Ed. Liza Knapp and Amy Mandelker. 2003.
Vergil's Aeneid. Ed. William S. Anderson and Lorina N. Quartarone. 2002.
Voltaire's Candide. Ed. Renée Waldinger. 1987.
Whitman's Leaves of Grass. Ed. Donald D. Kummings. 1990.
Wiesel's Night. Ed. Alan Rosen. 2007.
Works of Oscar Wilde. Ed. Philip E. Smith II. 2008.
Woolf's Mrs. Dalloway. Ed. Eileen Barrett and Ruth O. Saxton. 2009.
Woolf's To the Lighthouse. Ed. Beth Rigel Daugherty and Mary Beth Pringle. 2001.
Wordsworth's Poetry. Ed. Spencer Hall, with Jonathan Ramsey. 1986.
Wright's Native Son. Ed. James A. Miller. 1997.